Strive for a 5: Preparing for the AP® Psychology Examination

to accompany

Myers' Psychology for AP®
Second Edition

David G. Myers

Allison Herzig
Langley High School, Virginia

Nathaniel Naughton
Arlington Catholic High School, Massachusetts

Laura Brandt
Adlai E. Stevenson High School, Illinois

bfw
Worth

Strive for a 5: Preparing for the AP® Psychology Examination
by Alison Herzig, Nathaniel Naughton, and Laura Brandt
to accompany
Myers: *Psychology for AP®*, Second Edition

© 2014, 2011 by Worth Publishers

ISBN-13: 978-1-4641-5605-2
ISBN-10: 1-4641-5605-0

Printed in the United States of America.

Ninth   printing

BFW/Worth Publishers
41 Madison Avenue
New York, NY 10010

www.worthpublishers.com/MyersAP2e

Table of Contents

Preface

This book, *Strive for a 5: Preparing for the AP® Psychology Examination*, is designed for use with Myers' *Psychology for AP®*, Second Edition, by David G. Myers. It is intended to help you evaluate your understanding of the material covered in the textbook, reinforce the key concepts you need to learn, develop your conceptual understanding and communication skills, and prepare you for success on the AP® Psychology exam. This book is divided into two sections: a study guide section which will review each of the units in the textbook, and a test preparation section.

THE STUDY GUIDE SECTION

The study guide section is designed for you to use throughout your AP® Psychology course. As each module is covered in your class, you can use the study guide to help identify and learn the key concepts and terms.

After reading each unit in the textbook, use the study guide to practice problems and review questions to help you master the material and verify your understanding before moving on to the next unit.

This guide is organized to follow the formative assessment process. It provides a means for you to clearly identify what it is you need to learn, whether or not you have learned it, and what you need to do to close any gaps in your understanding before moving onto the next unit.

For each unit, the study guide is organized as follows:

Overview: The unit content is summarized to provide a quick overview of the material covered in the course.

Listing of modules: Each unit is broken into a handful of modules. This list identifies each of the modules within the unit.

Study Tip: Each unit provides a practical takeaway for you to strengthen your study skills. These tips will help you succeed in the course by getting more organized, practicing time management skills, and learning how to study more effectively.

Check Yourself: These high-level analysis questions, found at the very end of each unit, ensure that you have mastered the essential content in the unit. The questions here require you to think broadly and synthesize information from across all modules within the unit to properly answer them. If you have trouble answering the Check Yourself questions, you should definitely re-read the unit. The skills you develop to successfully answer these questions will help you with answering Free-Response Questions on the AP® exam!

For each module, the study guide is organized as follows:

Before You Read:

> MODULE SUMMARY: The module content is summarized to provide a quick overview of the material covered.

> KEY TERMS AND KEY NAMES: The key terms and people you will need to understand and be able to discuss are listed here, in order of presentation in the module. Many of these individuals are also included in the College Board's description for the AP® Psychology course. You should consider creating flashcards for each vocabulary term and key name.

While You Read: Use this section to help you actively read each module. This will aid in your understanding and retention of the material you're covering. Questions in this section are designed to help you focus on and start applying the key concepts you should master after reading the unit.

After You Read: Use this section to identify areas where you need to spend more time reading and studying the material in the module. The various types of questions in this section provide a thorough unit review that will help you really master the content.

THE TEST PREPARATION SECTION

The test preparation section of this guide is meant to help you better understand how the exam is constructed and scored, how to best study for the exam, and how to make sure you feature what you have learned when answering exam questions. Two practice exams are included to help you get a feel for the actual test.

As you are reviewing for the AP® exam, it is a good idea to read through the entirety of your answers in the guide and review the flashcards you have created of all the important key terms, contributors, and concepts you've encountered through the guide. When you feel confident you've mastered all the necessary concepts, take the first practice exam. Be sure to look closely at the questions you answered incorrectly and spend extra time with the concepts found in those questions. This will help you to fill any learning gaps you have before taking the second practice exam.

Please see your teacher for answers to all questions and practice exams in this guide.

We hope that your use of *Strive for a 5: Preparing for the AP® Psychology Examination* will assist you in your study of psychological science, help you earn a high score on the exam, and provide you with an interest and desire to further your study of psychology. Best wishes for a great year of studies and best of luck on your AP® Psychology exam!

Unit I

Psychology's History and Approaches

Overview

Psychology's historical development and current activities lead us to define the field as the science of behavior and mental processes. Unit I discusses the development of psychology from ancient times until today and the range of behaviors and mental processes investigated by psychologists in each of the various specialty areas. In addition, it introduces the biopsychosocial approach that integrates the three main levels of analysis followed by psychologists working from the seven major perspectives. Finally, an overview of the diverse subfields in which psychologists conduct research and provide professional services is given.

Modules

1 Psychology's History

2 Psychology's Big Issues and Approaches

3 Careers in Psychology

Tip #1
Vocabulary Cards

Making vocabulary cards can be a very useful tool in mastering all the new psychology jargon. See the example below for an example of the depth, detail, and content for your vocabulary card.

PSYCHOLOGY

The <u>scientific</u> study of <u>behavior</u> and
<u>mental processes</u>

What do we mean by <u>scientific</u>?

What do we mean by <u>behavior</u>?

What do we mean by **<u>mental processes</u>**?

?? Why is the word *human* absent from the definition?

Module 1

Psychology's History

Module Summary

Module 1 introduces the foundations of thought that influenced and directed the growth of psychology. From the earliest philosophers debating the duality of mind and body to the more recent scientific methods of inquiry, psychology has grappled with the question of being, doing and thinking. This module discusses the key contributions of scholars, philosophers and scientists across the ages and sets the stage for the remainder of the course.

Before beginning the module, take a moment to read each of the following terms and names you will encounter. You may wish to make vocabulary cards for each.

Key Terms	Key Names
empiricism	Socrates
structuralism	Plato
functionalism	Aristotle
experimental psychology	René Descartes
behaviorism	Francis Bacon
humanistic psychology	John Locke
cognitive neuroscience	Wilhelm Wundt
psychology	G. Stanley Hall
	Edward Titchener
	William James
	Charles Darwin
	Mary Whiton Calkins
	Margaret Floy Washburn
	John B. Watson
	B. F. Skinner
	Sigmund Freud
	Carl Rogers
	Abraham Maslow

While You Read

1-1 Complete the following chart with details to support each early theorist's beliefs about the nature of mind, body, and innate and acquired knowledge. One has been filled in to get you started.

> ⚠ More information is given on Locke, Decartes and Darwin in Module 2. Make sure to leave some space in the table and return to the two charts below later to add the additional information that will complete your chart.

Theorist/ Philosopher	Viewpoint
Socrates	
Plato	• *Knowledge is innate—born within us* • *Mind is separable from body and continues after the body dies*
Aristotle	
René Descartes	
Francis Bacon	
John Locke	

1-2 Complete the following chart detailing the contributions and important milestones each of the early psychologists made to the field.

Psychologist	Contribution or Milestone
Wilhelm Wundt	
G. Stanley Hall	
Edward Titchener	
Charles Darwin	
William James	
Mary Whiton Calkins	
Margaret Floy Washburn	

1-3   Complete the following chart with information about the developments in psychology from 1920 to the present.

Psychologist	Psychological Approach to Explaining Behavior and Mental Processes	Key Terms
John B. Watson		
B. F. Skinner	*You should observe and record people's behavior to understand them*	
Sigmund Freud		
Carl Rogers		*Growth potential*
Abraham Maslow		

2. According to your text, what is the definition of psychology?

After You Read

Module 1 Review

Complete the Matching Questions below to see if you have mastered the basics.

Terms or Names

_____ 1. Socrates

_____ 2. empiricism

_____ 3. Aristotle

_____ 4. structuralism

_____ 5. William James

_____ 6. functionalism

_____ 7. René Descartes

_____ 8. experimental psychology

_____ 9. Francis Bacon

_____ 10. behaviorism

_____ 11. John Locke

_____ 12. humanistic psychology

Definitions or Associations

A. British researcher who emphasized observation and experimentation

B. French philosopher who believed the mind and body are separate

C. Greek philosopher who believed that knowledge is innate

D. Greek philosopher who believed knowledge comes from experience

E. American functionalist

F. The view that knowledge originates in experience and science should rely on observation and experimentation

G. The field of psychology that believes only observable behavior is worthy of study

H. The field of psychology that conducts experiments to study behavior and thinking

I. An early school of thought that emphasized introspection as a tool to discover the structures of the mind.

J. An early school of thought that questioned how behavioral process function and enable an organism to adapt, survive and flourish

K. A British political philosopher who believed the mind at birth is a 'tabula rasa'

L. Psychological perspective that emphasizes growth potential of healthy humans

Module 2

Psychology's Big Issues and Approaches

Before You Read

Module Summary

Module 2 tackles the enduring question of the influence of nature and nurture on organisms. The various levels of analysis and the myriad subfields of psychology are presented as a means to interpreting, explaining, and predicting behavior. This module concludes with an overview of the SQ3R study method and some additional study tips.

Before beginning the module, take a moment to read each of the following terms you will encounter. You may wish to make vocabulary cards for each.

Key Terms

nature–nurture issue

natural selection

levels of analysis

biopsychosocial approach

behavioral psychology

biological psychology

cognitive psychology

evolutionary psychology

psychodynamic psychology

social-cultural psychology

psychometrics

basic research

developmental psychologists

educational psychologists

personality psychologists

social psychologists

applied research

industrial-organizational psychologists

human factors psychologists

counseling psychologists

clinical psychologists

psychiatrists

positive psychology

community psychologists

testing effect

SQ3R

While You Read

 2-1   Answer the following questions:

1. List a few of your more prominent traits: physical (for instance, eye color which is filled in for you), intellectual, personality, and so on that you feel either were inherited (nature) or arose from your environment (nurture).

Nature	Nurture
eye color	

Nurture works on what nature endows. (p. 10)

2. What do you think is meant by the statement above?

3. List and elaborate on at least two examples of your own traits—taken from your list above or new ones—that could make the above statement true in your life. For instance, if you wrote *"intelligence"* in the Nature column, discuss how your environment (nurture) contributed to or detracted from that trait.

⚠️ More information is given on Locke, Decartes and Darwin in this module. Remember to return to your charts in Module 1 and add the additional information to make them more complete.

2-2 Consider the levels of analysis and varying perspectives your author gives to explain the emotion of anger. Using the trait of shyness, apply the seven perspectives to explain why a person might be shy. One is done for you as an example.

Perspective	This person is shy because . . .
Behavioral	she learned that when she is quiet and avoids eye contact, other people leave her alone. She feels pleasure at being left alone to think her own thoughts and daydream so is rewarded for being shy.
Biological	
Cognitive	
Evolutionary	
Humanistic	
Psychodynamic	
Social-cultural	

2-3 Complete the chart below by providing the focus of each of the subfields of psychology.

Subfields of Psychologists	Focus
psychometrics	
developmental	
educational	
personality	
social	
industrial-organizational	
human factors	
counseling	
clinical	
psychiatrists	
positive	
community	

2-4   Answer the following questions:

1. According to Henry Roediger and Jeffrey Karpicke, what is the testing effect? Can you think of a time in your own studies when the testing effect has benefitted you?

2. Using the information from the text detailing the SQ3R study method, list the steps that you found yourself completing in the Unit thus far.

David Myers cites distributed (or spaced) practice and interleaving techniques as successful methods for study. In the space below, write out an example of how you would apply those techniques with your schedule this year. Include actual subjects and minutes of study in your plan. You may wish to make your own version of this chart, adding columns that have more meaning to you.

	SUBJECT	Monday	Tuesday	Wednesday	Thursday	Friday	Saturday	Sunday	TOTAL Time Allotted for Each Subject
1	AP Psych								
2									
3									
4									
5									
6									
7									
8									
TOTAL Time Spent Studying Subjects									

After You Read

Module 2 Review

Complete the Matching Questions below to see if you have mastered the basics.

Terms

_____ 1. biological perspective

_____ 2. educational psychology

_____ 3. developmental psychology

_____ 4. cognitive perspective

_____ 5. personality psychology

_____ 6. industrial-organizational psychology

_____ 7. behavioral perspective

_____ 8. counseling psychology

_____ 9. clinical psychology

_____ 10. social-cultural perspective

Definitions

A. The traits that govern our behavior and thoughts

B. Optimizing human behavior in workplaces

C. Genetic influence on individual differences

D. Ethnic and regional differences in behavior and mental processes

E. Influences on teaching and learning

F. Assists with daily problems of functioning

G. Life-span changes in our emotional, mental and physical abilities

H. Thoughts' and memories' impact on behavior

I. Effects of learning and environment on behavior and thoughts

J. Assesses and treats psychological disorders

Module 3

Careers in Psychology

Before You Read

Module Summary

Module 3 builds on the introduction of psychology's subfields from Module 2 and provides additional information regarding the vast opportunities and specialized focus of the varied career paths.

While You Read

3-1   Complete the two tables below:

Basic Research Subfields of Psychology	Examples of Work These Psychologists Do
Cognitive	
Developmental	
Educational	
Experimental	
Psychometric/ Quantitative	
Social	

Applied Research Subfields of Psychology	Examples of Work These Psychologists Do
Forensic	
Health	
Industrial-Organizational (I/O)	

Applied Research Subfields of Psychology	Examples of Work These Psychologists Do
Neuropsychology	
Rehabilitation	
School	
Sport	
Clinical	
Community	
Counseling	

After You Read

Module 3 Review

Complete the review questions below to see if you have mastered the basics.

Which psychologist would you consult with if you:

1. are a Major League Baseball player who is in a slump? _____

2. are a corporate executive that wants to increase employee morale? _____

3. work for the Centers for Disease Control and want to start a program to prevent the spread of sexually transmitted diseases? _____

4. want to develop a valid, reliable test to measure student performance in a school district?_____

5. want to reform the child-care institutions in this country? _____

6. suffer from schizophrenia? _____

7. have a child you suspect may have a learning disability? _____

8. just moved to a new town and are feeling out-of-place and sleeping more than usual? _____

9. want to make changes to the way you think about and perceive the world? _____

10. sustained a concussion in a soccer game and believe you may have a serious head injury? _____

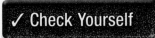

Now that you have mastered the basics, work through the problems below to see if you can *synthesize* what you have learned.

1. Describe one way in which Titchener's ideas of structuralism and James' emphasis on functionalism differ.

2. Discuss the arguments behaviorists Watson and Skinner may have had with James regarding the study of human behavior.

3. How might Sigmund Freud have differed from the behaviorists in his ideas of human behavior?

4. In what way did the theories of humanists Rogers and Maslow run counter to those of their predecessors, Freud and Watson?

5. In what way do the cognitivists agree with the early theorists' ideas of structuralism?

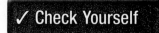 **Check Yourself**   Now that you have mastered the basics and can apply your knowledge, work through the case study below to see if you can *evaluate* and *analyze* using the basic material you have learned. You are not diagnosing the patient in the case, simply explaining her behavior through the lens of each listed approach.

> Norah is a 6-year-old girl who is often disobedient. She frequently throws temper tantrums and refuses to finish her meals. Her parents come to you, a well-respected psychologist in your town, asking for your thoughts on why they are having such difficulties with her. How would you explain Norah's behavior to her parents if you were a:

Humanist? It is obvious to me, as a humanist, that your daughter Norah's difficulties stem from…

Behaviorist? It is obvious to me, as a behaviorist, that your daughter Norah's difficulties stem from…

Psychoanalyst (Freudian)? It is obvious to me, as a psychoanalyst, that your daughter Norah's difficulties stem from…

In what ways might you find the four approaches above to be limiting in their ability to help you explain Norah's behavior?

Cognitivist? It is obvious to me, as a cognitivist, that your daughter Norah's difficulties stem from…

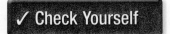 **Check Yourself**

Now that you have mastered the basics, work through the problem below to see if you can *synthesize* what you have learned.

A famous television and movie actor is repeatedly in and out of rehabilitation centers for drug and alcohol abuse. She began her career as the lead in a popular children's show and spent a decade starring in both Hollywood movies and television dramas. Now, in her late-twenties, she is a regular feature in the celebrity magazines and tabloids for her bizarre public outbursts, illegal behavior and edgy lifestyle. Finally, as a result of a court-order, she has sought psychological counseling and assessment. She is finding it hard to decide on a permanent psychologist because she is receiving conflicting explanations for her lack of functioning. Using your knowledge from Module 2, discuss how each of the perspectives/levels of analysis below might be utilized to explain the actor's behavior. Create specific examples that would apply.

1. A behaviorist:

2. A biopsychologist:

3. A cognitive psychologist:

4. An evolutionary psychologist:

5. A humanist:

6. A psychodynamic/psychoanalytic psychologist:

7. A socio-cultural psychologist:

Before You Move On

Use the checklist below to verify your understanding of the unit's main points.:

☐ Do I know the difference between structuralism and functionalism?

☐ Do I know the seven main approaches to understanding and explaining behavior?

☐ Do I know the subfields of psychology?

☐ Do I know the major historical figures in psychology from the ancient Greeks through the theorists of the 1900s?

☐ Do I know the definition of psychology?

☐ Do I know the careers available in psychology?

Unit II

Research Methods: Thinking Critically With Psychological Science

Overview

Psychology is defined as the scientific study of behavior and mental processes. While Unit I explored the origins of psychology and the contributions of early theorists and philosophers, psychology has evolved into a science-based, data-supported field. The empirical nature of the field is determined by the scientific method and the gathering of data to separate opinion and belief from demonstrable results. Unit II reviews the scientific method and the numerous research methods psychologists employ to study behavior and lays out the methodology and statistical reasoning that are modern psychology's underpinnings. Through the use of myriad examples, the distinction between beliefs and science is made clear.

Modules

Tip #2
Make Your Learning Fluid

Although your textbook and this accompanying study guide are arranged by "unit" and "module," the study of psychology is not easily segmented into parts. Psychology is a dynamic, ever-changing, and adapting science that overlaps and references all parts of life. As such, don't limit your understanding of a topic, theory, or key name to the sole chart you completed in Module 1, for instance. Throughout the course, when you can make a connection to previous content, return to that section and add a note or example. Keep YOUR learning fluid and unbound by unit or module distinctions. The more connections you make to previously learned material, the greater your recall of that material. This is called *elaborative rehearsal,* and we'll talk about that again in the Memory unit!

Module 4

The Need for Psychological Science

Before You Read

Module Summary

Module 4 lays the groundwork for future modules by pointing out the perception errors humans are known to make. The case is made for the use of empirical, science-based research to prove or disprove theories. A discussion of critical thinking ends the module.

Before beginning the module, take a moment to read each of the following terms you will encounter. You may wish to make vocabulary cards for each.

Key Terms

hindsight bias

critical thinking

While You Read

Answer the following questions/prompts.

1. Define hindsight bias.

2. Your text uses an example to illustrate hindsight bias: "After the football game, we credit the coach if a 'gutsy play' wins the game, and fault the coach for the 'stupid play' if it doesn't" (Myers, p. 31). How does this example illustrate hindsight bias?

3. Define overconfidence.

4. How are random events taken into consideration during both hindsight bias and overconfidence?

4-2

1. What are the three main components of the scientific attitude?

2. Why do you think skepticism is such an important part of the scientific attitude?

3. What is critical thinking? Give an original example from your own life of critical thinking.

After You Read

Module 4 Review

Complete the questions below to see if you have mastered the basics.

Read the situations below and identify whether the phenomenon of hindsight bias (HB), overconfidence (O), or the tendency to perceive patterns in random events (P) is at work. Mark your answer in the blank.

_____ **1.** Toni notices that the last four times she has been to the grocery store she has scored a parking place right up front! She knows she is on a lucky streak!

_____ **2.** Bruce is often called a Monday Morning Quarterback by his friends for saying he knew the Redskins should have put the rookie wide receiver in last Sunday's game.

_____ **3.** Janelle, a senior in high school with a 3.0 GPA, is filling out her college applications. When asked by her friends and family what schools she is applying to and what schools she thinks she will get into, she lists Princeton, Yale, Harvard and Stanford and says she thinks she will get into all of them, except maybe for Harvard, which is her reach school.

_____ **4.** Shreya and Steve break up. Their classmate, Iram, tells her mother that she knew all along the two of them were not going to make it.

_____ **5.** Fiona, a student in your class, is certain the instructor does not like her. For the last three class sessions, the instructor has not called on her to answer a question, even though her hand was raised.

Module 5

The Scientific Method and Description

Module Summary

Module 5 explains the process of moving from a theory to a hypothesis that is operationally defined and replicable. The module also introduces three descriptive research methods, the case study, naturalistic observation and surveys, and discusses the benefits and limitations of each. The module concludes by explaining the importance of selecting a random sample that represents the population being researched.

Before beginning the module, take a moment to read each of the following terms you will encounter. You may wish to make vocabulary cards for each.

Key Terms

theory

hypothesis

operational definition

replication

case study

naturalistic observation

survey

sampling bias

population

random sample

While You Read

5-1 Answer the following questions/prompts.

1. What is a theory? Give an example of a theory in your own life.

2. What is a hypothesis? Give an example from your own life of a hypothesis you might have.

3. Why is it essential to operationally define the variables in a study?

4. Why is replication so important in the research process?

5. David Myers presents the following example about the relationship between sleep and memory to show how a theory evolves into an operationally defined and replicable hypothesis. Study the text graphic, then test your understanding by filling in the blanks of the second graphic using the relationship between *smiling* and the *number of friends* people make.

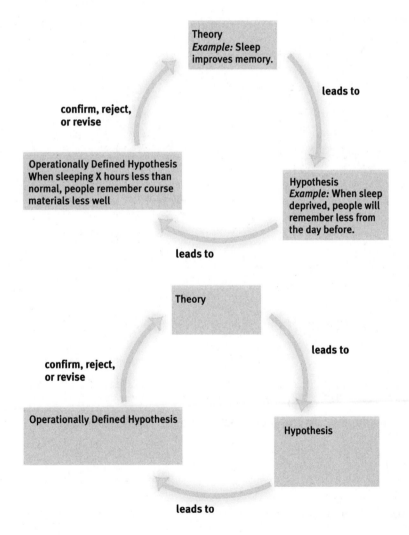

Can you identify the independent variable (IV) and the dependent variable (DV) in these situations?

    a. Sleep improves memory

        IV:

        DV:

    b. Relationship between smiling and number of friends

        IV:

        DV:

5-2 Complete the following chart. One box has been filled in for you to get you started. Then, answer the questions that follow.

Descriptive Research Method	Benefits	Drawbacks	Key Characteristics
Case Study			
Naturalistic Observation		*Does not explain behavior*	
Survey			

1. Why are descriptive research methods limited in their ability to explain behavior?

2. How can the phrasing of a survey question affect the responses given by those surveyed?

3. How would you draw a random sample of participants if you were surveying:

   a. your high school classmates?

   b. restaurant owners?

   c. music listeners?

After You Read

Module 5 Review

Complete the questions below to see if you have mastered the basics.

1. Read the statements below and identify them as either a theory (T) or a hypothesis (H):

   _____ a. Caffeine reduces the risk of developing Alzheimer's disease.

   _____ b. When smoking cigarettes, teens are more likely to recall geometry proofs.

   _____ c. Increase in television viewing results in decreased attention.

   _____ d. Flu vaccinations increase the risk of developing the flu.

   _____ e. Dogs see in color.

2. Read the following hypotheses and decide if there is an operational definition stated. If so, underline the operational definition.

   a. Pregnant women who consume 150 mg of caffeine daily have an increase in blood pressure.

   b. Dogs who overeat are more intelligent than those that do not.

   c. Instructors who smile ten times in their class have increased student participation.

   d. Students that break study sessions into five smaller 20-minute increments have higher grades on tests.

   e. Teenagers that sleep in have greater resiliency in life.

3. Read the statements below and decide which descriptive technique would be best utilized in each case: a case study (CS), naturalistic observation (NO) or survey (S). Write your answer on the blank.

   _____ a. A high school principal wants to determine whether she should use the building funds for a renovated student courtyard or a faculty exercise room.

   _____ b. An army doctor wants to see how soldiers are handling the transition back to civilian life.

   _____ c. A parent is curious to know how their child behaves when away from home at school.

   _____ d. An animal researcher wants to prove that squirrels run in packs as wolves do.

   _____ e. The school board in your town is trying to determine if teachers and students feel the building facilities are adequate and safe.

4. Identify the sampling flaw in the following three survey designs. Once you have identified the flaw, indicate you how would correct it.

   a. The principal at a school wants to survey the students to see if they would like increased lunch time in place of one academic course. He gives this survey to the freshman PE teachers to hand out to their classes.

      - flaw:

      - correction:

   b. A political campaign wants to poll potential voters to see how they feel about a candidate. They place calls to homes between the hours of 8:00 – 10:00 A.M. and again from 6:00 – 8:00 P.M.

      - flaw:

      - correction:

   c. The mayor wants input from the community on the planned festivities for the upcoming 4th of July celebration. She places a survey of options in the community paper and lists the phone number for citizens to respond with their answers.

      - flaw:

      - correction:

Module 6

Correlation and Experimentation

Before You Read

Module Summary

Module 6 adds correlation and experimentation to the list of research methods introduced in Module 5. The definitions and use of correlation coefficients and scatterplots are explained. The hazards of illusory correlations are pointed out and a thorough discussion of the experimental method is presented. The module concludes with a useful chart comparing and contrasting three of the primary research methods available to psychologists.

Before beginning the module, take a moment to read each of the following terms you will encounter. You may wish to make vocabulary cards for each.

Key Terms

correlation	random assignment
correlation coefficient	double-blind procedure
scatterplot	placebo effect
illusory correlation	independent variable
experiment	confounding variable
experimental group	dependent variable
control group	validity

While You Read

Answer the following questions/prompts.

 6-1

1. List two examples of a positive correlation between two variables. The first example should be from the text and the second example should be from your life.

2. List two examples of a negative correlation between two variables. The first example should be from the text and the second example should be from your life.

3. How is a scatterplot used to represent correlations between two variables?

4. The text author refers to a *New York Times* headline that states U.S. counties with high gun ownership rates tend to have high murder rates.

   a. Is this a positive or negative correlation?

   b. Why is the correlation positive or negative?

5. Draw a scatterplot below that would support your answer in #4. Be sure to correctly label the *x*- and *y*-axis.

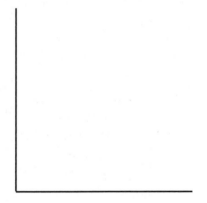

6. The text states that self-esteem correlates negatively with depression.

   a. Which of the following scatterplots could support that statement?

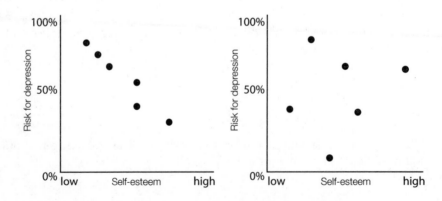

b. Why?

c. Based on the two scatterplots above, is it possible to say that low self-esteem causes depression? Why or why not?

d. Based on the two scatterplots above, is it possible to say that depression causes low self-esteem? Why or why not?

e. What point do you need to keep in mind regarding correlation and causation?

6-2

1. What is an illusory correlation? Give a real-life example of an illusory correlation.

2. Why should researchers (and people in general) be careful of illusory correlations?

6-3

1. David Myers presents two studies on the relationship between breast-fed babies and intelligence scores or social class. Working within that scenario, develop a hypothesis and show how the following terms would apply in an original experimental design that you create.

- Hypothesis:

- Experimental group:

- Control group:

- Random assignment:

- Double-blind procedure:

- Placebo effect:

- Independent variable:

- Dependent variable:

- Confounding variable:

2. A high school track coach is interested in the impact of carbohydrate consumption on running times in her athletes. She asks half of her team to eat a huge pasta dinner the night before a big meet and asks the other half of her team to eat a large steak and no carbohydrates. Identify the variables in this experiment.

- Independent variable:

- Dependent variable:

3. How do random sampling (from Module 5) and random assignment differ?

After You Read

Module 6 Review

Complete the questions below to see if you have mastered the basics.

1. Read the pairs of variables below and predict whether the correlation would likely be positive (P) or negative (N):

    _____ a. The number of fast food restaurants: the obesity rate in the U.S.

    _____ b. The average U.S. household income: annual gross profit reported by U.S. retailers.

    _____ c. The illiteracy rate: the presence of Head Start or early intervention education programs.

    _____ d. The number of hours spent commuting to and from work; the amount of dinners cooked at home from scratch.

    _____ e. Hours spent learning a skill; proficiency in the skill.

2. Look at the scatterplots below and identify the correlation as positive (P) or negative (N).

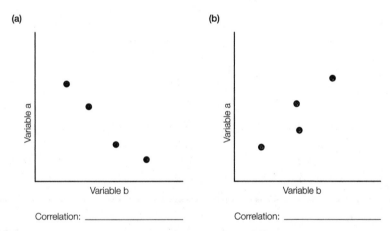

Correlation: _____   Correlation: _____

3. Which of the two scatterplots above has a strong correlation?

4. If a straight line represents a correlation coefficient of 1 and a complete random pattern represents a correlation coefficient of 0, what would you estimate the correlation to be

    a. in scatterplot (a)?

    b. in scatterplot (b)?

5. Give an example and an explanation of an illusory correlation in your life.

Module 7

Statistical Reasoning in Everyday Life

Before You Read

Module Summary

Module 7 describes the three measures of central tendency and discusses the usefulness of the two measures of variation. The concept of statistical significance is explained and the criteria necessary to generalize experimental results is introduced.

Before beginning the module, take a moment to read each of the following terms you will encounter. You may wish to make vocabulary cards for each.

Key Terms

descriptive statistics

mode

mean

median

skewed distribution

range

standard deviation

normal curve

inferential statistics

statistical significance

While You Read

Answer the following questions/prompts.

1. What are the three measures of central tendency, and what purpose does each of these measures serve?

2. Outliers, or extreme, "way-out" data that are significantly different from the majority of the data, have what effect on:

   a. the mean?

   b. the median?

   c. the mode?

3. Define what the range for a set of scores is, and identify the range of the following set: 29, 39, 40, 52, 55, 80.

4. What does the standard deviation tell us?

5. What would a large standard deviation indicate?

6. What would a small standard deviation indicate?

7. Using Figure 7.3 from the textbook, write the percentage of scores on a normal curve that fall within one standard deviation. Next, write the percentages that fall within two and three standard deviations.

8. Now that you have been introduced to the basics of descriptive statistics, review the following calculations and practice with the sample data below.

$$7, 15, 20, 4, 8, 5, 4$$

Measures of central tendency:

a. Calculate the mean, median and mode of the data above.

mean _____   median _____   mode _____

☞ *Point to note:* The mean can be pulled in the direction of the outliers, so often the median is a better measure of central tendency.

☞ *Point to note:*
- If there are an odd number of data, the median will be the number in the middle after the data is arranged from highest to lowest.

2, 4, ⬚6,⬚ 8, 10: 5 data points; median is 6

- If there are an even number of data, the median will be the mean (average) of the two middle numbers after the data is arranged from highest to lowest.

2, 4, ⬚6, 8⬚ 10, 12: 6 data points; mean is average of (6+8)/2, or 7

☞ *Point to note:* If more than one data point occurs with frequency, the data can be referred to as bimodal or multimodal.

Measures of variation: *How similar or diverse are the data?*

b. Calculate the range of the data. _____

☞ *Point to note:* When you take the highest number and subtract the lowest number, the result is the range.

c. Now find the standard deviation of the data, following the steps below.

1. Find the mean of your data
2. Find the difference between each number and the mean
3. Square each individual difference
4. Add up all of the squared numbers
5. Divide by the number of data points (This value is referred to as the variance. Variance is the average difference between individual data points in the distribution and the mean.)
6. Find the square root of the quotient from #5

You may use Table 7.1 from the text for reference (pg. 59) if you need help.

Data	Deviation from the mean	Squared deviation
7		
15		
20		
4		
8		
5		
4		
Mean of data:	Sum of squares:	

$$\sqrt{\frac{\text{Sum of squared deviations}}{\text{Number of scores}}} =$$

☞ *Point to note:* In a way, this is rather like taking the average of the average—a better way to decide how different data points are from each other.

7-2

1. What is the difference between descriptive statistics and inferential statistics?

2. What are the three principles to keep in mind when deciding to generalize from a sample?

3. In the field of psychology, what is the standard for deciding if a result is statistically significant?

4. What does it mean if a result is statistically significant?

After You Read

Module 7 Review

Complete the questions below to see if you have mastered the basics.

$$3, 6, 6, 8, 9, 22$$

1. Given the data set above, identify the

   a. mean _____   b. median _____   c. mode _____

2. Which measure of central tendency should be used to most accurately describe the data above? Why?

3. Using the data set above, identify the

   a. range _____   b. standard deviation _____

4. Assume a distribution of aptitude test scores forms a normal curve with a mean of 100 and a standard deviation of 15.

   a. Within which standard deviation will most of the scores fall?

   b. If a student scores a 120, within which standard deviation will that score fall?

   c. If a student scores within the second deviation, what is the possible range of the student's score?

5. Assume your class took a final exam in psychology in which the scores produced a normal curve with a mean score of 80 and a standard deviation of 5.

   a. 68% of the scores on the final exam would fall between _____ and _____.

   b. If a student scores within two standard deviations from the mean, what is the possible range of the student's score?

   c. What percentage of students may have scored either higher than 90 or lower than 70?

Module 8

Frequently Asked Questions About Psychology

Before You Read

Module Summary

Module 8 discusses the ethical issues that confront experimental researchers and offers guidelines that promote ethically sound experimentation. Additionally, the influence of culture on our behavior and mental processes and the application of experimental research across culture and gender is presented.

Before beginning the module, take a moment to read each of the following terms you will encounter. You may wish to make vocabulary cards for each.

Key Terms

culture

informed consent

debriefing

While You Read

As you read Module 8, answer the following questions/prompts.

8-1

1. According to the text, what is the purpose of an experiment?

2. Psychological science focuses less on _____ _____ than on seeking general principles that help _____ many behaviors.

3. What is meant by the statement you completed in #2?

8-2

1. What are WEIRD cultures?

2. Why does the text author bring up the topic of WEIRD cultures?

3. How does a collectivist culture differ from an individualist culture?

4. How do you think the text author's use of the image of Burkina Faso boys playing soccer on page 65 helps emphasize that behavior depends on one's culture?

8-3

1. Why do psychologists study animals?

2. What are the two issues the text author suggests arise from the debate on animal experimentation?

3. How have animals themselves benefitted from animal research?

1. List and define the four ethical principles discussed in this section.

1. According to the text author, is psychology free of value judgments? What examples are used in the text to support his contention?

2. Why do you think the text author included this section in this module?

After You Read

Module 8 Review

Complete the questions below to see if you have mastered the basics.

Read each situation below and decide which ethical guideline is not being followed.
Mark your answer(s) in the blank. More than one answer may apply.

Informed Consent (IC)
Protection from physical or emotional harm (H)
Confidentiality (C)
Debriefing (D)

_____ 1. A teacher in your school gives you a mandatory anonymous drug use survey to complete in class and tells you she cannot let you know why you are completing the survey because it would throw off her results.

_____ 2. You agree to participate in an experiment that is designed to measure your ability to lie in various circumstances. Under the direction of the researcher, you make false statements to your mother, your best friend, and your favorite teacher. The guilt you feel after lying to these influential and important people has you questioning your morals and values.

_____ 3. A psychologist in your town is invited to speak at career day at your school. You have been seeing the psychologist for more than a year for depression and attempted suicide. At career day the psychologist speaks of working with teen patients who are depressed and have attempted suicide and cites a few examples of his cases. Although he uses no names, you feel he is talking about you and run from the room embarrassed.

_____ 4. At the conclusion of a study testing memory and mood, you are released by the researcher, paid a small fee, and thanked for your time.

_____ 5. You are appointed to serve on the Institutional Review Board (IRB) at the research university where you teach, and will be screening research proposals to safeguard participant's well-being. A proposal is presented in which a researcher will be gathering data on the correlation between divorce and alcohol use disorder in celebrities. The proposal lists the research methodology, the sample population, and the manner in which the results of the study will be communicated. The researcher intends to write an article for a journal in the field, and also publish the results of the study in an entertainment magazine. He feels that if people know the actual names of the participants, they may take the results more seriously and so he intends to list the names in the entertainment article.

✓ Check Yourself

Now that you have mastered the basics, work through the problems below to see if you can *synthesize* what you have learned.

A local botanist believes that the town water supply contains contaminants that are killing the native plant life. She intends to make her case to the Board of Supervisors at the next town meeting in two months but wants to have hard data to support her case. She decides to conduct an experiment to test her theory. She begins by collecting 10 plant samples from the local park and places all 10 plants in a roped-off square area that receives ample light and will be undisturbed by park enthusiasts. Next, she places 10 scraps of paper numbered 1 to 10 in a hat, then pulls the scraps of paper at random, numbers the plants 1 to 10, and divides them into two groups. For six weeks, she waters 5 of the plants (plants 3, 5, 7, 9, and 10) using the town water supply and 5 of the plants (plants 1, 2, 4, 6, and 8) using bottled, distilled water. During the six weeks, she asks her neighbor and fellow plant lover to keep records of leaf condition (color, texture, strength) and stem and root conditions by counting the number of yellowed spots, wilted leaves, and withered offshoots. At the end of six weeks, she asks her neighbor to evaluate the 10 plants and he reports that plants 3, 5, 9, and 10 are yellowed, withering, and diseased.

a. What is the hypothesis in this situation?

b Which group of plants is the experimental group? The control group?

c. What method did the researcher use to randomly assign the groups?

d. How was a double blind procedure used?

e. Was a placebo used? If so, what was it?

f. What was the IV? The DV?

g. What is the operational definition of the IV? The DV?

h. What possible confounding variables might the researcher not have taken into account?

i. Was this experiment valid? Why or why not?

✓ Check Yourself   Now that you have mastered the basics, work through the problems below to see if you can *synthesize, evaluate,* and *analyze* what you have learned.

An instructor in an AP® Psychology course is trying to evaluate and analyze his test data to better hone his teaching methods and style to meet the needs of his students. After a quarter of collecting test data, the instructor has the following test averages for his 20 students:

89, 40, 82, 94, 93, 83, 73, 77, 49, 99, 78, 87, 86, 59, 90, 65, 60, 89, 73, 70

In order to help him assess his students' performance, he calls you, a psychometric statistical psychologist, to help him analyze the data and make a plan for improving his teaching. You compile the following data sheet to help the instructor with his goal.

Mean of the data:

Median of the data:

Mode of the data:

Range:

Variance:

Standard Deviation:

1. Based on the results of the data collection, how will you advise the instructor?

2. Which measure of central tendency should the instructor use to guide his analysis? Why?

3. How does the range and the standard deviation give you information to help advise the instructor?

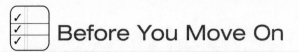

Before You Move On

Use the checklist below to verify your understanding of the unit's main points.

Do I know the difference between the types of descriptive research?

- [ ] case studies
- [ ] surveys
- [ ] naturalistic observation

- [ ] Do I know the purposes, benefits, and drawbacks to correlational studies and experiments?

Can I identify the components of an experiment?

- [ ] IV
- [ ] DV
- [ ] confounding variables
- [ ] control and experimental groups
- [ ] random assignment and random selection
- [ ] placebos
- [ ] experimenter bias

- [ ] Do I know the difference between reliability and validity?

- [ ] Do I know the importance of operational definitions in experimental research?

Do I know basic descriptive statistics?

- [ ] measures of central tendency
- [ ] range
- [ ] standard deviation

- [ ] Do I understand the difference between descriptive and inferential statistics?

- [ ] Do I know the ethical guidelines for conducting research on human and animal participants?

Unit III

Biological Bases of Behavior

Overview

At the core of what it means to behave and have mental processes is our biology. The brain's intricate and complex arrangement is what drives, compels, quiets, and consoles us. Unit III explores the mechanisms and processes by which we move our body, think about a friend, aim for a lofty goal or handle daily setbacks. The basics of neuroanatomy and neural transmission begin the unit, which then turns to a discussion of the nervous system as a whole. The endocrine system's role in regulating hormonal control of our body is discussed in detail, followed by a review of the various brain structures and their functions. Michael Gazzaniga's classic work with split-brain patients serves as the jumping off point to discuss hemisphere lateralization, plasticity, and neurogenesis, and both genetics and evolution are investigated as key foundations to the modern-day brain.

Modules

9 Biological Psychology and Neurotransmission

10 The Nervous and Endocrine Systems

11 Studying the Brain, and Older Structures

12 The Cerebral Cortex

13 Brain Hemisphere Organization and the Biology of Consciousness

14 Behavior Genetics: Predicting Individual Differences

15 Evolutionary Psychology: Understanding Human Nature

Tip #3
Use Mnemonic Devices to Remember Key Material

This unit is by far one of the most vocabulary-rich in the course. As you learned in Unit I, making useful and meaningful vocabulary cards with examples and references, questions and observations is a sure fire way to master the terminology. In addition, you will want to develop key mnemonic devices (memory tricks) to learn the structures and functions of the brain and nervous system. One such device is called the Method of Loci. (Loci is the plural of the Latin locus, meaning place or location.) You begin by visualizing a location you know well, such as your home. Then you insert items you wish to recall into various rooms and places in your 'home'. For instance, in this module you will be learning about the amygdala, a structure in the brain that plays a key role in extreme feelings such as rage and anger. Perhaps, in your visual 'home' you place an image of the amygdala (it doesn't have to actually look like an amygdala, try just placing the word) in your diary next to your bed. A diary is a place you might record emotions such as rage and anger. Following this idea, you might place your hypothalamus in the refrigerator. Any guesses as to the function of the hypothalamus? You'll find out in this unit!

Module 9

Biological Psychology and Neurotransmission

Before You Read

Module Summary

Module 9 revisits the early Greeks' philosophies as they relate to the mind-body connection and discusses the work of Franz Gall as one of the pioneers of the exploration of the brain and mind. The early contributions of the Greeks are debunked as the science of modern brain studies is introduced. A thorough discussion of neural transmission segues into neuroanatomy and neuronal function and ends with a brief introduction to neurotransmitters, agonists, and antagonists.

Before beginning the module, take a moment to read each of the following terms you will encounter. You may wish to make vocabulary cards for each.

Key Terms

biological psychology

neuron

dendrites

axon

myelin sheath

action potential

refractory period

threshold

all-or-none response

synapse

neurotransmitters

reuptake

endorphins

agonist

antagonist

While You Read

9-1   Answer the following questions.

1. Where in the body did Plato believe the 'mind' was located?

   The head / brain

2. How did Aristotle disagree with Plato?

   He thought it was in the heart

 Remember your charts from Module 1? Return now and add this additional information about Plato and Aristotle to make your chart more complete.

3. How did Franz Gall contribute to the mind-body question?

He created the idea of phrenology, the study of head shape to discover personality traits that led us to the idea of localization of function.

4. In what way was Franz Gall incorrect? In what way was he correct?

9-2   Answer the following questions, and complete the diagram and chart below.

1. What happy fact allows us to study animal brains to learn about human brains?

2. Fill in the chart below with the functions of these neural structures.

Structure	Function
dendrite	
cell body	
axon	
terminal branches	
myelin sheath	

3. Describe what the action potential is and why it is important to neural communication.

4. Use page 79 and Figure 9.3 to help you complete this paragraph describing the process of the action potential:

The fluid outside the axon membrane is largely made up of _____ charged ions but the fluid inside the membrane is primarily made up of _____ charged ions. This state is referred to as the _____ _____ . We refer to the axon's surface as _____ permeable since it will only allow particular ions to pass through. When a neuron fires, the axon membrane becomes permeable and _____ sodium ions flow into the cell. This _____ that part of the axon and then causes the next section of the membrane to become permeable. This occurs over and over down the line of the axon and serves to push the nerve impulse down the neuron. During the _____ _____ , the _____ ions are pumped back out of the cell and the axon returns to the original state of polarity, called the _____ _____ , prepared to fire again.

5. What is the difference between an excitatory nerve signal and an inhibitory nerve signal?

6. What is a threshold?

7. What happens when the level of neural stimulation above the threshold is increased? Why?

8. Create a metaphor or simile for the process of neural transmission.
   Neural transmission is like . . .

9-3   Answer the following questions.

1. What is a synapse?

2. How do neurons communicate with each other?

3. What is reuptake?

9-4   Answer the following questions/prompts.

1. Give an example of an agonist and describe how it functions in the nervous system.

2. Give an example of an antagonist and describe how it functions in the nervous system.

3. Describe how Botulin functions as an antagonist for acetylcholine.

4. What effect does the release of endorphins have on the body?

After You Read

Module 9 Review

Complete the diagram, then the section of matching questions below to see if you have mastered the basics.
Label and describe the function of the five main parts of the neuron.

NEURON

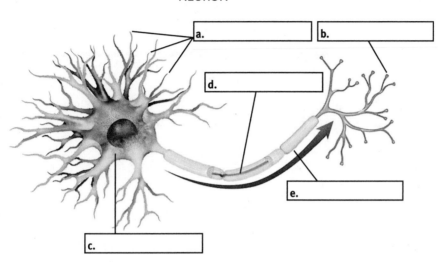

Terms

_____ 1. biological psychology

_____ 2. neuron

_____ 3. dendrites

_____ 4. axon

_____ 5. myelin sheath

_____ 6. action potential

_____ 7. refractory period

_____ 8. all-or-none response

_____ 9. threshold

_____ 10. synapse

_____ 11. neurotransmitters

_____ 12. reuptake

_____ 13. endorphins

_____ 14. agonist

_____ 15. antagonist

Definitions

A. Molecule that binds to a receptor and inhibits a response

B. Chemical messengers that cross the synapse between neurons

C. Level of physical stimulation required to trigger an impulse

D. Study of the links between biological and psychological processes

E. Reabsorption of the neurotransmitter by the sending neuron

F. Brief electrical charge that travels down an axon

G. Opiate-like neurotransmitters linked to pain control

H. Basic building block of the nervous system

I. A period of inactivity after a neuron fires

J. Receives neural messages and sends impulse to cell body

K. The junction between the axon tip of the sending neuron and the dendrites of the receiving neuron

L. Extension of neuron that passes messages through its branches to other neurons, muscles or glands

M. Neural reaction of either firing or not firing

N. Molecule similar to a neurotransmitter that triggers a response

O. Fatty tissue layer encasing the axon

Module 10

The Nervous and Endocrine Systems

Before You Read

Module Summary

Module 10 lays out the divisions and subdivisions of the nervous system and describes how each division helps us function. In addition, the nature and function of the endocrine system is discussed.

Before beginning the module, take a moment to read each of the following terms you will encounter. You may wish to make vocabulary cards for each.

Key Terms

nervous system

central nervous system

peripheral nervous system

nerves

sensory (afferent) neurons

motor (efferent) neurons

interneurons

somatic nervous system

autonomic nervous system

sympathetic nervous system

parasympathetic nervous system

reflex

endocrine system

hormones

adrenal glands

pituitary gland

While You Read

10-1 Complete the diagram and answer the prompts below.

1. Using the information from your text on the functional divisions of the human nervous system and Figure 10.1, fill in the chart below.

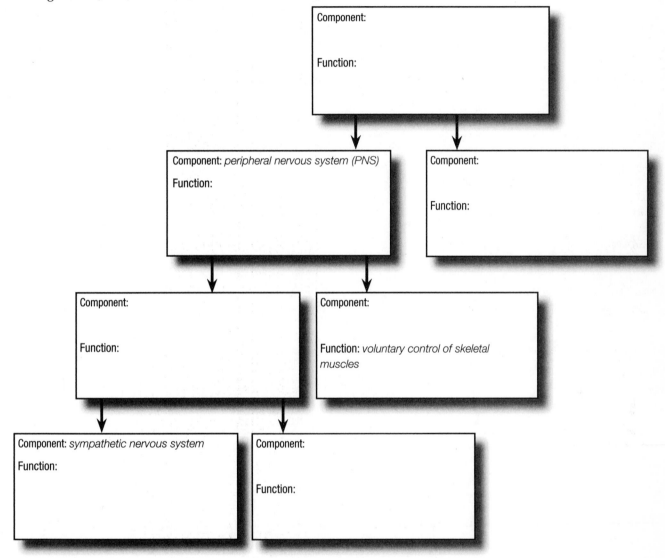

Component:

Function:

Component: *peripheral nervous system (PNS)*

Function:

Component:

Function:

Component:

Function:

Component:

Function: *voluntary control of skeletal muscles*

Component: *sympathetic nervous system*

Function:

Component:

Function:

2. Provide an example from your own life of when each of the subdivisions of the nervous system would be involved.

a. peripheral:

e. sympathetic:

b. central:

f. parasympathetic:

c. autonomic:

d. somatic:

3. Use Figure 10.2 to complete the chart below describing the physiological changes that occur when the sympathetic and parasympathetic nervous systems are stimulated. A few have been filled in for you.

	Effect When Sympathetic Nervous System Is Stimulated	Effect When Parasympathetic Nervous System Is Stimulated
Pupil of the eye		
Heart		
Stomach		
Liver	*Glucose is released by the liver*	*No effect*
Gallbladder	*No effect*	
Adrenal glands		*No effect*
Bladder		*Contracts*
Sex organs		

4. Label the diagram below with the three types of neurons used to carry reflex information to and from the spinal cord.

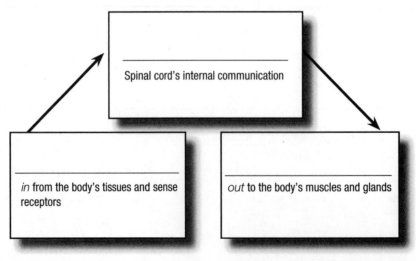

Spinal cord's internal communication

in from the body's tissues and sense receptors

out to the body's muscles and glands

10-2   Answer the questions and complete the chart below.

1. In what ways do the endocrine and nervous systems act similarly? In what ways do they act differently?

2. How does the endocrine system's release of hormones influence us?

3. Use the information from your text and Figure 10.5 to complete the chart of endocrine system structures and functions below.

Structure	Function
Hypothalamus	
	secretes female hormones
Adrenal glands	
	releases growth hormone, oxytocin, and other hormones
	affects metabolism
Testis	
	regulates the level of sugar in the blood
Parathyroid	

4. Why is the pituitary gland referred to as the "master gland"?

After You Read

Module 10 Review

Complete the questions below to see if you have mastered the basics.

1. After placing your hand on a hot stove, pain signals are sent from the sense receptors in your skin through _____ to the spinal cord where the signal is processed by _____ and finally to the muscles in your hand via the _____ , causing you to remove your hand from the stove.

2. When the morning announcements call for you to rise to recite the Pledge of Allegiance, the signal to stand up on your feet is sent by way of which system?

3. The control of your heartbeat is regulated by which system?

4. While taking your first AP® exam, a test that is causing you great anxiety, what physical reactions will your body have due to the sympathetic nervous system?

5. After finishing the AP® Exam and realizing you probably scored a 5 because you worked so hard to prepare this year, what physical reactions will your body have due to the parasympathetic nervous system?

Module 11

Studying the Brain, and Older Brain Structures

Before You Read

Module Summary

Module 11 begins the two-module exploration of brain structures by introducing the more primitive structures of the hind- and mid-brain. The functions of the brainstem structures, and the more evolved limbic system structures, are explained through detailed diagrams and examples. In addition, this module contains a thorough review of the scanning technologies that allow us to view inside the brain.

Before beginning the module, take a moment to read each of the following terms you will encounter. You may wish to make vocabulary cards for each.

Key Terms

lesion	medulla
electroencephalogram (EEG)	thalamus
CT (computed tomography) scan	reticular formation
PET (positron emission tomography) scan	cerebellum
MRI (magnetic resonance imaging)	limbic system
fMRI (functional MRI)	amygdala
brainstem	hypothalamus

While You Read

Complete the charts and answer the questions.

1. What does it mean to lesion the brain? Why is this procedure important in studying the brain?

2. As you learn about each of the methods used to scan the brain, complete the chart below.

Full name of brain scan technology	Abbreviation	Method Used to Produce Image
		electrodes placed on the scalp
	CT	
Positron emission tomography		
		magnetic fields and radio waves
	fMRI	

3. What do each of the brain scanning methods reveal or show us about brain function?

EEG:

CT:

PET:

MRI:

fMRI:

11-2

1. In general, what are the functions of the brainstem structures?

2. Complete the chart of brainstem structures below:

Structure	Function	Mnemonic Device to Remember Structure/Function
Medulla		
Pons		
Thalamus		
Reticular formation		
Cerebellum		

11-3

1. In general, what are the functions of the limbic system structures?

2. Complete the chart of limbic system structures below:

Structure	Function	Mnemonic Device to Remember Structure/Function
Amygdala		
Hippocampus		
Hypothalamus		
Nucleus accumbens		

3. What have experiments revealed about a dopamine-related reward pathway in humans?

☞   Use Figure 11.11 on page 101 to check your two charts above. Combine the information from
the text and the diagram to make sure your chart is as complete as possible.

After You Read

Module 11 Review

Complete the questions below to see if you have mastered the basics.

Terms

_____ **1.** EEG

_____ **2.** CT scan

_____ **3.** PET scan

_____ **4.** MRI

_____ **5.** fMRI

Definitions

A. Shows brain activity by tracking glucose absorption

B. Reveals brain damage through use of X-rays

C. Depicts brain structures through the use of magnetic fields and radio waves

D. Provides an amplified readout of brain waves by using electrodes on the scalp

E. Reveals brain activity and functioning by tracking increased oxygen-laden bloodflow

6. Use your knowledge of the hindbrain and limbic system structures to identify which structure(s) would be involved and what role they would play in the following task/function.

a. punting a football

b. hearing your stepdad call you home from playing outside

c. a cat arching its back and hissing at a potential predator

d. learning a set of new geometry theorems

e. returning again and again to a video game that you are having increased success playing

Multiple Choice

Circle the correct answer.

1. Identify the correct brain structure-function pairing.
   a. amygdala: thirst, sex and hunger
   b. cerebellum: conscious memories
   c. medulla: breathing and heart rate
   d. pons: aggression and fear
   e. hypothalamus: breathing and heart rate

2. In the final seconds of the Georgia-Florida game, the field-goal kicker accurately sends a 55-yard kick into the goal to score and GEORGIA WINS! Most likely, the precision and accuracy of this challenging kick was a result of neural functioning in the
   a. hippocampus
   b. hypothalamus
   c. medulla
   d. cerebellum
   e. amygdala

3. Which of the following senses does not send neural messages through the thalamus?
   a. taste
   b. smell
   c. touch
   d. sight
   e. hearing

4. In the climax of the Alfred Hitchcock thriller, *Psycho,* you are in a state of extreme fear. If viewed on a PET scan, which area of your brain would be bright white (or highly stimulated)?
   a. thalamus
   b. hippocampus
   c. cerebellum
   d. pons
   e. amygdala

5. At the movie theater, you feel a strong urge to eat popcorn and buy a drink. Most likely, this area of your brain is sending neural impulses influencing your thirst and hunger.
   a. hippocampus
   b. nucleus accumbens
   c. thalamus
   d. hypothalamus
   e. amygdala

Module 12

The Cerebral Cortex

Before You Read

Module Summary

Module 12 explores the lobes and association areas of the cerebral cortex. Detailed examples and illustrations elaborate on the motor and sensory functions of our brain's complex control center. The module concludes with a discussion of plasticity.

Before beginning the module, take a moment to read each of the following terms and names you will encounter. You may wish to make vocabulary cards for each.

Key Terms

cerebral cortex

glial cells (glia)

frontal lobes

parietal lobes

occipital lobes

temporal lobes

motor cortex

somatosensory cortex

association areas

plasticity

neurogenesis

Key Names

Paul Broca

Carl Wernicke

While You Read

Answer the following questions.

12-1

1. In general, what are the functions of the various cortex regions?

2. How do glial cells support neurons?

3. What are the four lobes of the cortex and what basic function does each serve?

4. A homunculus (literally meaning "little man") is a scaled figure used to illustrate physiological functions. In Figure 12.2, a somatosensory and motor homunculus is drawn to explain which functions of the body take up more or less space on the cortex. Using that diagram, answer the following questions:

   a. Which area(s) of the body is/are depicted as overly large in the motor cortex shown on the left of the diagram?

   b. Why would these structures need greater space in the motor cortex?

   c. What area(s) of the body is/are depicted as overly large in the somatosensory cortex shown on the right of the diagram?

   d. Why would these structures need greater space in the somatosensory cortex?

5. In which lobe is the motor cortex located? How does the location of the motor cortex help us to better understand the function?

6. In which lobe is the somatosensory cortex located? How does the location of the somatosensory cortex help us to better understand the function?

7. Why do you think the motor and somatosensory cortexes are located adjacent to one another?

8. In which lobe is the visual cortex located? How about the auditory cortex?

9. List three of the varied functions of the association areas.

10. How might the functions of #9 assist in debunking the myth that humans use only a minor percentage of our brains?

11. How does the case of Phineas Gage illustrate the function of the frontal lobe?

12. What role do Broca's area and Wernicke's area play in language?

12-2

1. What is plasticity and what are two instances in which it could occur?

2. What is the significance of plasticity?

3. Give two examples from the text of the brain's ability to reorganize or reassign brain functions.

4. How is neurogenesis different from plasticity?

After You Read

Module 12 Review

Complete the matching questions below to see if you have mastered the basics.

Terms

_____ 1. cerebral cortex

_____ 2. glial cells

_____ 3. motor cortex

_____ 4. somatosensory cortex

_____ 5. association areas

_____ 6. plasticity

_____ 7. neurogenesis

Definitions

A. Area at the rear of the frontal lobes that controls voluntary movements

B. The body's ultimate control and processing center that covers the cerebral hemispheres

C. Area at the front of the parietal lobes that processes body touch and movement sensations

D. Areas of the cortex involved in higher mental functions such as learning and speaking

E. Cells that support, nourish, and protect neurons

F. The brain's ability to reorganize after damage or build new pathways based on experience

G. The formation of new neurons

Label the lobes and identify the brain's hemispheres in the cross-section. Then, briefly describe each lobe's function below.

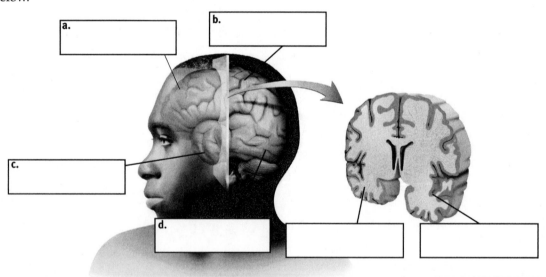

a.

b.

c.

d.

Module 13

Brain Hemisphere Organization and the Biology of Consciousness

Before You Read

Module Summary

Module 13 discusses the early and now classic work in split-brain patients that yielded vast information about the lateralization of the brain hemispheres. Detailed graphics and diagrams assist in conveying the key aspects of right- and left-brain functions. The module closes with the biology of consciousness and the explanation of dual processing.

Before beginning the module, take a moment to read each of the following terms and names you will encounter. You may wish to make vocabulary cards for each.

Key Terms	Key Names
corpus callosum	Michael Gazzaniga
split brain	Roger Sperry
consciousness	
cognitive neuroscience	
dual processing	

While You Read

Answer the questions and complete the charts below.

1. What is lateralization, and why is it important in the way our brain functions?

2. What is meant by the term *split brain*? Is it correct to refer to this condition as "having two brains"?

3. Fill in the chart below with some of the tasks served by each hemisphere of the brain. As you continue to read this module, return to this chart and add new information as you learn it.

Left Hemisphere Functions	Right Hemisphere Functions

4. Why do the tasks listed above lend themselves to the myth that we are "right-" or "left-"brained? Using the information regarding the brain structures and association areas you learned in the last two modules, address why this myth is erroneous.

5. What role does the corpus callosum play in relation to the two hemispheres?

6. Using Figures 13.2 and 13.3, and your knowledge of brain structures, explain step-by-step why Gazzaniga's patients were able to:

   a. say the word "ART"

   b. point to the word "HE" with their left hand

7. What is the relationship between handedness and speech processing?

8. How does split-brain research help us to understand the functions of our two brain hemispheres?

13-2

1. How is cognitive neuroscience changing the way we understand mental processes?

2. How does consciousness help humans survive?

3. What is dual processing? Give an example from the text of dual processing. Give an example from your own life of dual processing.

4. How does the example of the hollow face illusion (Figure 13.7) demonstrate dual processing?

After You Read

Module 13 Review

Answer the questions below to see if you have mastered the basics.

1. Jonathon undergoes an MRI and his doctor discovers a tumor in the left hemisphere of his brain. Which of the following functions may be impacted by this tumor?
    a. Jonathon's perceptual abilities
    b. the control of the left side of Jonathon's body
    c. Jonathon's ability to speak
    d. Johathon's ability to understand subtleties and inferences in literature or poetry
    e. Jonathon's understanding or "sense of self"

2. Myung Li was involved in a car collision and suffered severe injuries to the right side of her head. Her doctor has been giving her a battery of tests to determine to what extent her various functions are affected. In a remote-associates test in which Myung Li views three words (such as butter, fire and fruit) and is asked to produce a fourth word that would be able to pair with each of the three words to produce a new word, Myung Li is likely to
    a. modulate her speech when producing the answer.
    b. be able to quickly draw a picture of the word with her left hand.
    c. quickly produce the required word.
    d. be able to rapidly write the answer with her left hand.
    e. be unable to make the inference necessary to produce the word.

3. In Michael Gazzaniga's classic "HEART" experiment with split-brain patients, he found that patients were able to
    a. use their right hand to point to the word "ART."
    b. use their right hand to point to the word "HE."
    c. verbally express the word "HE."
    d. verbally express the word "HEART."
    e. use their left hand to point to the word "ART."

4. In a controlled replication of Gazzaniga's experiment, when shown an image of a frog in the left visual field and an image of a football in the right visual field, split-brain patients were able to correctly
    a. use their left hand to point to a picture of a football.
    b. use their right hand to point to a picture of a frog.
    c. use their left hand to point to a picture of a frog.
    d. use either hand to point to both the frog and the football.
    e. verbally express the word "FROG."

5. In order to reduce or eliminate epileptic seizures in patients, surgeons Philip Vogel and Joseph Bogen severed
    a. the amygdala.
    b. the corpus callosum.
    c. the hypothalamus.
    d. the limbic system.
    e. the cerebellum.

Module 14

Behavior Genetics: Predicting Individual Differences

Before You Read

Module Summary

Module 14 defines genes, and describes how behavior geneticists explain our individual differences. The potential uses of molecular genetics research are explored and the concept of heritability is explained. The interaction of heredity and environment and the relationship of heritability to individuals and groups are discussed.

Before beginning the module, take a moment to read each of the following terms you will encounter. You may wish to make vocabulary cards for each.

Key Terms

behavior genetics

environment

chromosomes

DNA (deoxyribonucleic acid)

genes

genome

identical twins (monozygotic)

fraternal twins (dizygotic)

molecular genetics

heritability

interaction

epigenetics

While You Read

Answer the following questions/prompts.

14-1

1. Using key terms from the text, complete the three analogies below:

   a. Your book of life: _____

   b. _____ : the chapters in your book

   c. words in the chapter: _____

2. Using #1 as a model, create your own analogy for the relationship between genes, chromosomes, and DNA.

3. Genes can either be _____ or _____ . What does this mean?

4. Why are psychologists interested in variations found at particular gene sites in humans?

5. Identical twins form from a _____ fertilized egg cell and are _____ identical. What are two important qualifications to the statement above?

6. Fraternal twins form from _____ fertilized eggs. They share a _____ _____ but are genetically no more similar than _____ _____ .

7. How are identical twins behaviorally more similar than fraternal twins?

8. Discuss the findings of Bouchard's twin studies.

9. What is a criticism leveled at Bouchard's studies?

10. According to the text, what is the rather counterintuitive finding regarding adoptive families versus biological families?

11. The environment shared by a family's children has virtually _____ discernible impact on their personalities.

   a. Describe what is meant by this statement, and why people are often surprised by this finding.

   b. In what ways does the statement above seem true for your family, extended family, or friends and their siblings?

14-2

1. What is molecular genetics? Why is it important to the study of human behavior?

2. What are some ways in which DNA gathering techniques are being used to help humans?

14-3

1. How is heritability defined?

2. As environments become more similar, heredity as a source of difference becomes

   _____ .

   Why is this the case?

14-4

1. "Heredity deals the cards; environment plays the hand." –C. Brewer, 1990 (p. 131)

   How does Charles Brewer's quote above explain the interaction between heredity and environment?

2. How is the example of two babies born with different genetic personalities used to explain how heredity and environment work together?

3. What does it mean to say that genes "react"? How might this cause **differences between traits of identical** twins?

4. What example from your own life can you give to show how heredity and environment work together

After You Read

Module 14 Review

Complete the questions below by noting whether the answer is *high* or *low* to see if you have mastered the basics of heritability.

1. Conor and Aidan, fraternal twins raised in the same home, have **many traits in common.** Both boys are outgoing, interested in building puzzles and playing soccer. However, Conor is compliant and easy-going, while Aidan is stubborn and rigid. Psychologists would gauge the heritability of this personality difference as _____ .
high or low

2. Students attending Japanese schools are often reported as having higher math and science scores than students attending American schools. The heritability of these math and science differences would likely be _____ .
high or low

3. Olivia and Dantelle are identical twins that were separated at birth and raised in two different homes. Olivia grew up in Georgia and Dantelle was raised in New York City. They each enjoy unflavored yogurt, pickles and horseradish, and both laugh with a distinctive throaty sound. Yet, Olivia is curious and inquisitive, while Dantelle seems uninterested in learning new things. The heritability of their personality differences would likely be _____ .
high or low

4. True or False? As environments become more similar, heritability of **differences between groups** from those environments increases.

5. True or False? If differences among people are mostly attributable to genes, then the heritability is closer to 0.

Module 15

Evolutionary Psychology: Understanding Human Nature

Before You Read

Module Summary

Module 15 discusses the concept of natural selection and adaptation in an evolutionary context and explores some of the work evolutionary psychologists do. The criticisms of evolutionary psychology and the responses from those that work in the field are presented. Lastly, the biopsychosocial approach to explaining behavior and mental processes is presented and explained.

Before beginning the module, take a moment to read each of the following terms and names you will encounter. You may wish to make vocabulary cards for each.

Key Terms

evolutionary psychology

natural selection

mutation

Key Name

Charles Darwin

While You Read

Answer the following questions/prompts.

15-1

1. How were researchers Belyaev and Trot able to produce domesticated foxes?

2. What are the larger implications of Belyaev and Trot's study?

3.

> No more than 5 percent of the genetic differences among humans arise from population group differences. Some 95 percent of genetic variation exists within populations. (Rosenberg et al, 2002 in Myers, p. 136)

    a. How does the text's author explain the statement above using the examples of Icelandic villagers and Kenyans?

    b. How might this statement be explained using a different group, for example, males and females?

4. How do contemporary scientists feel about Darwin's theory of natural selection?

5. What is the "second Darwinian revolution" and why is it significant?

6. How does evolutionary psychology explain behavior tendencies?

15-2

1. What arguments do evolutionary psychologists make that support men's increased interest in sex?

2. What arguments do evolutionary psychologists make that support women's increased interest in partnering and pairing?

3. What is significant about these presumed gender differences in mating preferences?

15-3

1. List three criticisms of evolutionary psychology.

15-4

1. Using Figure 15.1, discuss the three influences on individual development according to the biopsychosocial model.

2. Using the trait of aggressiveness, list possible

   a. biological components:

   b. social components:

   c. psychological components:

2. Why do you think the text author included this section in this module?

After You Read

Module 15 Review

Complete the matching questions below to see if you have mastered the basics.

Terms or Names

_____ **1.** evolutionary psychology

_____ **2.** natural selection

_____ **3.** mutation

_____ **4.** biopsychosocial approach

_____ **5.** Charles Darwin

Definitions or Descriptions

A. Evolutionary theorist

B. The study of the gradual change over time of behavior and the mind

C. A random error in gene application that leads to a change

D. The principle that inherited traits that contribute to reproduction and survival will most likely be passed on to succeeding generations

E. The belief that we are products of our genes, our environment, and our psychological decisions

✓ **Check Yourself**   Now that you have mastered the basics, work through the problems below to see if you can *synthesize, evaluate,* and *analyze* what you have learned.

> Samuel is a cross-country runner for your school and has qualified for the state cross-country meet. He has been training for years and is in top shape for the event. In order for Samuel to successfully perform at the meet, several key biophysiological functions will occur simultaneously—from the neural impulses his brain sends and the release of key neurotransmitters, to the structures of the central and peripheral nervous systems and endocrine systems.

1. Describe the neural transmission occurring in Samuel's body while he is warming up for the race. Be sure to include how a message moves through each part of a neuron and how messages communicate between neurons.

2. What neurotransmitters are likely being released at the synapse while Sam is competing at the meet?

3. Choose four brain structures and discuss how each structure is active in Samuel as he runs. Be sure to include how these particular brain structures are associated with Samuel and the cross-county meet.

4. What function are the three types of neurons serving as Samuel hears the signal to start the race?

   a. sensory (afferent) neurons:

   b. interneurons:

   c. motor (efferent) neurons:

5. What impact is each of the subdivisions of the nervous system having on Samuel as he warms up, competes, and cools down?

   a. somatic:

   b. sympathetic:

   c. parasympathetic:

6. Which glands of the endocrine system are active while Samuel competes, and which hormones do they release to help Samuel achieve his personal best time?

Before You Move On

Use the checklist below to verify your understanding of the unit's main points.

☐ Do I know the structures and functions of each part of a neuron?

☐ Do I know how neural transmission works within and between neurons?

☐ Can I accurately describe the processes involved in the action potential?

Do I understand the influence of drugs on neurotransmitters?

    ☐ Reuptake?

    ☐ Agonists?

    ☐ Antagonists?

☐ Do I know the divisions and subdivisions of the nervous system?

☐ Do I know the structures of the hind-, mid- and fore-brain and their functions?

☐ Can I name and identify the functions of the lobes of the brain and the cortexes included within each?

☐ Do I understand hemisphere lateralization and the information revealed from research on split-brain patients?

☐ Do I know the role of neuroplasticity in brain injury?

☐ Do I understand heritability?

☐ Do I understand how heredity and environment work together to drive behavior?

☐ Do I understand the evolutionary nature of our brain's development?

☐ Can I identify key contributors in the field of biopsychological research?

Unit IV
Sensation and Perception

Overview

Unit IV explains the sensory structures and physical mechanisms by which we take in information from our environment and attempt to make sense of it. Perceptual constancies and depth-perception cues are presented and numerous examples and illustrations aid with understanding. The unit provides detailed anatomy of the eye and ear, and reviews the processes by which the nose, tongue, skin receptors, and body positioning systems pick up sensory stimuli and convert it to electrical information for the brain. A distinction between sensation and perception is made and illustrated numerous times throughout the unit.

Modules

16 Basic Principles of Sensation and Perception

17 Influences on Perception

18 Vision

19 Visual Organization and Interpretation

20 Hearing

21 The Other Senses

Tip #4
Distribute Study Time and Fine Tune Focus

This unit begins by discussing the limitations of attention and the numerous distractions that impede our ability to focus on multiple tasks. Studying is a task that requires significant focus. Learning to focus your attention on the material you need to learn is a key strategy in the toolbox of academic success. You can increase attention to the task at hand by first locating a quiet space that you can dedicate to studying. Make certain to leave your cell phone off and out of sight and your computer off as well. Incoming texts and the lure of the Internet can be too tempting to pass on while studying! Set a time limit for your first study session, since a shorter time of 20–30 minutes is more productive than a longer time of 1–2 hours. At the end of the first session, step away from the material and treat yourself to either a walk around the block, a healthy snack and a glass of water, or 15 minutes of texting and checking in with friends. Then return to another study session of 30 minutes or so. You will learn in an upcoming unit about distributed practice, a learning strategy that breaks studying into smaller blocks over a longer period of time. Studies have shown us that we *learn better* and *retain more new information* when we break studying up into smaller batches over time. Cramming is OUT! Focus, quiet, short repeated study sessions and a small incentive are IN!

Module 16

Basic Principles of Sensation and Perception

Before You Read

Module Summary

Module 16 lays out the difference between sensation and perception and introduces the concepts of top-down and bottom-up processing. Multiple phenomena that influence our ability to attend to stimuli are discussed and studies of multi-tasking and distracted driving are used to drive home the point that human attention is a little-understood and complex process. The principles of thresholds and signal detection, as well as the development of Weber's Law and sensory adaptation, are reviewed.

Before beginning the module, take a moment to read each of the following terms and names you will encounter. You may wish to make vocabulary cards for each.

Key Terms

sensation

perception

bottom-up processing

top-down processing

selective attention

inattentional blindness

change blindness

transduction

psychophysics

absolute threshold

signal detection theory

subliminal

priming

difference threshold

Weber's law

sensory adaptation

Key Names

Gustav Fechner

Ernst Weber

While You Read

Answer the following questions/prompts.

16-1

1. How does the unit opening story of Heather Sellers explain why we study sensation and perception in psychology?

2. What is the difference between sensation and perception?

3. Define and give a real-life example of bottom-up processing.

4. Define and give a real-life example of top-down processing.

5. How do the processes of sensation and perception work together when we process from the bottom-up? How about top-down?

16-2

1. How does selective attention work?

2. How does the cocktail party effect function as an example of selective attention?

3. Discuss the findings and implications of two of the studies on the relationship between attention and accidents.

   a.

   b.

4. What do each of the following phenomena tell us about how humans attend to experiences around them? One has been filled in for you to get you started.

   a. pop out:

      Sometimes humans don't choose to attend to stimuli, it just "pops out," draws our eye (or ear) and demands our attention.

   b. inattentional blindness:

   c. change blindness:

   d. choice blindness:

6. Many people today claim to be "multitaskers," capable of processing multiple tasks at one time. Use your knowledge of this section on attention to respond to that claim.

16-3 .

1. What are the three steps basic to our sensory systems?

2. Define transduction.

3. What does the field of psychophysics research?

16-4 .

1. How might an eye doctor test for your absolute threshold for observing light?

2. Other than stimulus strength, what additional factor determines whether we will detect a sound, sight, taste, touch or smell stimulus? What is meant by that? Give an example.

3. What do signal detection theorists try to understand about human sensation? Be sure to elaborate your answer.

4. The textbook uses an example of detecting a text message to describe signal theory. Give an example from your own life of a stimulus or signal you are more likely to detect (hear, see, smell, and so on) than a friend or parent might be and why you would be more likely to detect it.

5. What determines if a signal is subliminal?

6. How does priming work? Give an example from your own life of a time you have primed someone else or been primed yourself to perceive stimuli in your environment.

7. What is a difference threshold and why is it important to humans?

8. What does Weber's law tell us about human perception?

9. If Jenny were lifting twenty pounds and added two pounds to her load, she would notice that it was heavier. According to Weber's law, how much weight would Jenny have to add to forty pounds of weight to notice the same difference?

16-5 .

1. Define and give an example from the text of sensory adaptation. Give an example from your own life of sensory adaptation.

2. Why can't a classmate who wears a lot of cologne notice that they are doing so?

3. How does sensory adaptation explain why television programming has the power to grab our attention?

After You Read

Module 16 Review

Answer the following questions to see if you have mastered the basics.

Identify whether each of the situations below represents the use of top-down (T) or bottom-up (B) processing:

_____ 1. A preschool child gives her father a picture she drew that day and he tries to decide what she has drawn by examining the lines of the picture.

_____ 2. A literature teacher instructs her students to locate the examples of sexism in the poem she assigns for homework.

_____ 3. On a long-distance road trip with his family, Joachim occupies himself by reading the license plates from passing cars. When he sees the plate "3DUC8R," Joachim quickly shouts out "EDUCATOR"!

_____ 4. An alien visitor to our planet takes detailed notes of "multi-sized boxes moving on four circular wheels" and suggests to his commander that they might be tools of communication on our planet.

_____ 5. A classmate shows you a hidden image 3D visual puzzle and tells you to find the fish.

Multiple Choice

Circle the correct answer.

1. If you can just notice the difference in brightness between two flashlights when one is using a 10-watt bulb and the other a 15-watt bulb, which of the following bulb wattages could you discriminate from a 100-watt bulb?
   a. 90-watt
   b. 120-watt
   c. 75-watt
   d. 60-watt
   e. 150-watt

2. When you enter your new teacher's classroom for the first time you take note of the ticking of the second hand on his wall clock and find it annoying. After a period of time in the classroom, you realize you are no longer hearing the tick-tick-tick of the clock. This occurrence is best explained by
   a. Weber's law.
   b. the signal detection theory.
   c. sensory adaptation.
   d. the difference threshold.
   e. the absolute threshold.

3. Ming-li's parents have to go out of town and are leaving her alone in the house for the first time. Being quite nervous, Ming-li is not at all pleased with staying alone. She hears every faint creak, whispered moan, soft whine, and shudder the house makes and is convinced each is an intruder. Her response to these noises is best explained by
   a. the signal detection theory.
   b. priming.
   c. absolute threshold.
   d. transduction.
   e. sensory adaptation.

4. While attending a magic show at your school's pep assembly, you are amazed at the skill and expertise of the tricks. Whether she makes the school mascot disappear, identifies your secret card from the deck, or arranges for your watch to come off your wrist, you are amazed and in awe of her talent. Your friend, an AP® Psychology student, recognizes that the magician has just made use of
   a. pop-outs.
   b. choice blindness.
   c. change blindness.
   d. inattentional blindness.
   e. transduction.

5. At a very crowded and noisy Homecoming Dance you hear your best friend calling your name from across the room. Your ability to hear your name in this situation is best explained by
   a. sensory adaptation.
   b. the cocktail party effect.
   c. priming.
   d. the difference threshold.
   e. transduction.

Module 17

Influences on Perception

Before You Read

Module Summary

Module 17 explains how our expectations, contexts, emotions and motivation influence our perception. The module also contains a lengthy discussion of extrasensory perception and the conclusions of researchers who have put ESP to the test.

Before beginning the module, take a moment to read each of the following terms you will encounter. You may wish to make vocabulary cards for each.

Key Terms

perceptual set
extrasensory perception
parapsychology

While You Read

Answer the following questions/prompts.

17-1

1. How does perceptual set relate to top-down processing (Module 16-1)?

2. How does the cartoon of the motorcycle officer on page 163 explain perceptual set?

3. Give an example from the text and one from your own life of perceptual set.

4. How do context effects relate to top-down processing (Module 16-1)?

5. How do our expectations, emotions, and motivations influence our perceptions?

 You have just learned more information about top-down and bottom-up processing. Recall the tip from Unit II, "Make Your Learning Fluid." Revisit Module 16-1, questions #3 and #4 now and add any additional information you have learned from this module to your response in that module. If you have additional examples to add, do that now.

17-2

1. Describe the relationship between sensation and perception that underlies a belief in ESP.

2. Cite research from the text that explains the scientific opinion regarding the existence of ESP.

After You Read

Module 17 Review

Answer the following questions to see if you have mastered the basics.

Discuss how perceptual set might impact how you perceive each of the following. The first one has been done for you.

1. Moviegoers burst into laughter when a black-leather-clad, large man on a Harley Davidson motorcycle shows up on the screen and begins to sing excerpts from the musical *The Sound of Music.*

   People assume, stereotypically, that motorcycle riders will not be familiar with musicals so they find it funny when their perception doesn't match the depiction in the film.

2. Your friend tells you that he learned all about backward masking of subliminal messages in rock songs and plays a few selections for you. He says you can clearly hear the word "Satan" and "devil" in the music.

3. You have heard advertising touting the nutritional benefits of a name-brand dog food and have purchased it for your puppy. After a few months of having your dog eat it, you tell your friends how healthy and full-of-life your dog seems.

4. You have asked your father repeatedly over the last few months if you can use the car to go meet friends. Despite being denied over and over, you approach him again and ask for the car. Expecting him to say *no* again, you actually hear him say *no* and walk off upset. Your father, puzzled, asks why you are upset that he finally said, "*Yes*, you can use the car."

5. Your older brother wants to make a chocolate dessert for your Stepmom's birthday, and you eagerly offer to help. The recipe calls for unsweetened baker's chocolate and you decide to trick your 5-year-old stepsister by offering her a taste of the whipped chocolate in the bowl. She excitedly dips her finger in!

6. A bank robber, using only his thumb and forefinger in his pocket as a weapon, is able to successfully rob multiple banks before he is caught.

Module 18

Vision

Module Summary

Module 18 provides very thorough coverage of the theories, physiology, and physics of vision. Physical properties of light waves and detailed drawings of the anatomy of the eye and visual processing systems of the brain explain the mechanisms by which we see color, recognize faces, and process visual information.

Before beginning the module, take a moment to read each of the following terms and names you will encounter. You may wish to make vocabulary cards for each.

Key Terms		Key Names
wavelength	cones	David Hubel
hue	optic nerve	Torsten Wiesel
intensity	blind spot	
pupil	fovea	
iris	feature detectors	
lens	parallel processing	
retina	Young-Helmholtz trichromatic	
accommodation	(three-color) theory	
rods	opponent-process theory	

While You Read

Answer the following questions, and complete the charts and diagrams below.

18-1

1. How large is the portion of light visible to humans related to the spectrum of electromagnetic energy?

2. What are the two physical characteristics of light and how do they determine our awareness of hue and intensity?

3. Trace the path of light through the eye as it enters the cornea, is transduced into neural energy, and ends in the visual cortex of the occipital lobe. Use Figures 18.3 and 18.4 as well as the information you learned in Module 12-1 to help with your diagram. Additionally, you may find you need some information from the beginning of Module 18-2.

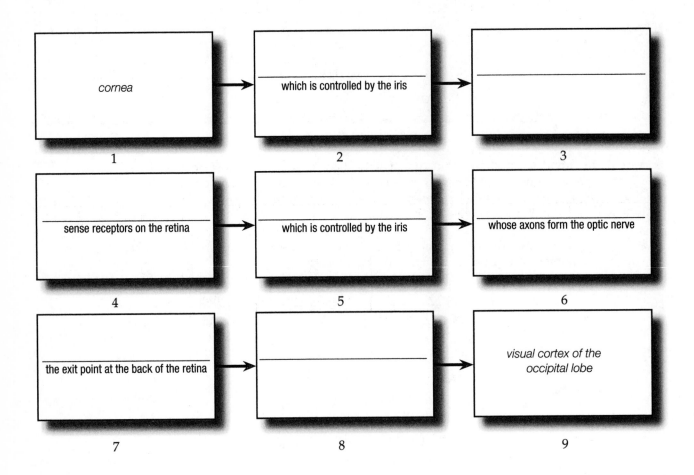

cornea	which is controlled by the iris	————————
1	2	3
———————— sense receptors on the retina	———————— which is controlled by the iris	whose axons form the optic nerve
4	5	6
———————— the exit point at the back of the retina	————————	*visual cortex of the occipital lobe*
7	8	9

4. Complete the chart below, using your own words to describe the function of each.

Structure	Function
cornea	
pupil	
iris	
lens	

Structure	Function
retina	
rods	
cones	
bipolar cells	
ganglion cells	
optic nerve	
blind spot	
fovea	

5. Why does human vision have a blind spot?

6. How does vision in the fovea relate to placement and quantity of rods and cones? How might the experience of nocturnal animals be different from humans with regard to their visual system's physiology?

7. Name three ways in which rods and cones differ.

18-2

1. Where are feature detectors located, and what is their function? How do feature detectors work together to portray a "whole" image?

2. Using fMRI scans, how are we able to tell if a person is looking at a "shoe, chair or face?"

3. How does parallel processing help us analyze a visual scene? How would the four subdimensions mentioned in the text allow you to see and perceive a person walking toward you on the street?

4. How might parallel processing be related to blindsight (described in Module 13)?

18-3

1. Discuss how the Young-Helmholtz trichromatic theory explains how we see and perceive color. Then discuss how it explains color blindness.

2. Explain how Hering's opponent-process theory adds to the explanation of how we see and perceive color.

3. Concerning the phenomenon of color blindness,

   a. what is the most common deficiency? _____

   b. what subgroup of humans is most impacted? _____

   c. what percentage of people are impacted? _____

4. Why do we see an afterimage when we look away at a white piece of paper after staring at a yellow and green flag, as in Figure 18.12?

After You Read

Module 18 Review

Complete the questions below to see if you have mastered the basics.

Terms

_____ 1. pupil

_____ 2. lens

_____ 3. cones

_____ 4. fovea

_____ 5. blind spot

_____ 6. iris

_____ 7. cornea

_____ 8. optic nerve

_____ 9. retina

_____ 10. rods

Definitions

A. receptor cells that are concentrated near the center of the retina and detect fine detail and color

B. protects the eye and bends light to provide focus

C. the central point in the retina, around which the eye's cones cluster

D. the light-sensitive inner surface of the eye containing the receptor cells

E. carries neural impulses from the eye to the brain

F. transparent structure behind the pupil that changes shape to help focus images on the retina

G. the point at which the optic nerve leaves the eye, no receptor cells are located there

H. receptor cells that detect black, white and grey and are necessary for peripheral and night vision

I. ring of muscle tissue that forms the colored portion of the eye and controls the size of the pupil opening

J. adjustable opening in the center of the eye through which light enters

Multiple-Choice and Short Answer Questions

1. Light waves with lower frequencies around 700 nanometers will produce which colors?

2. Frequency is to amplitude as _____ is to _____.

3. Why are cones, rather than rods, better able to detect fine detail?
   a. Cones are significantly more numerous than rods.
   b. Cones function better than rods in dim light.
   c. Cones have a direct connection to bipolar cells, whereas rods share bipolar cells with other rods.
   d. Cones are placed throughout the retina whereas rods are primarily concentrated along the fovea.
   e. Cones are placed around the blind spot whereas rods are concentrated within the blind spot.

4. In order to focus near and far objects on the retina, the lens changes its shape through a process called
   a. parallel processing.
   b. feature detecting.
   c. transduction.
   d. accommodation.
   e. after-imaging.

5. The Young-Helmholtz theory suggests that humans perceive color through
   a. cones on the retina that contain three different color receptors
   b. color receptors that are inhibited or stimulated by pairs of colors
   c. the focusing of the light wave along the section of the retina containing the most rods
   d. the pulses of electromagnetic energy that produce gamma rays
   e. the transduction of infrared waves in the visual cortex

Label the structures of the eye in the diagram below.

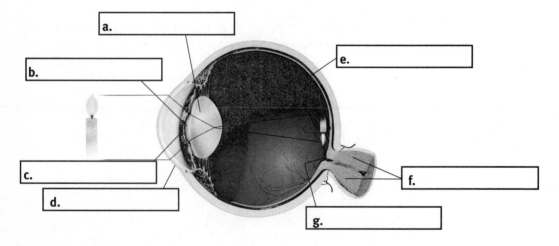

Module 19

Visual Organization and Interpretation

Module Summary

Module 19 reviews Gestalt principles of perceptual organization and discusses how depth cues, both monocular and binocular, are used to perceive the world in three dimensions. The module also introduces the way in which perceptual constancies aid in organization of visual information and the research on restored and restricted vision as it relates to the impact of experience on perception.

Before beginning the module, take a moment to read each of the following terms you will encounter. You may wish to make vocabulary cards for each.

Key Terms

gestalt	retinal disparity
figure-ground	monocular cues
grouping	phi phenomenon
depth perception	perceptual constancy
visual cliff	color constancy
binocular cues	perceptual adaptation

While You Read

Answer the following questions, and complete the charts and diagrams below.

19-1

1. How does the German word *gestalt* help explain how humans organize their perceptions?

2. How does the illustration of the Necker Cube in Figure 19.1 illustrate the difference between sensation and perception?

3. What is meant by the fundamental truth: *Our brain does more than register information about the world?* (p. 182)

4. Give an example from the text and one from your own life of figure and ground.

5. What are three examples of the principles we use to group stimuli? Explain and provide a real-life, nongeometric example of each.

   a.

   b.

   c.

19-2

1. Describe how depth perception helps us organize sensory input.

2. Referring to the work of Gibson and Walk or Campos et al., discuss our general understanding about the age and onset of depth perception in the human species. How does it differ in various animal species?

3. What insight can the visual cliff study give us regarding the nature–nurture debate?

4. How does retinal disparity occur and how does it help us perceive the depth of objects in our environment?

5. Explain how monocular cues differ from binocular cues. When might we use monocular cues rather than binocular cues?

6. How does the phi phenomenon create the perception of motion? Give an example of this phenomenon.

7. Using Figure 19.5, complete the chart below with the mechanism by which each monocular cue operates and a hand-drawn example of the illusion it creates. Your ability to draw is not essential—even a basic stick figure drawing can convey that you understand the cues.

Monocular Depth Cue	How It Helps Us Perceive Depth	Illustration
relative height		
relative motion		
relative size		
linear perspective		
interposition		
light and shadow		

19-3

1. Why is perceptual constancy referred to as a top-down process?

2. Complete the chart below. One has been filled in for you as an example.

Perceptual Constancy	How It Aids Our Perception of the Sensory Information From Our World
color	
brightness	
shape	*We perceive the form of familiar objects as constant even while our retinas receive changing images of them. The neurons in the visual cortex learn to associate different views of an object. A door opening seems to be changing shape, but we still perceive it as rectangular.*
size	

3. How do perceptual constancies help us organize our sensations into meaningful perceptions?

19-4

1. Explain how research on restored vision and sensory restriction helps us understand the importance of experience on perception.

2. What is meant by a "critical period," and how does the research on sensory restriction stress its importance?

3. How does the concept of perceptual adaptation inform our understanding of how humans perceive the sensations in our environment?

4. What evidence does the text provide to suggest that we can adapt to new ways of interacting with the world?

After You Read

Module 19 Review

Answer the following questions to see if you have mastered the basics.

> Use this story to answer questions 1–3. Maria is enrolled in a research project to determine how humans perceive depth. She is shown a set of 3 images and is asked to describe locations of people and objects in the images. Maria will be using a variety of monocular cues to detect depth in the images and respond to the researcher. Using the list of monocular cues below, discuss which are providing Maria with the information she needs to detect depth in each of the images and how it is functioning. Be sure to also discuss the "how" of your answer.

relative height	relative size	relative motion
interposition	linear perspective	light and shadow

1. Maria is shown the circle and square below. How would she describe the relationship of the square to the circle?

2. Maria is shown the two 3 ½ inch cups on a table below. How would she use two cues to describe the relationship of cup A to cup B?

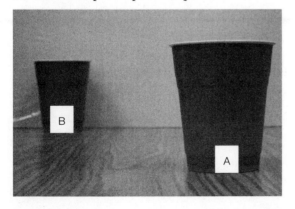

3. Maria is shown a long hallway of student lockers and is asked to imagine she was standing at Point A and then again at Point B while her friend remained at Point A. How would she describe her position in the hallway in relation to her friend in both instances?

friend

4. How would you discriminate figure from ground in the following instances?

   a. You are looking for a classmate in the cafeteria at lunch and remember she was wearing a red sweatshirt.

   b. You are listening intently for sounds that your newborn baby brother is upset.

   c. You are trying to identify the musical instruments used in a particular piece of music.

   d. You are trying to identify leaf types for your botany class.

   e. You are hoping to run into the boy you want to ask to Homecoming as you walk through the crowded halls during passing period.

Module 20

Hearing

Module Summary

Module 20 is a thorough discussion of the theories and physics of audition. The physical characteristics of sound waves and the mechanisms by which the structures of the ear process sound are explained in great detail. A distinction between types of hearing loss and an explanation of how we locate directionality of sound conclude the module.

Before beginning the module, take a moment to read each of the following terms and names you will encounter. You may wish to make vocabulary cards for each.

Key Terms

audition	sensorineural hearing loss
frequency	conduction hearing loss
pitch	cochlear implant
middle ear	place theory
cochlea	frequency theory
inner ear	

While You Read

Answer the following questions, and complete the chart below.

20-1

1. Discuss why David Myers' story of his mother's (and his own) hearing loss helps us to understand why we study audition in a psychology class?

2. Define the two physical characteristics of sound, and identify how they determine our awareness of loudness and pitch.

3. Using Figure 20.1, trace the path of sound waves through the ear beginning with the outer ear and ending with the auditory cortex of the temporal lobe.

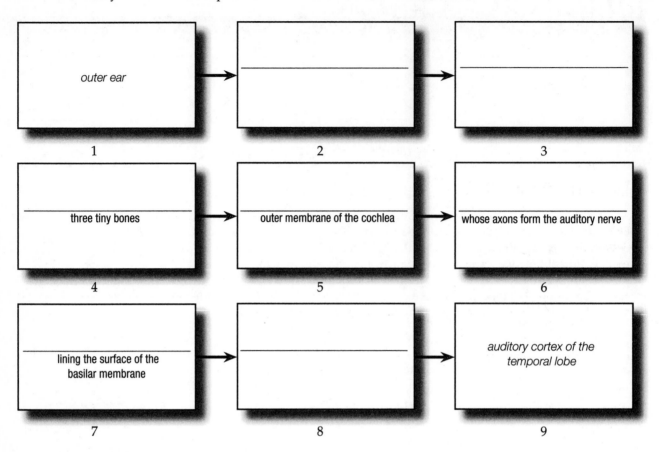

outer ear	_____	_____
1	2	3
_____ three tiny bones	outer membrane of the cochlea _____	_____ whose axons form the auditory nerve
4	5	6
_____ lining the surface of the basilar membrane	_____	auditory cortex of the temporal lobe
7	8	9

4. Complete the chart below, using your own words to describe the function of each

Structure	Function
eardrum	
ossicles (three tiny bones of the middle ear)	
oval window	

Structure	Function
cochlea	
basilar membrane	
auditory nerve	
semicircular canals	

5. Distinguish between sensorineural hearing loss and conductive hearing loss.

6. How might the different issues involved in hearing loss impact the treatment of each of these respective issues?

7. Consider Figure 20.2 and a typical day in your life. Estimate the highest decibel and source of sound you are exposed to on a daily basis.

8. In what way do the limitations of cochlear implants add to the explanation of the critical period theory discussed in Module 19-4?

20-2

1. How does von Helmholtz's place theory explain how we discriminate pitch?

2. How does the frequency theory suggest an alternative to the explanation of how we discriminate pitch?

3. Describe how the volley principle addresses the limitations of neural firing when explaining how we hear pitch.

20-3

1. How might the placement of our ears alongside our head make it difficult to hear sounds coming from certain locations? Explain.

2. How might our ability to locate sounds be different if we had one ear above our nose, as suggested by David Myers?

3. Discuss how the physical characteristics of sound, along with our own body's anatomy, works to help us determine directionality of sound.

After You Read

Module 20 Review

Complete the questions below to see if you have mastered the basics.

1. Frequency is to pitch as _____ is to _____ .
   a. amplitude; loudness
   b. wavelength; amplitude
   c. loudness; wavelength
   d. sound; light
   e. height; length

2. An older man diagnosed with sensorineural hearing loss most likely
   a. has a fracture in the bones of the middle ear.
   b. has a perforation on the eardrum.
   c. has wax buildup in the auditory canal.
   d. has spent too much time listening to high decibel sounds.
   e. has an ear infection.

3. What is the correct path of sound through the ear to the brain?
   a. stirrup, cochlea, basilar membrane, auditory nerve, auditory canal, eardrum
   b. auditory canal, eardrum, the bones of the middle ear, cochlea, basilar membrane
   c. eardrum, cochlea, auditory nerve, anvil, auditory canal
   d. auditory canal, basilar membrane, cochlea, oval window, hammer
   e. eardrum, auditory nerve, basilar membrane, oval window, the bones of the middle ear

4. The best explanation for how we understand and process the high pitch of a violin, with a frequency of more than 100 waves per second, comes from
   a. Helmholtz's place theory.
   b. the frequency theory.
   c. the volley principle.
   d. the transduction model.
   e. Brown's stereophonic theory.

5. Lashawna is exposed to a short wavelength with a tall/great amplitude. It is likely that she is perceiving
   a. a bright fuschia color.
   b. a loud bass guitar.
   c. a dusky green color.
   d. a soft cello.
   e. a very loud piccolo.

Module 21

The Other Senses

Module Summary

Module 21 concludes Unit IV with a review of the remaining senses of smell, taste, touch, and body positioning. Mechanisms by which each receives and conveys information to our brain about stimuli in our environment as well as the manner in which they interact makes up the majority of the module. A brief discussion of the gate-control theory and pain management techniques rounds out the module.

Before beginning the module, take a moment to read each of the following terms you will encounter. You may wish to make vocabulary cards for each.

Key Terms

gate-control theory

kinesthesia

vestibular sense

sensory interaction

embodied cognition

While You Read

Answer the following questions, and complete the charts and diagrams below.

21-1

1. What has research shown about the essential nature of touch?

2. What are the four basic sensations skin can detect?

3. Which of the skin sensations has identifiable receptors?

21-2

1. How does Melzack and Wall's gate-control theory serve as a model for how we feel and block pain signals?

2. Based on the information in the text about Ashlyn Blocker, what might be the benefits of experiencing pain?

3. Describe the effect of endorphins on pain.

4. How might the experience of pain be involved with the phantom limb syndrome?

5. What are the biopsychosocial influences on pain?

6. What have placebo studies revealed about the psychological aspects of pain?

7. What roles do acupuncture and virtual reality seem to play in pain relief?

21-3

1. Why do evolutionary psychologists see taste as adaptive?

2. What life experiences and choices impact the receptivity of taste buds?

3. Discuss the psychological influences on taste. How can our taste buds occasionally be fooled?

4. What is an evolutionary explanation for olfactory signals not processing first through the thalamus, as with other senses?

5. In what way are smells connected with memories and emotions?

21-4

1. Distinguish kinesthesia from your vestibular sense.

2. For which tasks might the kinesthetic system be most useful? When might the vestibular sense be most useful?

21-5

1. In what ways can the sense of smell change the perception of taste? Describe two additional examples of sensory interaction that you have experienced.

2. How does the McGurk effect illustrate how senses interact?

3. Give an example of how our bodily sensations and states can influence our cognitive perceptions and judgments.

After You Read

Module 21 Review

Circle the correct answers below to see if you have mastered the basics.

1. Which of the following senses receives information from the environment and does not pass signals through the thalamus to process?
   a. taste
   b. vision
   c. hearing
   d. smell
   e. body positioning

2. Which of the following sensations are detectable by skin?
   a. touch
   b. warmth
   c. cold
   d. pain
   e. all of the above

3. Your toddler refuses to eat the spinach and brussel sprouts that the rest of the family eats for dinner. The theory that over many generations, your toddler inherited the aversion to these bitter tastes would most likely be suggested by
   a. a cognitivist.
   b. an evolutionary psychologist.
   c. a behaviorist.
   d. a humanist.
   e. a psychoanalyst.

4. In order to receive a 10 on balance beam, the Olympic gymnast is best served by a highly functioning
    a. vestibular sense.
    b. kinesthetic nervous system.
    c. sense of smell.
    d. transduction.
    e. ganglion cell.

5. Which of the following is true about pain?
    a. No single stimulus produces pain.
    b. Pain diminishes when neurotransmitters such as endorphins are released.
    c. The brain can create pain.
    d. We edit our memories of pain.
    e. All of the above are true.

 **✓ Check Yourself**   Now that you have mastered the basics, work through the problems below to see if you can *synthesize, evaluate,* and *analyze* what you have learned.

> Two psychologists are discussing the processes and theories of sensation. One psychologist is adamant that the trichromatic theory of vision, the place theory of audition, and the kinesthetic system are the most useful in explaining human behavior. His companion believes strongly that the opponent-process theory of vision, the frequency theory of audition, and the vestibular system are the most useful in explaining human behavior.

Using your knowledge of Unit IV and specific terminology, make the case for each psychologist's argument, explaining the theories and their application to human behavior.

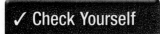 **✓ Check Yourself**   Now that you have mastered the basics, work through the problems below to see if you can *synthesize, evaluate,* and *analyze* what you have learned.

> Rodrigo is asleep in his home when a potential intruder begins to break into Rodrigo's home. Discuss how the following would impact Rodrigo's discovery of the potential intruder:

- signal detection theory:

- visual receptors:

- auditory receptors:

- interposition:

- perceptual set:

Before You Move On

Use the checklist below to verify your understanding of the unit's main points.

Do I know the basic principles of sensory transduction?

- [ ] absolute threshold
- [ ] difference threshold
- [ ] signal detection theory
- [ ] sensory adaptation

- [ ] Do I know the physical nature and mechanisms of light and sound waves?

- [ ] Can I identify the structures and functions of the eye, nose, ears, tongue, skin and kinesthetic and vestibular systems?
- [ ] Do I know the brain structures involved in vision, audition, gustation, olfaction, touch and body position?

- [ ] Do I know the characteristics of the two types of hearing loss?

- [ ] Do I know the Gestalt principles of grouping sensory input?

- [ ] Do I understand the ways in which binocular and monocular cues are involved in depth perception?

- [ ] Do I understand how psychological, biological and socio-cultural influences can impact sensation and perception?

- [ ] Do I understand the mechanisms and differences between top-down and bottom-up processing? Can I further point out examples of both in everyday situations?

- [ ] Do I understand the power and limitations of attention?

- [ ] Can I challenge common beliefs in ESP with concrete scientific arguments?

Do I know the historical researchers that influenced the study of sensation and perception?

- [ ] Fechner
- [ ] Hubel
- [ ] Weber
- [ ] Wiesel
- [ ] Helmoltz
- [ ] Hering

Unit V

States of Consciousness

Overview

Unit V begins with a historical overview of the growing importance of and research on consciousness. Various states of normal and altered consciousness, such as sleeping, dreaming, hypnosis, and drug use, are discussed and illustrated throughout the unit. Detailed information on sleep stages and the characteristics unique to each stage are presented in table form. Major sleep disorders (for example, insomnia and sleep apnea) are illustrated through charts, graphs, and images. The importance of sleep and its impact on learning, memory, and daily functioning is stressed. The unit concludes with a thorough discussion of drugs, their effects, and the processes by which these chemicals impact the central nervous system.

Modules

22 Understanding Consciousness and Hypnosis

23 Sleep Patterns and Sleep Theories

24 Sleep Deprvation, Sleep Disorders, and Dreams

25 Psychoactive Drugs

Tip #5
Unplug and Turn Off

Getting enough sleep is crucial to succeeding in school. If you are looking to improve your academic performance, sleep is one of the key factors that you can directly control. In this unit, you'll learn about the suprachiasmatic nucleus (SCN), which gauges the amount of light present and directs melatonin secretions to make you sleepy. It is easier to fall asleep when there is less light present. Exposure to light late in the night, such as your computer, electronic tablet, or TV screen, fools the SCN into thinking it is still daytime, which inhibits the release of melatonin. Shutting down the electronics and lowering lights in the room will help your body prepare you for sleep. Give yourself a break from these light sources about an hour or two before you hope to fall asleep and sleep will come easier to you.

Module 22

Understanding Consciousness and Hypnosis

Before You Read

Module Summary

Module 22 provides a definition and brief historical account of the increasing importance of the study of consciousness in psychology. The various states of consciousness are discussed here and current information on hypnosis is reviewed alongside a discussion of Ernest Hilgard's hypnotism experiments. The parallels between hypnosis and selective attention are illustrated with research studies.

Before beginning the module, take a moment to read each of the following terms and names you will encounter. You may wish to make vocabulary cards for each.

Key Terms	Key Names
consciousness	William James
hypnosis	Ernest Hilgard
posthypnotic suggestion	
dissociation	

While You Read

Answer the following questions/prompts.

22-1

1. List and elaborate on the historical factors that impacted the view of consciousness in the field of psychology.

22-2

1. What is one defining characteristic of someone who is easily hypnotized?

2. Discuss the evidence refuting some of the commonly held false beliefs about hypnosis.

3. List the ways in which hypnosis is used today in therapy and for pain reduction.

22-3

1. Explain the arguments that state that hypnosis is a social phenomenon.

2. Discuss the Stroop effect and how it supports the argument that hypnosis is a state of divided consciousness.

3. Summarize how Ernest Hilgard's work supports the idea of hypnosis as a divided consciousness.

4. John is a soccer player who sustained a serious injury during the game but was not aware of it and did not feel the pain from the injury until the game was over. Discuss how the idea of selective attention plays a role in his ability to not feel the pain.

After You Read

Module 22 Review

Choose the best answers to the following questions to see if you have mastered the basics..

1. Janice is under hypnosis and has held her arm in a bath of ice water for over 5 minutes. She reports that she can feel the cold, but is not registering the pain. Ernest Hilgard would say this was evidence of
   a. consciousness.
   b. a posthypnotic suggestion.
   c. cognitive appraisal.
   d. dissociation.
   e. perceptual illusions.

2. Mason is driving on his usual route home from work and thinking about the trouble he is having with his boss. Despite his distracting thoughts, he manages to get off at the right exit and heads for home. A theorist advocating dual-processing strategies would say this is most likely a result of
   a. the Stroop effect.
   b. posthypnotic suggestion.
   c. divided consciousness.
   d. the social influence theory.
   e. postural sway.

3. When one moment in time seems to flow into the next moment in time we experience what William James dubbed
    a. flow.
    b. postural sway.
    c. sensory deprivation.
    d. meditation.
    e. stream of consciousness.

4. If Dr. Choi, a psychologist, wanted to help one of his patients reduce his overeating behaviors and get control of his obesity, he might use hypnosis in the therapy session to offer a
    _____ _____ that would be carried out after his patient was no longer hypnotized.

5. When asked to read the word "BLUE" with letters colored in green many people find they take longer than if the letters were colored in blue. This phenomenon is referred to as the
    _____ _____ .

Module 23

Sleep Patterns and Sleep Theories

Before You Read

Module Summary

Module 23 explains circadian rhythms and how they impact on our sleep and daily functioning. Detailed charts and graphs illustrate the physical aspects and characteristics of each stage of sleep. The importance of REM sleep and its role in processing new learning is discussed, as well as current sleep theories.

Before beginning the module, take a moment to read each of the following terms you will encounter. You may wish to make vocabulary cards for each.

Key Terms

circadian rhythm	hallucinations
REM sleep	delta waves
alpha waves	NREM sleep
sleep	suprachiasmatic nucleus (SCN)

While You Read

Answer the following questions/prompts.

23-1

1. Define circadian rhythm and then use the timeline below to depict the ebb and flow of the typical human circadian rhythm.

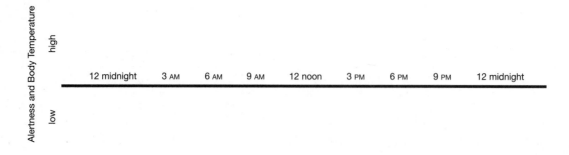

2. Explain how age and experience alter our circadian rhythms.

23-2

1. Complete the chart below.

Stage	Wave Name	Wave Characteristics	Characteristics or Common Behaviors of This Stage
Awake But Relaxed			
NREM-1			
NREM-2			
NREM-3			
REM			

2. Interpret the data from Figure 23.4 to describe three differences between the sleep of a young adult and that of older adults.

3. Use Figure 23.4 to describe how the time spent in each respective stage of sleep changes over the course of an 8-hour period of sleep.

23-3

1. Discuss the differences in sleep patterns and the need for sleep among humans.

2. Explain how biology and experience interact in our sleep patterns.

3. Explain the process by which the suprachiasmatic nucleus (SCN) and melatonin work to regulate sleep and wake cycles. Refer to Figure 23.5 for help.

4. How does artificial light from electronics and interior lighting distort the SCN-melatonin process you described above?

23-4

1. Sleep as protection from predators is most likely a view taken by which approach to psychology? Explain why.

2. Sleep as recuperation, repair, and a supporter of growth is most likely a view taken by which approach to psychology? Explain why.

3. Sleep as a memory rebuilder and nourishment for creative thinking is most likely a view taken by which approach to psychology? Explain why.

4. Hypothesize the reasons that the animals listed in Figure 23.6 need such varying amounts of sleep.

5. Explain how a regular night's sleep can also dramatically improve your athletic ability.

After You Read

Module 23 Review

Answer the following questions to see if you have mastered the basics.

1. Bob has just dozed off on the couch and is experiencing vivid sensory images. He is most likely
   a. in NREM-1 sleep.
   b. in NREM-2 sleep.
   c. in NREM-3 sleep.
   d. in REM sleep.
   e. still awake.

2. Jane is in NREM-3 sleep. As a sleep researcher you would expect to see which of the following?
   a. sleep spindles
   b. a hypnogogic jerk
   c. delta waves
   d. alpha waves
   e. momentary bursts of activity in her eyes

3. Justin doesn't understand why he often feels so tired in the early afternoon. As a psychology student learning about sleep, explain why this is normal.

4. Explain why REM sleep is referred to as paradoxical sleep.

5. The structure responsible for directing the pineal gland to increase and decrease its production of melatonin is the
   a. amygdala.
   b. adrenal gland.
   c. suprachiasmatic nucleus.
   d. basal ganglia.
   e. cerebellum.

6. Roberto is involved in a sleep study and researchers are recording the electrical activity of his brain as he sleeps. The researchers are likely using which type of brain scanning technology?
   a. PET scan
   b. CT scan
   c. EEG
   d. MRI
   e. fMRI

7. As Roberto sleeps, the researchers note that he is currently in NREM-2 sleep. They know this because on the EEG report they noticed
   a. delta waves.
   b. alpha waves.
   c. sleep spindles.
   d. theta waves.
   e. beta waves.

8. As 18-year-old Nathan sleeps through the night, he can expect that his
   a. time spent in REM sleep will decrease.
   b. time spent in NREM-3 sleep will increase.
   c. REM stage will occur right after his time in NREM-3 sleep.
   d. time spent in REM sleep will increase.
   e. REM stage will occur right before his time in NREM-3 sleep.

9. John is sleeping and is experiencing physiological arousal. His eyes are moving from side to side very quickly and his heart rate has risen sharply. John is currently in which stage of sleep?
   a. NREM-1
   b. NREM-3
   c. NREM-2
   d. REM
   e. delta sleep

Module 24

Sleep Deprivation, Sleep Disorders, and Dreams

Before You Read

Module Summary

Module 24 reviews the major sleep disorders and provides numerous examples of the impact of sleep loss on cognition and behavior. The major theories of dreams are presented and critiqued and common content of dreams is discussed.

Before beginning the module, take a moment to read each of the following terms and name you will encounter. You may wish to make vocabulary cards for each.

Key Terms		Key Name
insomnia	dream	Sigmund Freud
narcolepsy	manifest content	
sleep apnea	latent content	
night terrors	REM rebound	

While You Read

Answer the following questions/prompts.

24-1

1. Discuss the behavioral and emotional effects of sleep loss.

2. Describe how sleep deprivation impacts

   a. student performance in school:

   b. weight:

   c. health:

   d. job performance:

3. Explain specific research regarding the impact of sleep loss of as little as an hour on the frequency of auto accidents.

4. List and describe the symptoms and prevalence of the following sleep disorders:

   a. insomnia:

   b. narcolepsy:

c. sleep apnea:

d. night terrors:

c. sleepwalking:

d. sleeptalking:

5. Explain how night terrors differ from nightmares.

24-2

1. Discuss the research that supports the following quote from the text.

"For what one has dwelt on by day, these things are seen in visions of the night."

2. Explain how the brain's dual processing incorporates sensory stimuli into the dream.

3. Explain the current research regarding learning while we sleep.

24-3

1. Discuss how the definitions of manifest and latent content relate to the phrase from your text that in a dream, "a gun might be a disguised representation of a penis."

2. Explain Sigmund Freud's theory of wish fulfillment in dreams.

3. Discuss the function of dreams according to the information-processing perspective.

4. In what way do brain scans confirm the link between REM sleep and memory?

5. Explain the correlation between sleep and learning.

6. How might REM sleep function to develop and preserve neural pathways?

7. Explain the neural activation theory of dreaming.

8. Discuss how the cognitive development function of dreaming contrasts with the neural activation theory of dreaming.

9. Which of the dream theories summarized in Table 24.2 seem most credible to you? Why?

10. How does REM rebound suggest that the causes and functions of REM sleep are deeply biological?

After You Read

Module 24 Review

Choose the best answer to the following questions to see if you have mastered the basics.

1. Your new dorm mate at Sleep Disorders University tells you that he has insomnia. As a result, you can expect that he will
   a. sleewalk.
   b. have trouble falling or remaining asleep.
   c. scream out in his dreams.
   d. stop breathing in his sleep.
   e. act out his dreams.

2. Meanwhile, down the hall in your dorm, a young freshman student has repeatedly been found locked outside of his room in the middle of the night with no recollection of how he got there. You suspect that he may have
   a. sleep apnea.
   b. a sleeptalking disorder.
   c. a sleepwalking disorder.
   d. narcolepsy.
   e. night terrors.

3. The Resident Assistant at the University is well known for the loudness of his snore which can be heard down the hall. His roommate tells you that the RA wakes up repeatedly during the night but he doesn't recall any of the waking episodes in the morning. The most likely culprit in this case is
   a. narcolepsy.
   b. nightmares.
   c. night terrors.
   d. sleep apnea.
   e. insomnia.

4. John, a soccer player at the University, suffers from narcolepsy. You worry about his ability to play because one of the hallmarks of the disorder narcolepsy is that the sufferer
   a. is prone to sleepwalking as well.
   b. talks in their sleep.
   c. cannot remain asleep throughout the night.
   d. has great difficulty falling asleep.
   e. may lapse directly into REM sleep, causing him to lose all muscle tension.

5. Your friend lives on the floor above you and shares during a dorm meeting that she suffered from night terrors as a child. Knowing this you can expect that she
   a. primarily experienced this during her NREM-3 sleep.
   b. probably sees a therapist to deal with the memories of the disorder.
   c. suffers also from nightmares.
   d. is more prone to sleep apnea as well.
   e. is still experiencing the disorder today.

Use the following scenario to answer questions 6–10.

Justina dreamed last night that she was warding off villains in a life-or-death battle outside a fortified castle. In the dream, she attempted to cross the moat but saw that it was filled with grotesque swamp creatures with warty green skin and she recoiled in fear. Knowing there was only one way to reach safety, she flew over the top of the castle and landed among the weeds in the inner courtyard. She was surprised to run into her seventh period Geometry teacher, Ms. Hargroves, but seeing that her teacher had a spear, compass, and workbook with her, Justina knew they would prevail. Ms. Hargroves told Justina that the key to defeating the villains was to write the theorems from the homework on the castle walls as protection against the invaders. Justina scrambled to write the complicated theorems before the menacing villains closed in. Just when the towering castle walls were about to be sieged, Justina awoke from her dream with a start.

As a therapist who specializes in dreams, how would you interpret Justina's dream using

6. Freud's wish-fulfillment theory:

7. the information-processing theory:

8. the physiological function theory:

9. the neural activation theory:

10. the cognitive development theory:

Module 25

Psychoactive Drugs

Before You Read

Module Summary

Module 25 begins with an overview of the common misconceptions about addiction and a review of tolerance and withdrawal. The bulk of the module deals with each primary category of drugs: depressants (which include opiates), stimulants, and hallucinogens. Specific drugs in each category are highlighted and their effect on the central nervous system and behaviors is discussed.

Before beginning the module, take a moment to read each of the following terms you will encounter. You may wish to make vocabulary cards for each.

Key Terms

substance use disorder	stimulants
psychoactive drug	amphetamines
tolerance	nicotine
addiction	methamphetamine
withdrawal	Ecstasy (MDMA)
depressants	hallucinogens
alcohol use disorder	LSD
barbiturates	near-death experience
opiates	THC

While You Read

Answer the following questions/prompts.

25-1

1. What role do tolerance, addiction, and withdrawal play in substance abuse disorders? Explain how the three are connected.

2. According to the text, in what ways has the concept of addiction been stretched too far? In what ways is the idea of addictive behaviors just beginning to be explored?

3. What are your own opinions on the discussion of addictions?

4. Discuss how drug use can turn to abuse and then to a substance abuse disorder.

25-2

1. Define depressants and give three examples of drugs in this category.

2. List the effects of depressants on the central nervous system.

3. Explain and give examples of how alcohol impacts

   a. neural processing:

   b. memory:

   c. self-awareness and self-control:

4. How do the expectations of drinking alcohol influence behavior? Briefly address how this relates to the placebo effect discussed in Unit I.

5. What are the effects of barbiturates on the central nervous system?

6. List three common opiates and explain their effect on the central nervous system. Explain how these impact the levels of endorphins in the body.

7. How does addiction to pain medication occur biochemically?

25-3

1. Define stimulants and give three examples of drugs in this category.

2. List the effects of stimulants on the central nervous system.

3. Explain the relationship between nicotine use and the release of neurotransmitters in the brain.

4. Discuss the forces and influences teens in particular are subject to when considering whether or not to begin smoking.

5. What are the benefits to quitting smoking?

6. Use Figure 25.4 and the text to explain the effect of cocaine on neural transmission.

7. Discuss the long-term effects of cocaine use on a person's behavior.

8. How is the expectation effect of using cocaine similar to that of using alcohol?

9. Explain the impact of methamphetamine at the neural synapse.

10. Discuss how Ecstasy (MDMA) has both stimulant and hallucinogenic properties.

11. What are the potential long-term effects of using Ecstasy?

25-4

1. Define hallucinogens and give two examples of drugs in this category.

2. What is the primary effect of hallucinogen use?

3. Describe the emotions and visual imagery associated with use of LSD.

4. Relate the visual images experienced under LSD use with those reported by survivors of near-death experiences, temporal lobe seizures, or prolonged periods of isolation. What point is the author trying to make with this discussion?

5. Explain the negative effects of marijuana use on mood and memory.

6. Discuss how the body metabolizes and eliminates marijuana differently from alcohol.

7. In what situations is marijuana use being decriminalized? What is your opinion on the legalization of marijuana for medical use? sHow about recreational use?

After You Read

Module 25 Review

Answer the following questions to see if you have mastered the basics.

1. Complete the chart below.

Drug	Category	Effect on CNS	Behavioral Impact
Alcohol			
Caffeine			
Methamphetamine			
Nicotine			
LSD			
Heroin			
Barbiturate			
Cocaine			
Marijuana			
Ecstasy			

2. Jonathan has injured himself on the rugby field and is feeling a great deal of pain in his leg. Which of the following drugs would be appropriate for him to take to reduce the pain?
   a. Caffeine
   b. Nicotine
   c. An opiate
   d. LSD
   e. A depressant

3. Nita is at a party and is drinking a great deal of alcohol. Which of the following is NOT an expected effect of the increasing alcohol in her bloodstream?
   a. It will slow her neural processing, slurring her speech.
   b. It can disrupt memory formation and Nita may not recall portions of the night.
   c. It can decrease her self-control, making it likely she will act impulsively.
   d. It can reduce frontal lobe control, causing Nita to say things she normally would filter.
   e. It will increase her ability to concentrate and judge the situation she is in.

4. Which is a physiological effect of nicotine use?
   a. Depressing the activityv in the brain
   b. Decreased heart rate and blood pressure
   c. Increased appetite for carbohydrates
   d. Reduced circulation to extremities
   e. Increase in the release of neurotransmitters that cause stress

5. Theresa and Sydney are at a party and using a drug. They seem to have a great deal of energy and are feeling very loving toward all the partygoers. They have been dancing nonstop for hours and are feeling very thirsty. Theresa and Sydney are most likely using
   a. Ecstasy.
   b. marijuana.
   c. heroin.
   d. a barbiturate.
   e. a depressant.

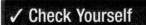 **✓ Check Yourself** Now that you have mastered the basics, work through the problems below to see if you can *synthesize, evaluate,* and *analyze* what you have learned.

You are a psychologist with a thriving drug addiction and sleep disorders practice. A patient has just come to see you complaining of myriad symptoms and seeking your help. Your patient has been fired from his last three jobs because he arrives late to work consistently, falls asleep at his desk, and seems highly agitated around co-workers. In addition, he forgot to turn in several of his assigned projects and reports missing the due dates for others because he simply did not remember the projects had due dates. In your capacity as a psychologist, you review your checklist on drug and sleep disorders and narrow down your possible diagnosis by ruling out the disorders that would not produce these behaviors and highlighting those that would. Fill in your checklists on the next page for this patient, then make and support your diagnosis.

Disorder	Behaviors I Would Expect	Patient Exhibits (✓)
Insomnia		
Narcolepsy		
Sleep apnea		
Night terrors		

Drug Use Category	Behaviors I Would Expect	Patient Exhibits (✓)
Stimulant		
Depressant		
Opiate		
Hallucinogen		

My diagnosis: This patient might be having difficulty with _____ .

Support for my diagnosis:

☑ **Before You Move On**

Use the checklist below to verify your understanding of the unit's main points.

☐ Can I describe various states of consciousness and their impact on behavior?

Can I discuss the aspects of sleeping and dreaming?
☐ Stages and characteristics of the sleep cycle
☐ Theories of sleep and dreaming
☐ Symptoms and treatment of sleep disorders

☐ Can I describe the historic and contemporary uses of hypnosis?

☐ Can I explain hypnotic phenomena?

☐ Can I identify the major psychoactive drug categories and classify specific drugs, including their psychological and physiological effects?

☐ Can I discuss drug addiction, tolerance, and withdrawal?

☐ Can I identify the major figures in consciousness research?

Unit VI

Learning

Overview

How we learn is one of humanity's most enduring questions and Unit VI defines and identifies four basic forms of learning: operant, classical, observational, and cognitive learning. This unit explores the early work and research of behaviorists Ivan Pavlov and B. F. Skinner, along with the more recent contributions of Edward Tolman and John Garcia. Significant time is spent comparing the applications of operant and classical conditioning to our real life of work, school and home. Alternate methods of learning, such as latent learning and cognitive maps, are examined and compared to classical and operant conditioning. Albert Bandura's research on modeling behavior and the research into mirror neurons and empathy are also reviewed.

Modules

Tip #6
Reinforce Yourself!

How perfect to study about learning while you are striving to be a better learner! Now is the time to put operant conditioning principles into play. This unit teaches positive reinforcement methods that can be used to increase repetition of desired behavior. You will find it simple to set up reinforcements to develop good study habits, and become a life-long learner. First, as we discussed in Tip #4, break your studying into small, 30 minute chunks. After each chunk of study time, reward yourself with some positive reinforcement. Rewards are relative (that is known as the Premack Principle) so make sure the reward works for you. It might be a food treat, an internet or texting break, a run around the block, or some quiet reflection outdoors. Whatever works to motivate you is great! Then, when you receive your desired score on a quiz or test, give yourself another positive reinforcement: perhaps a movie night, time with friends, or time to read a book you enjoy. Over time, you will find that you have developed stronger study habits and you won't need to reward yourself every time (remember this when you reach reinforcement schedules later in this unit!).

Module 26

How We Learn and Classical Conditioning

Module Summary

Module 26 defines learning and identifies some basic forms of learning. The components of classical conditioning and behaviorism's view of learning are presented alongside a discussion of the specific processes of acquisition, extinction, spontaneous recovery, generalization and discrimination. The module concludes with an explanation of the applications and evidence of the importance of Ivan Pavlov's and John B. Watson's work.

Before beginning the module, take a moment to read each of the following terms and names you will encounter. You may wish to make vocabulary cards for each.

Key Terms

learning

habituation

associative learning

stimulus

cognitive learning

classical conditioning

behaviorism

neutral stimulus (NS)

unconditioned response (UR)

unconditioned stimulus (US)

conditioned response (CR)

conditioned stimulus (CS)

acquisition

higher-order conditioning

extinction

spontaneous recovery

generalization

discrimination

Key Names

Ivan Pavlov

John B. Watson

While You Read

Answer the following questions/prompts.

26-1

1. Your text defines *learning* as the process of acquiring new and relatively enduring information or behaviors. Why would a behavior or information have to endure in order to be considered learned?

2. List three behaviors you have learned since middle school. (Remember . . . : enduring behaviors = learned.)

3. The text states that we learn by association or linking two sequential events. Refer to two of the learned behaviors you listed in #2 and detail the process of how you associated the events leading to each.

   Behavior #1:

   Behavior #2:

4. List and include a brief explanation of each of the three types of learning described in your textbook.

   a.

   b.

   c.

5. A circus lion repeatedly receives a smack on the nose just after the trainer walks into the cage. The lion shrinks from the trainer's slap each time and eventually cowers in the corner of the cage when the trainer enters. What would a behaviorist call this increased withdrawal response? Explain your answer.

26-2

1. Define and give an example from your own life of classical learning.

2. Why were Pavlov's findings so important to behaviorism?

3. Complete the table below with the term, definition, and example from Pavlov's classic experiment. One has been filled in for you.

Component	Full Term	Definition	Pavlovian Example
US			
UR	*unconditioned response*	*an unlearned, naturally occurring response to an unconditioned response*	*salivation to the food in the mouth*
NS			
CS			
CR			

4. Using Figure 26.4 and the chart in #3, properly label the two associative learning examples below.

   a. A young man and woman who are in love listen to Beyoncé's love songs when they drive around together. Later, when the young man is alone in the car, he hears Beyoncé on the radio and thinks lovingly of his girlfriend and the great times they have together.

     US:

     UR:

     NS:

     CS:

     CR:

   b. Look at Figure 26.1 and correctly label the components of the classically conditioned relationship between thunder and lightning.

     US:

     UR:

     NS:

     CS:

     CR:

26-3

1. How does higher-order conditioning differ from the initial acquisition of the stimulus-response relationship?

2. Write two examples that demonstrate how higher-order conditioning can be applied to example #4a (Beyoncé tunes) and #4b (thunder and lightning) above.

3. Give an example from your life of higher-order conditioning.

4. How did Ivan Pavlov extinguish the conditioned response (CR) in his dogs? Use classical conditioning terms in your response.

5. Give an example from your school life of how generalization can be adaptive.

6. How can generalization be maladaptive?

7. Define discrimination in classical conditioning. Then, describe how a researcher would teach an animal to discriminate between relevant and irrelevant stimuli. Use classical conditioning terms in your response.

26-4

1. Complete the chart below to apply the principles of classical conditioning to the three examples discussed in the text.

Component	Example #1 Former Drug User	Example #2 Body's Immune System	Example #3 Little Albert
US			
UR	*craving*		
NS		*taste*	
CS			
CR			*fear*

After You Read

Module 26 Review

Label the five basic components of classical conditioning in each of the scenarios below.

1. Ahmed is a mediocre student in school and over the years has received many lectures from his parents about his poor study habits. He received another report card full of Cs and Ds today, and he knows that once his parents come home from work they will want to lecture him again. To distract himself from his nervousness, he plays his video games for several hours but later, as he hears the garage door open, Ahmed's heart begins to race.

US:

UR:

NS:

CS:

CR:

2. As a child, Charlotte was an avid reader who spent hours buried deep in classic and exciting literature. Her favorite reading spot was in the back yard in her swing under a strong oak tree. Years later, as an adult, Charlotte is looking through a magazine selling tree swings and feels the rush of good memories.

   US:

   UR:

   NS:

   CS:

   CR:

3. Your history instructor enjoys incorporating student projects into the class. You, however, typically do poorly on projects and prefer to learn from lectures. When your instructor creates a project, she produces the guidelines on colored paper to make it stand out. Today, as she enters the class, you see that she has a stack of colored paper in her hands and immediately you become agitated and upset.

   US:

   UR:

   NS:

   CS:

   CR:

In the following two scenarios, label the five basic components of classical conditioning and then respond to the prompt that follows it.

4. a. Each time you come home from school, you head to the kitchen to fill up your dog Lassie's food bowl. Lassie excitedly devours her food with her tail swinging. You notice after a few weeks that Lassie has conditioned your arrival home from school with a filled food bowl and eagerly comes running to the door to greet you when you come in.

   US:

   UR:

   NS:

   CS:

   CR:

   b. After learning about higher-order classical conditioning, you become interested in teaching Lassie to respond to additional cues. Describe how you will teach Lassie to associate two new neutral stimuli with being fed.

5. **a.** Your 2-year-old cousin AnnaBeth giggles delightedly every time her father picks her up and tosses her into the air. Now each time she sees her father, she feels great love and enjoyment at being with him.

  US:

  UR:

  NS:

  CS:

  CR:

  b. Using the principle of generalization explain why AnnaBeth now runs up to her friends' fathers with the same delight and excitement with which she approaches her father.

  c. Using the principle of discrimination, explain how you can teach AnnaBeth only to respond this way to her father.

Choose the best answers to the following questions.

6. The repeated presenting of the conditioned stimulus without being followed by the unconditioned stimulus will result in
   a. discrimination of the unconditioned response.
   b. generalization of the conditioned response.
   c. extinction of the neutral stimulus.
   d. extinction of the conditioned response.
   e. generalization of the unconditioned response.

7. Which of the following best defines spontaneous recovery?
   a. The reappearance of a weakened conditioned response.
   b. The reappearance of the original unconditioned stimulus.
   c. The recovery of the generalized response.
   d. The extinction of the original neutral stimulus.
   e. The immediate resurgence of the unconditioned stimulus.

8. A pigeon pecking at an orange oval and not a red circle in order to receive a food reward is an example of
   a. shaping.
   b. extinction.
   c. stimulus generalization.
   d. stimulus discrimination.
   e. acquisition.

9. A behaviorist would most likely explain the pigeon's behavior above as a result of
    a. being reinforced for desired behaviors.
    b. brain structures that detect color variations.
    c. unconscious avian instincts for color.
    d. a free choice the pigeon made to prefer orange to red.
    e. a deficit of cones along the retina for color detection.

10. Grandpa and Grandma Jackson's 4-year-old grandson Chandler frequently has temper tantrums to get his way when he comes to visit. Tired of giving into him, Chandler's grandparents choose to ignore his outbursts and not give in to his demands, and after a while they notice that Chandler is no longer misbehaving. Grandma and Grandpa Jackson succeeded by applying the behaviorist principles of
    a. stimulus discrimination.
    b. stimulus generalization.
    c. cognitive learning.
    d. positive punishment.
    e. extinction.

Module 27

Operant Conditioning

Module Summary

Module 27 defines and describes operant conditioning and presents the difference between positive and negative reinforcement. B. F. Skinner's experiments and their importance to behavioral psychology are disscussed. The basic types of reinforcers and the schedules in which those reinforcers most affect behavior are reviewed. This module also includes a detailed discussion of punishment and its effect on behavior as well as how it differs from negative reinforcement. The module wraps up with a discussion of the controversy surrounding B.F. Skinner's views of human behavior.

Before beginning the module, take a moment to read each of the following terms and names you will encounter. You may wish to make vocabulary cards for each.

Key Terms		Key Names
operant conditioning	conditioned reinforcer	Edward Thorndike
law of effect	reinforcement schedule	B. F. Skinner
operant chamber	continuous reinforcement	
reinforcement	partial (intermittent) reinforcement	
shaping	fixed-ratio schedule	
discriminative stimulus	variable-ratio schedule	
positive reinforcement	fixed-interval schedule	
negative reinforcement	variable-interval schedule	
primary reinforcer	punishment	

While You Read

Answer the following questions/prompts.

27-1

1. How is operant conditioning different from classical conditioning? Describe these differences in your own words.

2. Give an example from your own life of operant conditioning.

3. What is another way to state Thorndike's law of effect?

4. What is a Skinner box and what is its purpose?

5. List two specific behaviors you have learned (remember: enduring = learned) and the type of reinforcement (negative or positive) you received for each of them in the following four situations:.

    a. as a student

        (1)

        (2)

    b. as a member of your family

        (1)

        (2)

    c. as a friend

        (1)

        (2)

6. How does the process of shaping work? Describe how one of your behaviors has been shaped.

7. Design an experiment that would use the principles of shaping to teach a particular behavior to a person or animal in your life.

27-2

1. How does positive reinforcement differ from negative reinforcement?

2. Give an example (that is not mentioned in the text) of negative reinforcement.

3. Give an example from your life in school of a situation where positive and negative reinforcement both work to strengthen a particular behavior.

4. How do primary and conditioned (secondary) reinforcers differ?

5. Give an example of a conditioned (secondary) reinforcer in your life.

6. In what ways is a human's response to immediate and delayed reinforcers different from that of a rat?

7. Are there circumstances in which people are drawn to immediate reinforcers even though they know it might not be to their benefit? Explain.

27-3

1. Explain why an animal trainer would prefer using intermittent reinforcement schedules to continuous reinforcement schedules when teaching a lion to perform in a circus act. Are there times the trainer would prefer using continuous reinforcement? Explain.

2. Complete the chart below.

Reinforcement Schedule	Definition	Example From Text	Original Example
Continuous			
Fixed-ratio			
Fixed-interval			

Reinforcement Schedule	Definition	Example From Text	Original Example
Variable-ratio			
Variable-interval			

3. If the intent of conditioning is to create an enduring response, which of the five methods in your chart above is the best schedule to follow to reinforce desired behavior? Why? Which method of partial reinforcement would lead to the quickest extinction of desired behavior? Explain.

4. Describe the typical patterns of response under fixed-interval, fixed-ratio, variable-interval, and variable-ratio schedules of reinforcement.

27-4

1. How does a punisher differ from a reinforcer?

2. Explain, using examples to illustrate your response, how punishment differs from negative reinforcement?

3. How is positive punishment different from negative punishment? Give an example of each in your response.

4. Sometimes what seems to be punishment is actually reinforcement. (Consider the misbehaving child who is sent to his room to calm down and now has access to all of his favorite toys.) How can you determine if a behavior has been reinforced or punished?

5. What are four drawbacks of physical punishment?

   a.

   b.

   c.

   d.

6. As the author notes at the end of 27-4, many threats of punishment can be more effective when rephrased positively. Therefore, complete the author's prompt from the text here: "If you don't get your homework done, I'm not giving you money for a movie!" would be better phrased as . . .

☞   Note to remember: Punishment tells you what not to do; reinforcement tells you what to do.

27-5

1. Why did Skinner's ideas provoke controversy?

2. Now that you have studied B. F. Skinner's operant principles, how would you attempt to

   a. influence your classmate to study more thoroughly for tests?

   b. shape your teacher's treatment of you?

   c. increase the likelihood of having your stepmother say "Yes" more frequently to your requests to drive her car?

3. Use the chart below to give an example of how you would use each of the following four types of operant conditioning techniques to train your dog to pick up the newspaper off of the driveway.

	Reinforcement	Punishment
Positive		
Negative		

After You Read

Module 27 Review

Complete the following questions by identifying which response is being applied to shape the behavior of the subject in each example.

> Positive reinforcement
>
> Negative reinforcement
>
> Positive punishment
>
> Negative punishment

1. Juanita asks a useful and timely question in class and her teacher responds, "I am glad you asked that, Juanita." Juanita soon regularly raises her hand to contribute in class.

2. Dante cannot sit still in his kindergarten class and his teacher tells him he will have to remain inside while the other students go out for recess. Dante learns to sit still.

   How is Dante's behavior being reinforced?

   How is the teacher's behavior being reinforced?

3. Finnegan, your cat, has begun to bite more frequently. You read that if you squirt him with water from a spray bottle, he will learn not to repeat that behavior.

4. After promising your parents that you will follow the school rules and not use your cell phone in class, you check your text messages during Algebra and have your phone confiscated by the teacher. When your parents find out, they take your cell phone from you for 2 weeks. When you finally get your phone back, you do not check your texts in class any longer.

5. You are hoping that if you take a different route to your 5th period class each day, you can avoid the kid who has been bullying you. When you do not see them in the new hall, you feel relieved and take that route from now on.

Complete the following questions by identifying which intermittent reinforcement schedule is being applied to shape behavior

> Variable-ratio
>
> Variable-interval
>
> Fixed-ratio
>
> Fixed-interval

6. The local pet store offers a discount for buying dog food by the case, and if you save ten UPC bar codes on each case, you can receive a free case from the supplier. How is your dog food buying behavior being reinforced?

7. Your neighbors just had a new baby and are learning to be parents for the first time. They decide not to respond to every cry their new infant makes but instead allow the baby to fuss and cry for a while before they go to see what is wrong. From the baby's perspective, on what schedule is her crying behavior being reinforced by her parents' attention?

8. Tien has been unsuccessfully trying for years to perfect his golf game. Each time he decides to give up the game for good, he makes a beautiful shot that lands precisely where he wants it to and finds that he wants to continue perfecting his game.

9. Sasha works for a shoe store that pays her weekly and likes that she doesn't have to make a quota or sell a certain number of shoes in order to get paid. Her check comes every week regardless of how many customers come in and this gives her time to text on her phone, or finish homework in the back of the store.

10. On the other hand, Sasha's friend Monty works next door at the suit shop and receives a bonus for every 3 suits he sells. As he is trying to save for college, the bonus could really come in handy and this compels Monty to work hard to learn about suits and perfect his sales techniques so that he can sell more of them.

Module 28

Operant Conditioning's Applications, and Comparison to Classical Conditioning

Before You Read

Module Summary

Module 28 offers an application of the theories presented in Modules 26 and 27 and identifies key areas in home, work, and school where operant principles can be used. In addition, the module presents an easy-to-understand chart of the characteristics that distinguish operant from classical conditioning.

Before beginning the module, take a moment to read each of the following terms you will encounter. You may wish to make vocabulary cards for each.

Key Terms

biofeedback

respondent behavior

operant behavior

While You Read

Answer the following prompts, and complete the diagram below.

28-1

1. Give an example (that is not mentioned in the text) of how operant principles can be applied

    a. in school

    b. in sports

    c. at work

d. at home

e. for self-improvement

2. How does biofeedback work to reduce tension headaches?

3. In what way are the principles of operant conditioning illustrated in the use of biofeedback to train people to reduce stress?

28-2

1. Using the information in Table 28.1 and the material in Modules 26 and 27, complete the Venn diagram below on the similarities and differences between operant and classical conditioning. Use your own words when possible.

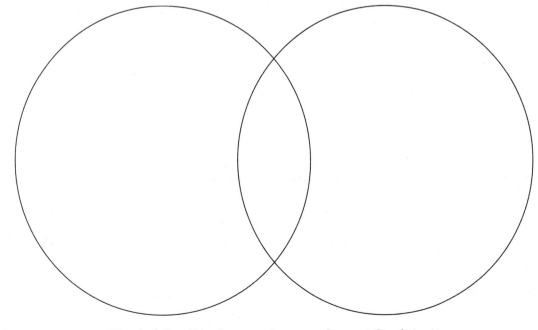

Classical Conditioning   Operant Conditioning

After You Read

Module 28 Review

Answer the prompt to see if you have mastered the basics.

1. Shereen suffers from high levels of anxiety regarding academics and sports. As a psychology student, you know she can use operant conditioning principles to reduce her anxiety and increase her performance in both school and sports. Describe how Shereen can utilize a type of punishment, a type of reinforcement, and a specific schedule of reinforcement to modify her anxious behaviors.

2. Specify how you would apply the three operant principles listed in the previous question to a behavior in your own life that you would like to change.

Module 29

Biology, Cognition, and Learning

Before You Read

Module Summary

Module 29 explains how biological constraints and cognitive processes affect classical and operant conditioning. A detailed discussion of how different methods of coping with personal problems and feeling control over your life can impact people's health and behavior concludes the module.

Before beginning the module, take a moment to read each of the following terms and names you will encounter. You may wish to make vocabulary cards for each.

<u>**Key Terms**</u>

cognitive map
latent learning
insight
intrinsic motivation
extrinsic motivation
coping

problem-focused coping
emotion-focused coping
learned helplessness
external locus of control
internal locus of control
self-control

<u>**Key Names**</u>

John Garcia
Robert Rescorla
Edward Tolman

While You Read

Answer the following questions/prompts.

 29-1

1. Summarize and explain the importance of John Garcia's work with taste aversion in rats.

2. Complete the chart below with components from Pavlov's work with dogs, Garcia's work with rats, and the work on sheep-eating coyotes.

Component	Example #1 Pavlov's Dogs	Example #2 John Garcia's Rats	Example #3 Sheep-eating coyotes
US		radiation or drugs	
UR	drooling		
NS			sheep
CS			
CR			

3. What is an evolutionary explanation for the development of taste aversions in both humans and animals?

4. What does it mean when psychologists say that there are biological constraints on classical conditioning?

5. What are the biological constraints on operant conditioning?

6. Shayna wants to put operant principles to use to train her pet gerbil to stand on its hind legs and raise its right paw in order to get food. Based on your knowledge of biological constraints on learning, how would you advise her?

29-2

1. What are the limitations of classical conditioning in addressing the cognitive processes of humans?

2. Summarize and discuss the importance of Robert Rescorla's work with rats' responses to tones and shocks. Relate this to the idea of a variable-ratio schedule of reinforcement and explain why this schedule is the best to prevent extinction.

3. How do cognitive processes impact operant conditioning? Why is this important to understand when training humans or animals?

4. Summarize Edward Tolman's work with rats in a maze. What does this research teach us about learning?

5. Give an example from your own life of latent learning.

6. How does insight learning differ from latent learning?

7. How does intrinsic motivation differ from extrinsic motivation? Give examples (that are not mentioned in the text) of intrinsic and extrinsic motivation.

29-3

1. How does problem-focused coping differ from emotion-focused coping? Provide a specific example and explain how each can impact individuals in different ways.

29-4

1. Summarize and discuss the importance of Martin Seligman's work with harnessed dogs. How does the issue of control impact the behavior of the dogs?

2. How can humans learn helplessness?

3. Describe how a student in high school might develop learned helplessness in one or more of her classes.

4. What is the relationship between learned helplessness and stress and health problems?

5. How does an internal locus of control differ from an external locus of control? How do each of these impact stress and health levels?

6. As defined by the text, what is self-control? How can high levels of self-control impact the outcome of a situation? Provide a specific example.

7. How is self-control depleted? Strengthened?

After You Read

Module 29 Review

Complete the Matching Questions below to see if you have mastered the basics.

Terms or Names

_____ 1. John Garcia

_____ 2. insight

_____ 3. problem-focused coping

_____ 4. emotion-focused coping

_____ 5. learned helplessness

_____ 6. external locus of control

_____ 7. internal locus of control

_____ 8. self-control

_____ 9. Robert Rescorla

_____ 10. Edward Tolman

Definitions or Associations

A. the hopelessness and passive resignation an animal or human learns when unable to avoid repeated aversive events

B. the ability to control impulses and delay short-term gratification for greater long-term rewards

C. the perception that chance or outside forces beyond our personal control determine our fate

D. showed that an animal can learn the predictability of an event

E. attempting to alleviate stress directly-by changing the stressor or the way we interact with that stressor

F. tested cognitive maps in rats

G. attempting to alleviate stress by avoiding or ignoring a stressor and attending to emotional needs related to one's stress reaction

H. a sudden realization of a problem's solution

I. tested taste aversion in rats

J. the perception that you control your own

Answer the following questions.

11. When a well-learned route in a maze is blocked, rats sometimes choose an alternative route, acting as if they were consulting a _____ _____ .

12. Animals may learn from experience even when reinforcement is not available. When learning is not apparent until reinforcement has been provided, _____ _____ is said to have occurred.

13. The desire to perform a behavior for its own sake is called _____ _____ , while motivation to seek external rewards and avoid punishments is called _____ _____ .

14. The researcher(s) most likely to challenge Ivan Pavlov's concept of the simplistic and mechanistic associations dogs seem to make between two stimuli would be
    a. Robert Rescorla through his work on the cognitive component of associative learning.
    b. Charles Tolman through his research on latent learning.
    c. B. F. Skinner because of his work on shaping pigeons.
    d. John Garcia with his studies on taste aversion in rats.
    e. John B. Watson and Rosalie Rayner based on their work with Little Albert.

15. As a soon-to-be college student you have decided that although you feel education is important, it does not make much sense to overemphasize it. You have heard from students who graduated before you and you believe that getting into college is more a matter of luck than a reflection of hard work and study. Your beliefs most illustrate
    a. latent learning.
    b. learned helplessness.
    c. an external locus of control.
    d. an internal locus of control.
    e. self-control.

Module 30

Learning by Observation

Module Summary

Module 30 describes the process of observational learning and the impact of mirror neurons. A discussion of modeling, both prosocial and antisocial, and its impacts on human behavior concludes the module.

Before beginning the module, take a moment to read each of the following terms and names you will encounter. You may wish to make vocabulary cards for each.

Key Terms

observational learning

modeling

mirror neurons

prosocial behavior

Key Name

Albert Bandura

While You Read

Answer the following questions/prompts.

30-1

1. Summarize and explain the implications of Albert Bandura's work with the Bobo doll and the modeling of aggression.

2. How does vicarious reinforcement or punishment differ from modeling?

3. What are mirror neurons and how do they work? What is their significance in life?

4. How does the work with mirror neurons explain children's theory of mind?

30-2

1. What are some outcomes of prosocial modeling? Provide an example from your life.

2. What are some outcomes of antisocial modeling? Provide an example from your life.

3. Connect the work of Bandura to the question of media violence.

   a. How would his research support the view that media violence triggers violent behavior?

   b. Suggest two alternative explanations for the existence of this violent behavior.

After You Read

Module 30 Review

Select the best answers below to see if you have mastered the basics.

1. After viewing adults kick and throw an inflatable Bobo doll around a room, children who are purposely frustrated and then placed in a room with the same Bobo will be most likely to
   a. attempt to make up for the poor adult treatment of Bobo by playing nicely with it.
   b. invent new and unique ways to treat Bobo.
   c. kick and throw Bobo as the adults did.
   d. ignore Bobo and choose other more appropriate toys.
   e. fear that the adults will treat them as they treated Bobo.

2. According to Bandura's research on vicarious reinforcement and punishment, we are especially likely to learn from people we perceive to be
   a. similar to ourselves.
   b. successful.
   c. admirable.
   d. likable.
   e. all of the above.

3. Mirror neurons are believed to play a role in
   a. everyday imitation and observational learning.
   b. facial recognition.
   c. personal self-esteem.
   d. occipital lobe visual processing.
   e. language.

4. When Jennie was trying to learn to play baseball, her mother noticed that she was holding the bat wrong. Jennie's mom said, "Here, Jennie, let me show you how you hold it." This method of teaching is best explained by
   a. cognitive maps.
   b. observational learning.
   c. vicarious learning.
   d. classical condtioning.
   e. latent learning.

5. Which of the following is an example of a prosocial behavior that might be learned through modeling?
   a. Justin acts like a bully to the kids at school after watching his favorite TV character bully on a TV show.
   b. Manahil learns to lie by watching her older brother get away with it.
   c. Emma learns to tease her cousin James by watching her aunt tease him as well.
   d. Ahad learns to care for his younger brother by watching his father feed and change him.
   e. Melissa thinks women are incapable of a career in business because all the important women in her life are stay-at-home mothers.

 Now that you have mastered the basics, work through the problems below to see if you can *synthesize, evaluate,* and *analyze* what you have learned.

1. Apply the principles of operant, classical, and observational learning, and your knowledge of psychological vocabulary, to explain

   Taste aversion:

   Superstitious behavior:

   Learned helplessness:

2. Austin is a teenager who has been suspended from school for possessing illegal substances. He has a long history of acting out, enraged resistance to adult authority and other antisocial behaviors. Suggest how the following can be used to address Austin's behavioral problems:

   • biofeedback
   • coping strategies
   • self-control

3. Interpret the graphs below and show how they depict the components of classical and operant conditioning. Be sure to incorporate correct usage of psychological terms.

   a. Discuss how the graph below, based on Pavlov's experiments with salivating dogs, demonstrates generalization and discrimination.

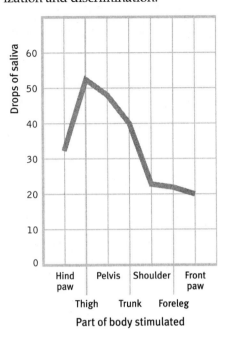

   b. Discuss how the graph below demonstrates extinction and spontaneous recovery.

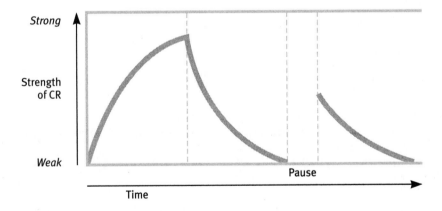

c. Discuss how the graph below demonstrates the impact of various reinforcement schedules on learning.

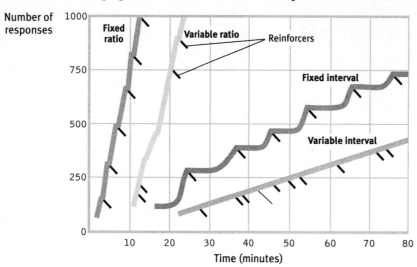

d. Discuss how the graph below demonstrates Thorndike's law of effect.

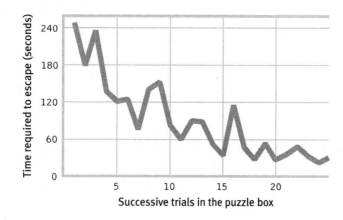

4. Draw a graph that would show the results of Seligman's experiments with learned helplessness. Be certain to label the x-axis and y-axis correctly.

☑ Before You Move On

Use the checklist below to verify your understanding of the unit's main points.

☐ Do I know the difference between classical conditioning, operant conditioning and observational learning?

Can I describe the basic components of classical conditioning?

    ☐ acquisition

    ☐ extinction

    ☐ spontaneous recovery

    ☐ generalization

    ☐ discrimination

    ☐ higher-order learning

Can I describe the basic components of operant conditioning and their effects on behavior?

    ☐ positive reinforcement

    ☐ negative reinforcement

    ☐ positive and negative punishment

Do I understand the difference between schedules of reinforcement?

    ☐ continuous

    ☐ partial (intermittent): fixed-interval, fixed-ratio, variable-interval, variable-ratio

☐ Can I provide examples of how biological constraints create learning predispositions?

☐ Can I describe the characteristics and differences between insight learning, latent learning and social learning?

☐ Can I apply learning principles to explain emotional learning, taste aversion, superstitions and learned helplessness?

☐ Can I describe how operant conditioning techniques can be used for behavior modification?

☐ Can I describe how biofeedback, coping strategies, and self-control can be used to address behavioral problems?

Can I describe the work of:

    ☐ Albert Bandura

    ☐ John Garcia

    ☐ Ivan Pavlov

    ☐ Robert Rescorla

    ☐ B. F. Skinner

    ☐ Edward Thorndike

    ☐ Edward Tolman

    ☐ John B. Watson

Unit VII

Cognition

Overview

Unit VII brings the topics of memory, thought, and language together under the umbrella of cognition. The first half of the unit discusses how memories are encoded, stored and retrieved, as well as theories of retrieval failure and forgetting. Elizabeth Loftus' work on the reliability of eyewitness testimony is presented in the section on memory construction, and tips to improve memory are provided. The unit continues with an overview of how thoughts are derived, how we process and make sense of concepts in our world, and how creativity results from myriad cognitive processes. The aids and detriments to problem solving are reviewed followed by a presentation of the mechanisms of decision making. Finally, the unit closes with a review of language formation and the relationship between language and thought.

Modules

31 Studying and Building Memories

32 Memory Storage and Retrieval

33 Forgetting, Memory Construction, and Memory Improvement

34 Thinking, Concepts, and Creativity

35 Solving Problems and Making Decisions

36 Thinking and Language

Tip #7
Form Study Groups

It is often said that we learn best by teaching others. And nowhere is that truer than in studying for your psychology exams! If you are looking to improve your understanding and retrieval of key psychological knowledge, form a small study group of like-minded students. Include a variety of people because sometimes a classmate may really understand a concept you struggle with and sometimes you are the one who can readily explain a tough concept. Arrange a place to meet and practice quizzing each other on the material. Remember to include applications of the terms and theories, not just definitions. Use the extremely helpful and practical suggestions from Modules 31 and 33 to help you remember key concepts. One group member can make a study outline, one can lead the review, one can develop quiz questions and roles can rotate at the next study session. And of course, don't forget the pizza!

Module 31

Studying and Building Memories

Before You Read

Module Summary

Module 31 offers a definition of memory and explains how psychologists describe the human memory system. The module distinguishes between explicit and implicit memories and explains how sensory, short-term, and working memory function. A section on the difference between effortful processing and automatic processing is presented and a description of the levels of processing and their effect on encoding closes the module.

Before beginning the module, take a moment to read each of the following terms and names you will encounter. You may wish to make vocabulary cards for each.

Key Terms

memory
encoding
storage
retrieval
parallel processing
sensory memory
short-term memory
long-term memory
working memory
explicit memory
effortful processing

automatic processing
implicit memory
iconic memory
echoic memory
chunking
mnemonics
spacing effect
testing effect
shallow processing
deep processing

Key Names

Richard Atkinson
Richard Shiffrin
George A. Miller

While You Read

Answer the following questions/prompts.

 31-1

1. Compare the definition of memory to the definition of learning (from Unit VI).

2. How has research on memory's extremes helped us understand how **memory works?**

31-2

1. The analogy of a computer system is often used to illustrate the **different parts of memory. The keyboard is** where we *encode* new information, the CPU (or main hard drive) is **where we** *store* information, and the monitor is where we *retrieve* information.
encoding: keyboard
storage: CPU
retrieval: monitor

Now create your own analogy and explain why each part of the **memory system corresponds with the** analogy you have selected.

encoding:

storage:

retrieval:

2. How could a file cabinet full of file folders fit the analogy above?
encoding:

storage:

retrieval:

3. Define and give an example of parallel processing.

4. Define the Atkinson and Shiffrin model of memory and the information-processing model. Compare how Atkinson and Shiffrin's model of memory is similar to and dissimilar from the information-processing model. Which model do you most agree with and why?

5. Give an example of how you encoded, stored and retrieved a psychology term or concept from any previous unit.

6. Imagine you are trying to remember a math formula. Using Figure 31.2, show how each of the stages in the model would be applied to memorize the math formula.

7. Explain why "working memory" is a more useful term for the way we process memory.

8. Teachers are sometimes asked to put their classroom lecture notes online for students to view later. According to Sparrow et al., why might this result in decreased memory for the material?

31-3

1. Explain how explicit and implicit memories are produced and processed. Be sure to discuss how the two types of memory are different.

2. How do the terms *declarative* and *nondeclarative* apply to explicit and implicit memory? Provide your own example for each category.

31-4

1. In your own words, explain how we automatically process:

Space:

Time:

Frequency:

2. How can effortful processing become more automatic over time?

31-5

1. Define *sensory memory.*

2. Discuss how echoic and iconic memory operate in sensory memory. Provide examples of each in your own life.

31-6

1. Compare the capacity of short-term memory to that of working memory.

2. What have we learned about our ability to focus on more than one event at a time? Support your answer with an example from your own life.

31-7

1. List and give three examples of effortful processing strategies.

2. Explain how organizing new material into categories helps us recall it.

3. Explain why chunking and mnemonic devices are useful in aiding memory. Provide an example of how you have used each of these in your own experiences.

4. How does the spacing effect relate to distributed practice and recall?

5. Discuss why it is more advantageous to practice retrieval of information than to reread material.

6. Explain how you can put the principles of distributed practice, the spacing effect and the testing effect to use in studying for the test on this unit.

31-8

1. Explain, using examples and definitions, how shallow processing differs from deep processing.

2. How does *meaning* help aid retrieval or reduce the encoding time and effort?

3. Discuss how the self-reference effect aids recall.

After You Read

Module 31 Review

Complete the Matching Questions below to see if you have mastered the basics.

Terms

_____ 1. short-term memory

_____ 2. working memory

_____ 3. explicit memory

_____ 4. effortful processing

_____ 5. iconic memory

_____ 6. echoic memory

_____ 7. long-term memory

_____ 8. implicit memory

_____ 9. sensory memory

_____ 10. automatic processing

Definitions

A. activated memory that holds a few items briefly before the information is stored or forgotten

B. a momentary sensory memory of visual stimuli; a photographic or picture-image memory lasting no more than a few tenths of a second

C. the relatively permanent and limitless storehouse of the memory system

D. the immediate, very brief recording of sensory information in the memory system

E. a momentary sensory memory of auditory stimuli; if attention is elsewhere, sounds and words can still be recalled within 3 or 4 seconds

F. a newer understanding of short-term memory that focuses on conscious, active processing of incoming auditory and visual-spatial information, and of information retrieved from long-term memory

G. memory of facts and experiences that one can consciously know and "declare"

H. encoding that requires attention and conscious effort

I. retention independent of conscious recollection

J. unconscious encoding of incidental information such as time, space and frequency

11. Explain how chunking could be used to remember this long string of letters:

TSAFBICIAIRSNSADOJDOE

12. Devise a mnemonic device to remember the four lobes of the brain (learned in Unit II).

13. Janice, a classmate in your psychology class, wants to improve her memory for the material in the course. She has been staying up late, pulling all-night study sessions the night before tests, and getting up early to reread the chapter before quizzes. Use the concepts of the spacing effect, the testing effect, and deep processing to advise Janice of a better way to study.

14. Katrina is a talkative student in your class. The teacher is halfway through a detailed explanation of the causes of the Civil War when Katrina leans over to tell you about a joke she saw online. The teacher stops in the middle of her explanation and accuses Katrina of not listening. Katrina defensively retorts, "I was listening and I can prove it. You just said the most significant cause of the Civil War was the inequity in wealth between the slave-holding states and the non-slave-holding states." The teacher apologized because that was indeed what she had just said. Katrina smirked in victory, but as a psychology student, you understand that something else occurred. Explain why Katrina was able to repeat word-for-word what the teacher had been saying.

Module 32

Memory Storage and Retrieval

Module Summary

Module 32 describes the capacity of our long-term memories and the roles of various brain structures in memory processing. Also discussed are how emotions and changes at the synaptic level affect our memory processing. The module closes with a description of how external cues, internal emotions, and order of appearance influence memory retrieval.

Before beginning the module, take a moment to read each of the following terms and names you will encounter. You may wish to make vocabulary cards for each.

Key Terms

hippocampus

flashbulb memory

long-term potentiation (LTP)

recall

recognition

relearning

priming

mood-congruent memory

serial position effect

Key Names

Eric Kandel

Hermann Ebbinghaus

While You Read

Answer the following questions/prompts.

32-1

1. Discuss our current understanding of the limits of long-term memory.

2. How do we process and store memories?

32-2

1. Discuss the frontal lobe's role in processing particular types of memory.

2. Explain how the hippocampus functions in the encoding of explicit memories.

3. Describe the role that sleep plays in memory consolidation.

32-3

1. Apply your knowledge of classical conditioning to the situation in which a patient becomes afraid of a tack. Identify the unconditioned stimulus (US), unconditioned response (UR), neutral stimulus (NS), conditioned stimulus (CS) and the conditioned response (CR).

2. Discuss how the cerebellum plays a role in memory processing.

3. Explain the role of the basal ganglia in procedural memory.

4. Briefly explain infantile amnesia.

32-4

1. How does the amygdala play a role in memory processing?

2. Give an example from your own life of a flashbulb memory. Discuss the meaning of the term "flashbulb" in this context. Are flashbulb memories implicit or explicit? Explain.

3. Answer the Try This from page 332: Which do you think is more important—your experiences or your memories of them? Explain your thinking.

32-5

1. Summarize and discuss the importance of the work of Kandel and Schwartz with the sea slug *Aplysia* as it relates to memory processing.

2. Explain the meaning of and list the support for long-term potentiation as a physical basis for memory. Provide an example of how this process may be disrupted.

32-6

1. Discuss the difference between the three measures of retention. Give an example of each from your own life.

2. Use Figure 32.6 and information from the text to summarize and analyze the results of Ebbinghaus' work with memory.

32-7

1. Use Figure 32.7 and information from the text to provide a new example of priming.

2. In what ways can context aid memory recall?

3. Explain how state-dependent memory differs from context-dependent memory.

4. How does mood-congruent memory influence the retrieval and recall of other memories? How has this worked in your own experiences?

5. Use Figure 32.9 and information from the text to explain how the primacy and recency effects relate to the serial position phenomenon. Create a new example that illustrates your explanation.

After You Read

Module 32 Review

Answer the following questions to see if you have mastered the basics.

1. The brain structure shown to be essential in laying down new explicit memories of names, images and events is the
   a. amygdala.
   b. hippocampus.
   c. cerebellum.
   d. basal ganglia.
   e. hypothalamus.

2. The brain structure shown to be necessary in the development of implicit memories for skills, particularly classically conditioned reflexes, is the
   a. basal ganglia.
   b. hippocampus.
   c. amygdala.
   d. cerebellum.
   e. hypothalamus.

3. Implicit procedural memories for motor movement or skills like riding a bike seem to be a function of the
   a. amygdala.
   b. hippocampus.
   c. hypothalamus.
   d. frontal lobes.
   e. basal ganglia.

4. Which of the following is a typical example of a flashbulb memory?
   a. the scrambled eggs you had for breakfast this morning
   b. the daily homework assignment from your psychology teacher
   c. your first kiss
   d. the shirt you wore to school yesterday
   e. the chores your parent asked you to complete after school

5. Which of the following is NOT a measure of retention?
   a. recall
   b. recognition
   c. relearning
   d. retrieval
   e. long-term potentiation

6. Jim has just memorized the following list of words for his 3rd grade spelling test: host, most, coast, boast, ghost. When asked by a classmate, "What do you put in a toaster?" Jim replies "Toast!" "No, silly!" said his friend. "You put bread in a toaster!" What psychological process caused Jim to reply incorrectly?
   a. long-term potentiation
   b. priming
   c. serial position effect
   d. implicit memory
   e. recall

7. Leila is studying an alphabetical list of thirty African countries. She has a test tomorrow in her 4th grade history class and hopes to remember all thirty. According to the serial position effect, it is most likely that Leila will
   a. remember the countries at the beginning of the list, but not the end.
   b. recall the countries at the end of the list only.
   c. remember all thirty correctly.
   d. recall the countries at the beginning and end of the list, but not as many from the middle.
   e. remember the countries from the middle of the list, but not as many from the beginning or the end.

8. Danielle has just broken up with her long-time boyfriend and is feeling quite down. Her friends are trying to cheer her up, but are having a hard time. According to the research on memory, in her current emotional state, what memories is Danielle most likely to recall? Why?

9. John robbed three banks, stashed the money in a secret place in the woods, then jumped into the getaway car and raced off. Due to his erratic state, he got into a car accident and has suffered trauma to his brain. After leaving the hospital, John still remembered how to drive a car and find his way home. He did not have memory of the bank robbery or the hiding spot of the loot. Discuss which brain structures may have been damaged and which remained undamaged in John's accident and the reasons for your answer.

10. Jorge is preparing for a psychology test and tells you he really hopes the test is in essay format so he'll get a better grade. Based on your understanding of measures of retention, how would you respond to Jorge?

Module 33

Forgetting, Memory Construction, and Memory Improvement

Before You Read

Module Summary

Module 33 explains how we forget and how misinformation, imagination, and source amnesia distort our recollection and our ability to discern true memories from false. The module discusses Elizabeth Loftus' work on eyewitness testimony and discusses the controversies surrounding claims of repressed and recovered memories. The module concludes with tips on using memory research to improve your studies.

Before beginning the module, take a moment to read each of the following terms and names you will encounter. You may wish to make vocabulary cards for each.

Key Terms

anterograde amnesia   repression

retrograde amnesia   misinformation effect

proactive interference   source amnesia

retroactive interference   déjà vu

Key Names

Hermann Ebbinghaus

Elizabeth Loftus

While You Read

Answer the following questions/prompts.

33-1

1. Discuss how forgetting can actually be helpful and efficient.

2. Explain how anterograde amnesia differs from retrograde amnesia, and use personal examples to support your explanation.

3. Summarize the theories that address the reasons we forget:

   a. encoding failure:

   b. storage decay:

   c. retrieval failure:

   d. proactive interference:

   e. retroactive interference:

   f. motivated forgetting/repression:

4. Briefly summarize the work of Hermann Ebbinghaus on the retention and recall of nonsense syllables.

5. Using Figure 33.2 and information from the text, draw a basic cartoon illustrating Ebbinghaus' forgetting curve.

33-2

1. Summarize and discuss the importance of Elizabeth Loftus' work on the misinformation effect. How might the misinformation effect impact those testifying as eyewitnesses in crime? How might lawyers use the misinformation effect to their favor in a criminal case?

2. Provide an example of a time in your life when you have fallen victim to the misinformation effect.

3. Explain how source amnesia affects our formation of memory.

4. How does source amnesia help explain déjà vu?

5. What difficulties arise in trying to sort real memories from false memories? Why is it that false memories often seem to be so vivid and strong?

33-3

1. Summarize and discuss the implications of research on children's eyewitness descriptions.

2. In what circumstances have children been shown to be reliable eyewitnesses?

3. Discuss the controversy surrounding repressed or constructed memories of abuse.

4. How has the American Psychological Association (APA) helped to negotiate this controversy?

33-4

1. Show how the seven tips provided in the text can be applied to your study of psychology. Give specific examples, timeframes, and terminology that support your application.

   a. rehearse repeatedly:

b. make the material meaningful:

c. activate retrieval cues:

d. use mnemonic devices:

e. minimize interference:

f. sleep more:

g. test your own knowledge:

After You Read

Module 33 Review

Answer the following questions to see if you have mastered the basics.

1. Rashad has recently been in a car accident and suffered damage to his brain, which has him hospitalized and involved in rehabilitative therapy. He can recall his childhood and other memories from his past, but is having difficulty learning the names of his nurses, doctors and aides and cannot recall from one day to the next what he did the day before. Most likely Rashad is suffering from
   a. the forgetting curve.
   b. anterograde amnesia.
   c. retrograde amnesia.
   d. storage decay.
   e. proactive interference.

2. Samantha cannot recall her childhood, her name, or most of the events that occurred prior to the trauma that caused her brain damage. She does, however, seem to be making good progress in her therapy and has learned the names of her doctors and nurses. Samantha's condition is likely
   a. retroactive interference.
   b. anterograde amnesia.
   c. misinformation effect.
   d. retrograde amnesia.
   e. motivated forgetting.

3. In Ebbinghaus' studies involving recall of nonsense syllables he found that
   a. memories stored in childhood are more easily retrieved.
   b. memory for new information fades fast and is completely lost.
   c. subjects still attempted to chunk the syllables into meaningful units.
   d. memory for new information fades fast then levels off over time.
   e. relearning was improved by working memory.

4. Troy just moved to a new school in the middle of his junior year. He is given a locker combination but keeps entering the combination from his old locker before he remembers his new combination. This occurrence is referred to as
   a. retroactive interference.
   b. encoding failure.
   c. anterograde amnesia.
   d. proactive interference.
   e. retrograde amnesia.

5. The sense that "I've been in this exact situation before" is referred to as
   a. reconstructive memory.
   b. déjà vu.
   c. source amnesia.
   d. proactive interference.
   e. mood-congruent memory.

6. Studies by Loftus and Palmer on the misinformation effect, in which people were quizzed about a film of an accident, indicate that
   a. when quizzed immediately, people can recall very little, due to the stress of witnessing an accident.
   b. when questioned as little as one day later, their memory was very inaccurate.
   c. most people had very accurate memories as long as 6 months later.
   d. people's recall may easily be affected by misleading information.
   e. people could recall the first and last events of the film, but not the middle.

7. Lindsey has a vivid memory of swimming with dolphins when she was a young girl, but her mother denies that this ever occurred. Her mother explained that Lindsey watched many movies about dolphins and visited them frequently at the aquarium as a toddler, but did not actually swim with them herself. The best explanation for Lindsey's constructed memory is
   a. retroactive interference.
   b. source amnesia.
   c. déja vu.
   d. proactive interference.
   e. retrieval failure.

8. When he was a young boy, Montel lied to people he respected. This caused him a great deal of distress but he felt he had no choice. Years later, when asked if he lied as a child, Montel reported being a pretty honest kid. A psychoanalytic psychologist would likely explain Montel's self-censoring of this painful and anxiety-provoking memory as
   a. source amnesia.
   b. proactive interference.
   c. anterograde amnesia.
   d. recall failure.
   e. repression.

9. Caitlin is learning French in college after spending her high school years studying Spanish. Initially, she has difficulty learning the new French words as the Spanish words keep getting in the way. However, over the course of the semester Caitlin becomes much more fluent in French and can no longer even recall the Spanish word for the same item. Which is the best explanation for Caitlin's experience in world languages?
   a. Initially, her recall of the Spanish terms was blocked through proactive interference and recall of the French words is blocked through retroactive interference.
   b. In the beginning, Caitlin was not encoding the terms effortfully and later in the semester she began encoding the terms automatically.
   c. Caitlin was impacted by the misinformation effect in the beginning of the semester but as that passed, she was able to learn the French words.
   d. Initially, Caitlin's recall of the French was blocked through proactive interference, and eventually, recall of the Spanish vocabulary is blocked through retroactive interference.
   e. Initially, Caitlin's recall of the French vocabulary was blocked by retroactive interference, but toward the end of the semester, the Spanish vocabulary was blocked by retroactive interference.

10. Bruck and Ceci's work on children's eyewitness descriptions and accuracy of recollection showed
   a. children's recollections can be easily skewed by suggestive interviewing techniques.
   b. older children tend to recall events more vividly than younger children.
   c. preschoolers are the least likely to produce false stories when asked.
   d. psychologist specializing in interviewing children have tools that help detect real from false memories.
   e. children were especially accurate when they talked about the incident with adults prior to the interview.

Module 34

Thinking, Concepts, and Creativity

Before You Read

Module Summary

Module 34 defines and reviews the functions of cognition and identifies the factors associated with creativity.

Before beginning the module, take a moment to read each of the following terms and name you will encounter. You may wish to make vocabulary cards for each.

Key Terms		Key Name
cognition	creativity	Robert Sternberg
concept	convergent thinking	
prototype	divergent thinking	

While You Read

Answer the following questions/prompts.

34-1

1. Discuss how concepts simplify cognition. Provide an example of a concept from the text and one of your own creation.

2. Explain how a prototype aids in the formation of concepts.

3. Discuss the problems that arise when an object, person, or event does not fit our prototype.

34-2

1. Explain how the processes of convergent and divergent thinking contribute to creativity.

2. Using Robert Sternberg's five components of creativity, consider whether you self-identify as creative. Support or refute each of the components with a specific example from your life.

3. How do intelligence and creativity co-mingle to impact one's success?

4. Briefly explain the components that make up creativity.

5. Explain, using the material in this module, how it may be possible to increase creativity.

After You Read

Module 34 Review

Complete the questions below to see if you have mastered the basics.

1. Place the words below in either the Concept or Prototype category of the chart. Then, add one concept and one prototype of your own. Two have been filled in for you.

couch	Red Delicious apple	robin	laugh
sing	Jay-Z	flower	4-door sedan

Concept	Prototype
laugh	*Jay-Z*

2. Devon is part of a consumer survey group and is being asked to think of as many ways as he can to improve gas mileage in a new line of vehicles. Devon's responses require _____ thinking.

3. In Geometry class, Chantal is asked for the answer to a problem on the board. Her response requires _____ thinking.

4. What are the five components of creativity, according to Robert Sternberg?

5. When forming a concept, people often develop a best example, or _____ , of a category.

Module 35

Solving Problems and Making Decisions

Before You Read

Module Summary

Module 35 describes the cognitive strategies that assist and hinder our problem-solving abilities. The module explains heruristics and algorithms as problem-solving strategies and discusses how overconfidence, belief perseverance, and framing influence our decisions and judgments. The module closes with a description of intuition and the ways in which smart thinkers utilize this ability.

Before beginning the module, take a moment to read each of the following terms and names you will encounter. You may wish to make vocabulary cards for each.

Key Terms

		Key Names
algorithm	representative heuristic	Wolfgang Köhler
heuristic	availability heuristic	Amos Tversky
insight	overconfidence	Daniel Kahneman
confirmation bias	belief perseverance	
mental set	framing	
intuition		

While You Read

Answer the following questions/prompts.

1. Discuss and give an example of how algorithms differ from heuristics as problem-solving strategies.

2. How have you personally used an algorithm and a heuristic as problem-solving strategies?

3. How does insight relate to problem solving?

4. Explain, using definitions and real-life examples, the ways in which confirmation bias and mental set can impede the ability to problem solve.

5. How might confirmation bias and mental set relate to one's political views?

35-2

1. Briefly summarize and give an example of the representativeness heuristic.

2. Use the data from Figure 35.4 to summarize and give an example of the availability heuristic.

3. How does the concept of overconfidence influence your decisions or judgments in both helpful and detrimental ways? Give an example of overconfidence impacting a decision in your life.

4. Define and give an example of belief perseverance. How is it different from confirmation bias? Provide your own example of belief perseverance.

5. Explain the power of framing in influencing our cognitions. Provide an example of how framing could be a powerful persuasion tool in negotiating with your parents for a later curfew.

35-3

1. How does intuition fit into the larger discussion of cognition? What does it mean that intuition is often implicit?

After You Read

Module 35 Review

Complete the questions below to see if you have mastered the basics.

Terms

_____ 1. algorithm

_____ 2. heuristic

_____ 3. insight

_____ 4. confirmation bias

_____ 5. mental set

_____ 6. representative heuristic

_____ 7. availability heuristic

_____ 8. overconfidence

_____ 9. belief perseverance

_____ 10. framing

Definitions

A. a tendency to search for information that supports our preconceptions and to ignore or distort contradictory evidence

B. a tendency to approach a problem in one particular way because the approach has been successful in the past.

C. the way an issue is posed; how an issue is phrased can significantly affect decisions and judgments

D. a sudden realization of a problem's solution

E. a simple thinking strategy that often allows us to make judgments and solve problems efficiently but may sometimes lead to the wrong conclusion

F. judging the likelihood of things in terms of how well they seem to represent, or match, particular prototypes

G. clinging to one's initial conceptions after the basis on which they were formed has been discredited

H. a methodical, logical rule or procedure that guarantees solving a particular problem

I. the tendency to be more confident than correct, to overestimate the accuracy of our beliefs and judgments

J. estimating the likelihood of events based on their availability in memory

11. Keisha is told that her new geometry instructor will be flexible, nurturing, and soft-spoken. When she arrives to class on the first day, Keisha is somewhat surprised to discover her instructor is a man. Most likely Keisha applied _____ in her vision of her new instructor.
    a. the representativeness heuristic
    b. belief perseverance
    c. confirmation bias
    d. mental set
    e. the framing effect

12. Barrett's parents are divorced and several of his friends' parents are divorced as well. In a class discussion about marriage and compatibility, Barrett shares his opinion that the divorce rate is on the rise and that most marriages will not remain intact over time. It is likely Barrett's opinion is influenced by
    a. overconfidence.
    b. a mental set.
    c. the representativeness heuristic.
    d. belief perseverance.
    e. the availability heuristic.

13. The tendency to minimize the arguments that contradict our opinions and accept information that supports them is known as
    a. framing.
    b. confirmation bias.
    c. mental set.
    d. representativeness heuristic.
    e. insight.

14. When Tim and Ali were dating, he learned that she liked to receive flowers after they had a fight. Years later, Tim dates another woman and after having a fight, he stops by the florist to order a bouquet of flowers. Tim is likely affected by which cognitive occurrence?
    a. confirmation bias
    b. mental set
    c. representativeness heuristic
    d. insight
    e. availability heuristic

15. Simran is running for class officer and has to present a compelling speech in front of the student body. She is adamant about the illiteracy problem in her 2000-student school and wants to drive home the statistics that demonstrate the pervasiveness of the problem. Having studied psychology last year, Simran adds the following points to her speech:
    "22% of our classmates failed the end-of-year reading exam last spring."
    "Schools like ours that have implemented literacy support programs have shown a 17% increase in student's reading ability"
    It is apparent from these inclusions, that Simran understands the power of
    a. confirmation bias.
    b. overconfidence.
    c. intuition.
    d. algorithms.
    e. framing.

Module 36

Thinking and Language

Before You Read

Module Summary

Module 36 concludes Unit VII by tying thought and cognition to language acquisition. The milestones and acquisition processes of language development are reviewed and the brain areas involved in language processing and speech are identified. The module concludes by describing the relationship between language and thinking and discussing the value of thinking in images.

Before beginning the module, take a moment to read each of the following terms and names you will encounter. You may wish to make vocabulary cards for each.

Key Terms		Key Names
language	two-word stage	Steven Pinker
phoneme	telegraphic speech	Noam Chomsky
morpheme	aphasia	Paul Broca
grammar	Broca's area	Carl Wernicke
babbling stage	Wernicke's area	Benjamin Lee Whorf
one-word stage	linguistic determinism	

While You Read

Answer the following questions/prompts.

36-1

1. Discuss the various forms of communication that could be considered language.

2. Explain how phonemes differ from morphemes.

3. Can you think of a phoneme that is also a morpheme?

4. Consider the word *incomprehensible*. List the phonemes and morphemes that make up this word.

5. Which sentence below is an example of poor syntax and which exhibits faulty semantics? Explain your answer.

  a. Sluggish calendars advise immediate butchers.

  b. Lunch disturbs eaten hastily digestion.

36-2

1. Explain how infants develop receptive language. How is this different from productive language?

2. List and describe the stages involved in productive language. In your description, include the characteristics and an example of what children can say in each respective stage.

36-3

1. Briefly address Noam Chomsky's view regarding how children acquire language.

2. What does current research reveal about the importance of the critical period in language development?

3. Based on the research presented in the text, what advice would you give a friend who is hoping to raise her new son to be multilingual?

4. How might the results differ for your friend's son above and her parents who have just immigrated and are trying to learn a new language?

36-4

1. Briefly explain aphasia.

2. Using examples, explain the roles of Broca's and Wernicke's areas on language and speech processing. How do the two effects differ?

3. Discuss how the brain divides its mental functions into subfunctions.

36-5

1. Explain Whorf's linguistic determinism and discuss why it may be too extreme of a hypothesis in explaining the relationship between language and thinking.

2. What evidence does the text provide that we may interpret the world differently because of our language?

3. In what situations might we tend to think in images? Discuss how thinking in images can be valuable and what the limitations might be.

After You Read

Module 36 Review

Circle the correct answers below to see if you have mastered the basics.

1. The concept of linguistic determinism is most closely associated with
   a. Steven Pinker.
   b. Carl Wernicke.
   c. Benjamin Whorf.
   d. Paul Broca.
   e. Noam Chomsky.

2. Consider the word *unbuttoned.* Which of the following is true of this word?
   a. It has 4 morphemes and 8 phonemes.
   b. It has 3 morphemes and 9 phonemes.
   c. It has one morpheme and 10 phonemes.
   d. It has 4 morphemes and 5 phonemes.
   e. It has 3 morphemes and 4 phonemes.

3. Carlos was born into a Spanish-speaking household and as an infant he made many babbling sounds that could be identified as Chinese or Swahili, in addition to those that sounded Spanish. Now, as an adult, Carlos cannot distinguish the sounds in any language but Spanish. The explanation for this occurrence is likely that
   a. he cannot retrieve the sounds due to retroactive interference.
   b. he wasn't exposed to any other languages but Spanish and lost his innate ability to hear and produce sounds and tones outside his native language.
   c. Carlos was exposed to too many other languages in school.
   d. he is missing a portion of his hippocampus, which is essential for memory of words.
   e. Chinese and Swahili words have too many morphemes and are hard to pronounce.

4. Two-year-old Claudia is finishing dinner in her high chair. She says, "Me, down" to her mother. Her mother understands that Claudia is finished and wants to be taken out of her chair and set down to play. Claudia is displaying
   a. telegraphic speech.
   b. receptive language.
   c. babbling.
   d. a morpheme.
   e. a phoneme.

5. Stephanie sustained left temporal lobe damage in an athletic injury and has just returned home from a long stay in the hospital. Her mother asks her to check on the dinner cooking in the oven and Stephanie responds, "The boy didn't jump as fast and the turtle should have known it". Stephanie's misunderstanding of her mother's request and her subsequent meaningless response is most likely caused by
   a. linguistic determinism.
   b. Broca's aphasia.
   c. a critical period for language.
   d. Wernicke's aphasia.
   e. universal grammar constraints.

✓ Check Yourself   Now that you have mastered the basics, work through the problems below to see if you can *synthesize*, *evaluate*, and *analyze* what you have learned.

Carly is a social studies teacher at a new school and will be welcoming students into the classroom next week. She has just received her student roster for the course and finds the following students listed:

Short-Term Memory Maria

Hippocampus Damage Holly

Retroactive Interference Inez

Divergent Thinking Daniel

Mental Set Monty

Linguistic Determinism Diego

Using definitions and examples, discuss the specific obstacles and limitations each student will face in Carly's class.

Before You Move On

Use the checklist below to verify your understanding of the unit's main points.

- [ ] Do I understand the difference between different types of cognitive processes (for example, effortful versus automatic processing; deep versus shallow processing; focused versus divided attention)?

Can I describe the psychological and physiological systems of memory?
- [ ] short-term memory
- [ ] working memory
- [ ] long-term memory
- [ ] explicit memory
- [ ] implicit memory
- [ ] procedural memory
- [ ] semantic memory
- [ ] episodic memory

Can I describe the principles that support memory?
- [ ] encoding
- [ ] storage
- [ ] retrieval

- [ ] Do I understand how biopsychosocial factors facilitate language acquisition, development, and usage?

- [ ] Can I identify the aids and obstacles to problem solving?

- [ ] Can I list the characteristics of creative thought and thinkers?

Can I describe the research findings of:
- [ ] Noam Chomsky
- [ ] Benjamin Whorf
- [ ] Hermann Ebbinghaus
- [ ] Elizabeth Loftus
- [ ] George A. Miller
- [ ] Wolfgang Köhler

Unit VIII

Motivation, Emotion, and Stress

Overview

Unit VIII explores the motivations and emotions that drive our behavior, and examines the health effects of intense or prolonged emotions such as anger and stress. The unit begins by explaining the contrasting theories of motivation and applies them to common motivations: hunger, sex, and affiliation. The unit then explores the theories of emotion and explains the differences between the James-Lange, Cannon-Bard, and Schachter and Singer two-factor theory, as well as introducing two newer theories of emotion. Our ability to communicate nonverbally with facial expressions and gestures is explained in Module 42 and research into cultural similarities and differences in emotional expression is discussed. The unit concludes with two modules covering the impact of stress on health and the prevalent illnesses impacted by stress, such as cancer, AIDS, and depression.

Modules

37 Motivational Concepts

38 Hunger Motivation

39 Sexual Motivation

40 Social Motivation: Affiliation Needs

41 Theories and Physiology of Emotion

42 Expressed Emotion

43 Stress and Health

44 Stress and Illness

Tip #8
Reduce Stress by Reducing "Busy-ness"

Reducing stress is not always as easy as it sounds. There are many demands placed on you by family members, teachers, coaches, and of course, yourself! How to balance all of these demands and still find time for quiet reflection, a fun game of Monopoly, a walk in your local park, or just staying healthy is the challenge. It may seem like there is never enough time to finish all of your schoolwork and chores and still have time for you. You can work to reduce your overall load and that starts by taking a look at your schedule. Evaluate the courses you are taking and the homework load each of those courses requires. Is it right for you? Could you make some changes this year or register for different courses next year to provide more time for rest, fun and that all-important sleep? How many clubs or outside activities are you involved in? Do you actually get fulfillment and enjoyment from each of them or might you cut back on a few? Carefully choosing your daily scheduled activities with stress reduction in mind can make a big difference on your overall well-being. Give it a try!

Module 37

Motivational Concepts

Before You Read

Module Summary

Module 37 defines motivation and introduces four main theories of motivation. Key terms like homeostasis and instinct are explained in detail.

Before beginning the module, take a moment to read each of the following terms and the name you will encounter. You may wish to make vocabulary cards for each.

Key Terms

motivation

instinct

drive-reduction theory

homeostasis

incentive

Yerkes-Dodson law

hierarchy of needs

Key Name

Abraham Maslow

While You Read

Answer the following questions/prompts.

37-1

1. How do psychologists define *motivation*?

2. Describe some of the nature and nurture factors that influence motivation.

3. Complete the chart below.

Perspective/Theory	Key Terms	Key Contributors	Summary
Instinct/Evolutionary			
Drive-Reduction		*none mentioned*	
Arousal			
Hierarchy of Needs			

4. Briefly summarize the strengths and weaknesses of each theory as described by Table 37.1.

5. Explain and use a new example to illustrate the relationship between a need, a drive, and a behavior.

6. How does the body try to maintain homeostasis?

7. How do incentives pull behavior from an organism?

8. Explain why different levels of arousal might be required for tasks of different difficulty. Use the following figure as a guide.

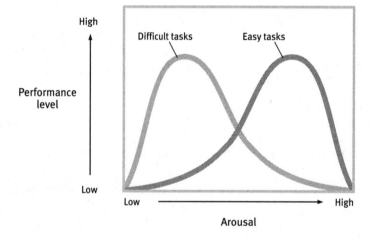

9. Consider a typical day in your life. Using Figure 37.3, provide one example from your day of how you are motivated to meet each of the needs described in Maslow's hierarchy. The chart below is provided for your work.

Maslow's Need	My Example
physiological	
safety	
belongingness and love	
esteem	
self-actualization	
self-transcendence	

After You Read

Module 37 Review

Select the best answers to see if you have mastered the basics.

1. Every day, after a long day of work, Juan heads out to practice his sky-diving maneuvers. He often spends weekends jumping out of planes and bungee jumping. Which of the following motivation theories most correctly explains why Juan enjoys these risky behaviors?
   a. drive-reduction theory
   b. instinct theory
   c. arousal theory
   d. evolution theory
   e. incentive theory

2. Mohandas Gandhi and Alice Paul are two historical figures who often fasted or used hunger strikes as a means of gaining attention to their cause. Their motivations refute which of the following theories of motivation?
   a.   hierarchy of needs
   b.   instinct theory
   c.   drive-reduction theory
   d.   arousal theory
   e.   incentive theory

3. Studies have shown that newborn waterfowl, when presented with a model of a bird with a short neck like a hawk, who are a threat to them, were more prone to try to escape from the area than when they were shown a bird model with a long neck like that of a goose. The young waterfowl's motivation to try to flee from this natural predator is best explained by which theory?
   a.   arousal theory
   b.   drive-reduction theory
   c.   incentive theory
   d.   instinct theory
   e.   homeostasis theory

4. A survivalist has been in the forest for over two weeks and is out of food and water. In desperation, she has begun eating leaves and various insects and can think of nothing more than satisfying her hunger. Which of the following theories would best explain her motivation to eat these items?
   a.   instinct theory
   b.   drive-reduction theory
   c.   incentive theory
   d.   arousal theory
   e.   Yerkes-Dodson theory

5. Martin is a brain surgeon with an extremely successful track record for treating a wide variety of brain damage in his patients. Each difficult surgery he undertakes requires painstaking precision, patience and skill. According to new research into optimal arousal, what would Martin's optimal arousal level be prior to beginning a new operation?
   a.   moderate
   b.   low
   c.   high
   d.   very high
   e.   somewhat high

Module 38

Hunger Motivation

Module Summary

Module 38 describes the physiological, cultural, and situational factors that influence hunger and motivate eating behavior. The module concludes with a discussion of the physiology and environmental factors affecting obesity.

Before beginning the module, take a moment to read each of the following terms you will encounter. You may wish to make vocabulary cards for each.

Key Terms

glucose
set point
basal metabolic rate

While You Read

Answer the following questions/prompts.

38-1

1. Explain how Cannon and Washburn's work established one factor that pushes or drives hunger.

2. Describe the role of glucose in triggering hunger.

3. Explain the effects on hunger and eating behavior when stimulating or destroying the appetite suppression areas of the hypothalamus.

4. Explain the impact of the set point on hunger and energy output.

5. Why might the term *set point* be too limiting in explaining weight gain and loss? How might a person attempt to increase his or her basal metabolic rate?   **OK?**

6. Use Figure 38.4 and the text to complete the chart.

Appetite Hormone	Location of Secretion	Effect on Hunger
Insulin		
Ghrelin		
Orexin		
Leptin		
PYY		

38-2

1. How might memory impact our desire to eat?

2. Discuss the cultural influence on eating behaviors.

3. Explain how geography and the environment in which a culture lives can impact food choice and taste.

    Gven that culture is covered in 2 and a culture
    doesn't live, how aboult "people live"

4. How do the following impact eating behavior and weight?

    Group size:

    Portion size:

    Food variety:

38-3

1. List one social and one physiological/health consequence of being overweight or obese.

2. What role do set (or settling) point and metabolism play in obesity?

3. What role do genetics play in obesity?

4. What role do environmental factors play in obesity? What information in the Close-Up can help you make better choices regarding what you eat?

After You Read

Module 38 Review

Answer the following questions to see if you have mastered the basics.

1. Keisha is experiencing hunger pangs and stomach contractions as the lunch break nears. Fill in the chart below to indicate which of the hormones in Keisha's body are being secreted.

Hormone	Being Secreted Yes	No
Ghrelin		
Orexin		
Leptin		
PYY		

Choose either increases or decreases for the fill-in-the-blank questions below.

2. As blood glucose _____ , hunger increases.

3. As body weight rises, hunger _____ and energy expenditure _____ .

4. As food intake decreases, basal metabolic rate _____ and energy expenditure

   _____ .

5. When an overweight or obese person's body weight drops below its set point, the person's hunger

   _____ and metabolism _____ .

Module 39

Sexual Motivation

Before You Read

Module Summary

Module 39 describes the phases of the human sexual response cycle and lists the various dysfunctions that disrupt it. In addition, the module explains the impact of hormones and environmental stimuli on human sexual motivation.

Before beginning the module, take a moment to read each of the following terms and names you will encounter. You may wish to make vocabulary cards for each.

Key Terms

sexual response cycle

refractory period

sexual dysfunction

estrogens

testosterone

Key Names

William Masters

Virginia Johnson

While You Read

Answer the following questions/prompts.

39-1

1. Briefly summarize the work of Masters and Johnson in the 1960s.

2. Complete the chart.

Stage of Sexual Response Cycle	Physiological Changes
Excitement Phase	
Plateau Phase	
Orgasm	
Resolution Phase	

3. Discuss three sexual dysfunctions that impair sexual arousal or functioning.

   a.

   b.

   c.

4. Briefly address how the APA determines if a given experience/behavior is qualified as a sexual dysfunction.

39-2

1. Discuss the impact of estrogens and testosterone on sexual motivation.

2. Discuss the biopsychosocial factors impacting sexual motivation.

3. Explain how external and imagined stimuli impact sexual motivation. How can these materials have a detrimental effect on sexual behavior?

After You Read

Module 39 Review

Select the best answers to see if you have mastered the basics.

1. Which shows the correct order of the phases of the sexual response cycle?
   a. excitement, orgasm, plateau, resolution
   b. plateau, excitement, orgasm, resolution
   c. excitement, plateau, orgasm, resolution
   d. plateau, orgasm, excitement, resolution
   e. excitement, plateau, refractory period, orgasm, resolution

2. At a routine doctor appointment, a woman tells her physician that she rarely experiences orgasm with her husband of twenty years. The physician is most likely to tell her she has a sexual dysfunction called
   a. exhibitionism.
   b. premature ejaculation.
   c. erectile disorder.
   d. fetishism.
   e. female orgasmic disorder.

3. Which of the following is the correct relationship between the sex hormone and its effect on sexual behavior?
    a. lower testosterone levels result in increased interest in sex
    b. estrogens peak during ovulation
    c. testosterones peak during ovulation
    d. estrogens decline right before ovulation
    e. women's sexual interest rises as testosterone levels decrease

4. The period of time following orgasm in which a man cannot achieve another orgasm is referred to as
    a. a plateau.
    b. a sexual dysfunction.
    c. the sexual response cycle.
    d. the exhibition phase.
    e. the refractory period.

5. Findings regarding men's and women's interest in sexually explicit materials show that
    a. women experience only half as much arousal as men.
    b. women report nearly as much arousal to the materials as men.
    c. women report twice as much arousal to the materials as men.
    d. women experience no arousal while men experience high arousal.
    e. women report men experience decreased arousal when viewing materials.

Module 40

Social Motivation: Affiliation Needs

Before You Read

Module Summary

Module 40 presents evidence that supports the benefits of affiliating and explains the pain of being shut out of social interactions. The module also tackles the timely subject of Internet social connections, exploring the ways in which this novel technology impacts us both positively and negatively.

While You Read

Answer the following questions/prompts.

1. Using real-life examples, summarize what is meant by our need to "affiliate."

2. Summarize the benefits of belonging. Suggest an additional benefit of your own.

3. What are some behavioral effects of being excluded?

4. Briefly summarize the work of Baumeister et al. and Twenge et al. on the effects of rejection on behavior.

40-2

1. Cite specific information from the text to prove or disprove these statements:

    a. American teens have not readily adopted cell-phone use.

    b. People who report being lonely also report higher amounts of time spent online.

    c. Most heavy users of cell phones have lower grades.

    d. Person-to-person communication is no longer a predictor of life satisfaction.

    e. The images online users post are very unlike their actual personalities.

f. Narcissistic people have many more "friends" on social networking sites and more pictures posted of themselves.

2. How can the recommendations provided in the Close-Up on Managing Social Networking help you have a healthy relationship with both social media and the outside world?

After You Read

Module 40 Review

Answer the following prompt to see if you have mastered the basics.

> You are a parent raising a pre-teen daughter who is desperate to have her first cell phone. She argues that all of her friends have a phone and since she does not currently have one, she misses out on all the gossip and invitations to parties. In addition, you have not yet allowed her to have a presence on a social networking site, although many of her friends are signed up. Because you are an authoritative parent, you want to consider all of the benefits and drawbacks to your daughter's request and therefore you make the following "pro/con" list. In the "pro" column, list the reasons your daughter should have a cell phone and social networking access and in the "con" column list the reasons she should not. Be sure to address affiliation needs and the influences of social networking as described in the module.

Pro	Con

Module 41

Theories and Physiology of Emotion

Before You Read

Module Summary

Module 41 describes how arousal and expressive behaviors interact in emotional situations and discusses the link between emotional arousal and the autonomic nervous system. The role of consciously interpreting and labeling emotions in our understanding and experiencing of them is explained, and is followed by an examination of whether different emotions activate different physiological and brain-pattern responses. The module concludes with a review of the effectiveness and limitations of polygraph technology in detecting lies.

Before beginning the module, take a moment to read each of the following terms and names you will encounter. You may wish to make vocabulary cards for each.

Key Terms

emotion

James-Lange theory

Cannon-Bard theory

two-factor theory

polygraph

Key Names

William James

Stanley Schachter

While You Read

Answer the following questions/prompts.

Use these three words to answer questions 1 and 2.

| emotion | physiological arousal | bodily response. |

1. Place the three words in the box above in the order they would occur according to the James-Lange theory of emotion.

2. Place the three words in the box above in the order they would occur according to the Cannon-Bard theory.

3. Think of an example of a stimulus that produces an emotional response. Use both the James-Lange and the Cannon-Bard theory to explain why that emotion occurred.

41-2

1. What is the additional component Schachter and Singer add to the James-Lange and Cannon-Bard theories? Discuss how important you think that component is to emotional theory.

2. Place the following four words in the order they would occur according to Schachter and Singer's two-factor theory.

emotion   stimulus   physiological arousal   cognitive label.

3. Briefly summarize Schachter and Singer's experiment with epinephrine in the waiting room. What is the key component that causes participants to create the label for the emotion they are experiencing?

4. In what way does the work of Zajonc, LeDoux, or Lazarus contradict the work of the previous theorists?

41-3

1. What role do the sympathetic and parasympathetic nervous systems play in emotional arousal?

2. What are the physiological changes that occur in the sympathetic and parasympathetic nervous systems as a result of emotional arousal?

3. Consider the following figure. How does the Yerkes-Dodson law explain emotional arousal?

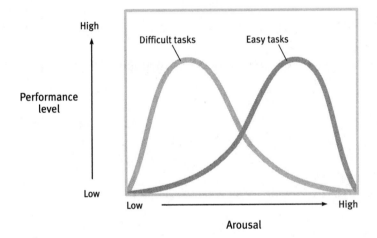

41-4

1. Discuss the relationship between different emotions and the

   a. presence of brain structure stimulation (be sure to include the insula, amygdala, prefrontal cortex, and frontal lobe):

   b. presence of facial feature change:

   c. physiological responses:

41-5

1. Briefly summarize the arguments against the effectiveness of polygraphs.

2. Why are polygraphs so popular on TV if evidence shows them to be so wrong?

3. What physiological information does a polygraph test attempt to collect to determine if participants are telling the truth or lying?

After You Read

Module 41 Review

Answer the following questions to see if you have mastered the basics.

Decide which theory of emotion best explains each scenario below. Write JL for the James-Lange theory, CB for the Cannon-Bard theory, and SS for Schachter and Singer's theory.

_____ 1. Shelby had tears streaming down her cheeks and became sad.

_____ 2. Daneen was out walking in a strange neighborhood at night when a man turned the corner and began walking toward her. Daneen recognized that her breathing and heart rate were accelerating and decided she must be afraid. Fearfully, she crossed over to the other side of the street.

_____ 3. The next day, Daneen was out walking in her own neighborhood when a man turned the corner and began walking toward her. Daneen recognized that her breathing and heart rate were accelerating and decided she must be excited. She screamed with delight as she ran to greet her father who just arrived from a long trip.

_____ 4. Ji-hoon is walking between classes at school when he encounters a student who has been bullying him. Immediately, his pulse increases and he begins to sweat as he is overwhelmed by fear.

_____ 5. Angelo noticed that his heart was racing and began shaking with fear.

Use the following scenario to answer questions 6 through 10.

> You are hoping to ask a girl in your next class if she will accompany you to the school dance. You are very nervous and excited. Address the impact the autonomic nervous system will have on each of the bodily processes described below as you enter the room to pop your question.

6. What role does your liver play? Why?

7. How will your lungs assist you in asking your question? Why?

8. What is happening with your digestion? Why?

9. What is happening to your pupils? Why?

10. What is happening with your sweat glands? Why?

Module 42

Expressed Emotion

Module Summary

Module 42 describes the nonverbal communication of emotion and discusses cultural and gender differences in this form of expression. The impact of facial expressions on our emotions is explained by the facial feedback effect.

Before beginning the module, take a moment to read each of the following terms you will encounter. You may wish to make vocabulary cards for each.

Key Terms

facial feedback effect

health psychology

While You Read

Answer the following questions/prompts.

42-1

1. Cite three examples from the text to support the following statement: "Humans communicate and detect emotion nonverbally."

    a.

    b.

    c.

2. Explain how a Duchenne smile differs from a feigned smile.

3. Why is it often difficult to tell when someone is being dishonest?

4. Briefly summarize how the research findings suggest men and women recognize and experience emotion differently from one another.

42-2

1. Explain how different nonverbal cues convey emotion across cultures. Provide a specific example for each and address how each can be interpreted correctly or incorrectly based on one's culture.

   a. gestures:

   b. facial expressions:

   c. music:

2. Why are smiles and expressed emotions social as well as emotional?

42-3

1. Using original examples, discuss how facial expressions can actually influence emotion. Explain why this is counterintuitive.

2. Define and give an example of the facial feedback effect.

3. Briefly explain the behavior feedback phenomenon.

4. On which specific areas does health psychology focus?

After You Read

Module 42 Review

Answer the following questions to see if you have mastered the basics.

1. Patrick is new to the school and is eager to meet new people and make new friends. Use your understanding of the facial feedback effect to offer Patrick advice on meeting his goal.

2. Hakim is new to your school, having just arrived from Ethiopia where he has lived since he was born. He is worried that he will have trouble being accepted here as people may not understand his facial expressions and may misinterpret them. Based on your understanding of culture and emotional expression, address Hakim's concern.

3. As a photographer, you are interested in having your subjects look as real and authentic as possible. When your models put on a smile for the camera you notice that it seems artificial and staged. You suggest they use a Duchenne smile for better pictures. The models don't take psychology and do not understand the reference. Explain to the models what you mean by the term and how it differs from the smile they are currently making for you.

4. Your best friend is upset with you over this text you sent last night.

Ur speech 2day made me LOL

You intended the text to be funny, but your friend interpreted it seriously, thinking you were laughing at her. Demonstrating your understanding of nonverbal communication, explain to her why she misinterpreted your text. Then, indicate how you could modify your text to make sure your friend knew you were joking.

Module 43

Stress and Health

Module Summary

Module 43 identifies events that provoke stress responses and describes how we respond and adapt to stress. This module makes the distinction between a stressor, a stress reaction, and stress. Hans Selye's general adaptation syndrome is explained in the context of possible responses to stress.

Before beginning the module, take a moment to read each of the following terms and name you will encounter. You may wish to make vocabulary cards for each.

Key Terms

stress

general adaptation syndrome (GAS)

tend-and-befriend response

Key Name

Hans Selye

While You Read

Answer the following questions/prompts.

 43-1

1. Use an example from your own life to explain the difference between a stressor, a stress reaction, and stress.

2. Explain how stressors can have positive effects. What stressors in your life have positive effects?

3. Discuss the negative effects of stress. What negative effects of stress have you experienced?

4. List and give an example from your life of the three types of stressors. Provide a hypothetical example if you have not experienced one of the types.

    a.

    b.

    c.

5. Use the diagram below to explain the three phases of the general adaptation syndrome (GAS). Create a hypothetical example to illustrate each of the three phases.

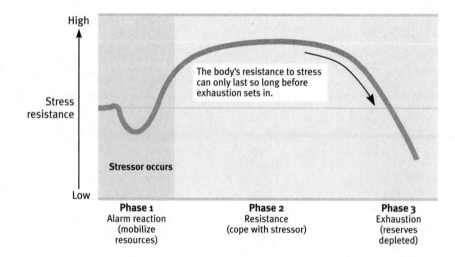

6. Discuss common reactions to extended stress.

7. Explain the tend-and-befriend response to stress.

After You Read

Module 43 Review

Answer the following question to see if you have mastered the basics.

> Ethan, a junior in high school, is the captain of the hockey team and attends practice every afternoon for three hours and tournament games out of town most weekends. He is being scouted by colleges in the area and hopes to be offered an athletic scholarship to play hockey, since his family does not have enough money to send him to college. In addition, he is taking three Advanced Placement® classes and two honors classes at school in the hopes of getting an academic scholarship to help pay his college tuition. Juggling all these demands has cost Ethan a lot of sleep. He has a lot riding on his grades and athletic performance this year; however, the sustained pressure of keeping up with the athletic and academic requirements is overwhelming him. He got a D– on his last test and his coach yelled at him for not running as fast during conditioning. He has begun to develop a cold and is feeling grouchy and uptight.

Identify the stressor, stress reaction, and stress in this scenario, then apply Hans Selye's work with the general adaptation syndrome to Ethan's case. Discuss the changes that might occur as Ethan moves through the three phases of the GAS.

Module 44

Stress and Illness

Before You Read

Module Summary

Module 44 explains the link between stress and illness. It discusses the relationship between cancer, AIDS, and depression with stress and highlights the personality types of people who are more prone to coronary illness.

Before beginning the module, take a moment to read each of the following terms you will encounter. You may wish to make vocabulary cards for each.

Key Terms

psychophysiological illness

psychoneuroimmunology

lymphocytes

coronary heart disease

Type A personality

Type B personality

While You Read

Answer the following questions/prompts.

44-1

1. Explain why the newly adopted term *psychophysiological illness* is a better description of the effects of stress-related illness than *psychosomatic*.

2. Complete the chart below.

Immune Cell	Action Against Invaders

3. Discuss the link between stress and illness in general.

4. Discuss the increased impact stress has on someone suffering from AIDS.

5. Explain the relationship between stress and cancer.

44-2

1. What is the relationship between stress and heart disease?

2. Explain the personality characteristics and impact on health of someone who is

   a. Type A:

b. Type B:

3. Discuss how depression is linked to stress and heart disease.

After You Read

Module 44 Review

Select the best answer to see if you have mastered the basics.

1. Coralee has just been diagnosed with cancer. Which of the following pairs of cells are at work in her immune system trying to fight off the cancerous cells?
   a. B and T lymphocytes
   b. B lymphocytes and macrophages
   c. T lymphocytes and natural killer cells
   d. macrophages and B lymphocytes
   e. natural killer cells and macrophages

2. Boone is a highly stressed adult working in the high-paced field of advertising. He works long hours, often all seven days of the week, and consistently has a deadline to meet. According to stress researchers, it is likely that Boone will
   a. develop a Type B personality.
   b. catch colds more often than nonstressed people.
   c. heal faster from wounds.
   d. contract HIV.
   e. develop cancer.

3. Which of the following statements is true regarding AIDS?
   a. Once acquired, stress does not impact the progression of the disease.
   b. AIDS kills quite rapidly.
   c. AIDS is most prevalent in males in Western Europe and women in Africa.
   d. Stress gives people AIDS.
   e. AIDS is contracted first, followed by HIV.

4. Which of the following statements is false regarding cancer?
   a. NK cells search out and destroy cancer cells.
   b. Stress creates cancer cells.
   c. Stress can impact a person's ability to fight off cancer.
   d. Some people are at increased risk for cancer a year after experiencing depression.
   e. Some people are more at risk for colon cancer when under workplace stress.

5. Pamela is a partner in a law firm and is known to be a competitive and verbally aggressive co-worker. She is easily angered and impatient and expects all of her employees to report exactly on time, work precisely the required number of hours, and put in overtime work on demand. According to studies on stress and heart disease, how might Pamela be typified and what health issues might she encounter?
   a. It is more likely that she will have a heart attack being a Type B personality.
   b. Pamela is less likely to have a heart attack since she is a Type B personality.
   c. She is a Type A personality and less likely to have a heart attack.
   d. Pamela is a Type A personality and more likely to have a heart attack.
   e. Pamela has a higher risk of heart failure but does not fit in either Type A or B category.

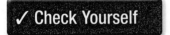 Now that you have mastered the basics, work through the problem below to see if you can *synthesize*, *evaluate*, and *analyze* what you have learned.

> Caitlin is shipwrecked and abandoned on the eastern side of a deserted island. The island is rich with varied food sources and materials to make a shelter. Caitlin has seen many strange animals on this island and is often unsure of her safety. She has been focused solely on survival and has been alone for over a month, but is now planning to hike to the western side of the island over the next few days to see if there are any other people on the island.

Describe how each of the following will impact her ability to survive on this island:

- Drive-reduction theory

- Glucose

- Affiliation needs

- Schachter and Singer two-factor theory

- Universal emotions

- Stress impact on the immune system

Before You Move On

Use the checklist below to verify your understanding of the unit's main points.

☐ Do I understand basic motivational concepts (for example, instincts, incentives, intrinsic versus extrinsic motivation, and so on), and do I know how to apply the concepts?

☐ Can I describe the biological theories of motivation and use the correct terms in my descriptions (for example, needs, drives, homeostasis)?

Can I describe the basic components and compare and contrast the strengths and weaknesses of the different motivational theories?

☐ Drive-reduction theory

☐ Arousal theory

☐ Maslow's hierarchy of needs

Can I describe classic research findings of specific motivations?

☐ Hunger

☐ Sex

☐ Affiliation and aggression

Can I discuss theories of stress and the effects of stress on psychological and physical well-being?

☐ General adaptation syndrome (GAS) theory

Can I compare and contrast the major theories of emotion?

☐ James-Lange

☐ Cannon-Bard Thalamic

☐ Singer and Schachter two-factor

☐ Can I explain how culture shapes emotion and discuss the impact body language has on emotion?

Can I describe the research and findings of:

☐ William James

☐ Abraham Maslow

☐ Stanley Schachter

☐ Hans Selye

Unit IX

Developmental Psychology

Overview

Unit IX tackles the enduring questions of how we develop cognitively, physically, and socially. The revealing research of Jean Piaget, Erik Erikson, Harry Harlow, and Mary Ainsworth, among others, is presented to frame the abilities and traits that develop in our attachment, cognition, and self-concept. Outside environmental influences such as parenting and peer groups are also reviewed. This unit reviews the infancy, childhood, adolescent, and adult phases of physiological growth and decline. A significant portion of the unit is devoted to examining the impact gender development has on the individual and attention is paid to the factors influencing teen sexuality and sexual orientation and identity.

Modules

Tip #9
Develop a Study Schedule or Routine

In Units IV and VI we talked about the importance of distributed practice and reinforcement in the development of study skills. To add on to those tips, it is a good idea to establish a study routine that you can abide by. You can use the calendar of study provided in Unit I or make a new one now. You should schedule time to study for each of your courses as well as time for a reward break. Each day when you return from school, you will know your routine and can stick with it. Take your peak energy times into account so that you can schedule rigorous study times then. Make certain to designate the few hours before your desired sleep time as a no-electronics time. Studies have shown that increased exposure to computers close to bedtime makes it more difficult to fall asleep. Use those last hours to read from your text or assigned book instead.

Module 45

Developmental Issues, Prenatal Development, and the Newborn

Before You Read

Module Summary

Module 45 begins the unit on development by posing three engaging questions about the way in which we grow cognitively, emotionally, socially, and physically. The module continues by presenting the basic physiology of prenatal development and gestational changes, as well as one primary teratogen that can impact development. A concluding discussion with numerous research findings on the abilities of newborns takes to task William James' famous assertion that newborns are a "blooming, buzzing confusion."

Before beginning the module, take a moment to read each of the following terms you will encounter. You may wish to make vocabulary cards for each.

Key Terms

developmental psychology	teratogens
zygote	fetal alcohol syndrome (FAS)
embryo	habituation
fetus	

While You Read

Answer the following questions/prompts.

45-1

1. Give an example from your life of how your genetic inheritance (nature) interacted with your experience (nurture) to influence your development.

2. Give an example from your life of a part of your development that was gradual and continuous. Then, give an example that was abrupt and discontinuous.

3. Which of your traits has persisted throughout your life? How have you changed as you have grown older?

4. Using developmental psychology's three major issues, create a thesis statement that discusses how they interact and explain a person's development.

45-2

1. Describe the changes that occur in prenatal development from conception through birth. Be sure to include the three distinct stages and the developments in each.

2. Define and give an example of a *teratogen*. Write down two additional examples of teratogens not mentioned in the text.

3. Why would maternal alcohol consumption have an epigenetic effect on the fetus?

45-3

1. Briefly list and describe the newborn's reflexes.

2. Discuss how habituation is used to understand a newborn's competencies.

3. What are some newborn competencies researchers have been able to demonstrate? Why do researchers spend time researching newborn competencies?

After You Read

Module 45 Review

Answer the following questions to see if you have mastered the basics.

Identify the prenatal stage of development: zygote (Z), embryo (E), or fetus (F) represented by the characteristics below.

_____ 1. Two days after conception, cell division begins to occur.
_____ 2. Entering the fourth month after conception, it weighs approximately 3 ounces.
_____ 3. Cells begin to differentiate and specialize structure and function.
_____ 4. At 40 days, the spine is visible and arms and legs begin to grow.
_____ 5. In the third month, facial features, hands and feet have formed.

Module 46

Infancy and Childhood: Physical Development

Before You Read

Module Summary

Module 46 describes the ways in which brain and motor maturation impacts development. The general stages of motor progression as well as a discussion of infantile amnesia assist in understanding maturation.

Before beginning the module, take a moment to read the following term you will encounter. You may wish to make a vocabulary card.

Key Term

maturation

While You Read

Answer the following questions/prompts.

1. Summarize the growth of neurons in the brain from the fetal stage to puberty.

2. In what way is motor development dependent on maturation?

46-2

1. Based on the information in this section, how might you reply to a friend who insists he remembers events clearly from his first and second years of life?

After You Read

Module 46 Review

Complete the questions below to see if you have mastered the basics.

1. Define and explain the mechanism of *maturation*.

2. Define *infantile amnesia* and explain two studies of this phenomenon.

Module 47

Infancy and Childhood: Cognitive Development

Before You Read

Module Summary

Module 47 introduces the esteemed Jean Piaget and his research on cognitive development in children. His proposed four stages of cognition in children are fully explained. Exceptions to his stages, along with newer findings, are also discussed to show where portions of Piaget's theory could be expanded. The scaffolding and language work of Lev Vygotsky is briefly discussed as an alternative theory to Piaget's. Finally, a special Close-Up section dealing with autism spectrum disorder reviews the unique challenges in cognitive growth experienced by children with autism spectrum disorder.

Before beginning the module, take a moment to read each of the following terms and names you will encounter. You may wish to make vocabulary cards for each.

Key Terms

cognition

schema

assimilation

accommodation

sensorimotor stage

object permanence

preoperational stage

conservation

egocentrism

theory of mind

concrete operational stage

formal operational stage

autism spectrum disorder

Key Names

Jean Piaget

Lev Vygotsky

While You Read

Answer the following questions/prompts.

47-1

1. What did Jean Piaget teach us about how children reason differently from adults?

2. Explain how a child might assimilate and accommodate a schema for a car when presented with a truck.

3. Complete the chart below detailing Piaget's stages of cognitive development.

Stage	Approximate Age Range	Name and Description of Tasks to Be Mastered	Key Words
Sensorimotor			
Preoperational			
Concrete Operational			
Formal Operational			

4. What are two examples of how Piaget underestimated young children's competence in the sensorimotor stage?

5. Describe the research that showed symbolic thinking may appear at an earlier age than Piaget suggested.

6. Discuss the ways in which Lev Vygotsky's views on the cognitive development of children differ from Jean Piaget's.

7. How can Piaget's findings on children's cognitive development be used by babysitters to better understand the thoughts of small children?

47-2

1. What is one explanation for the increase in autism spectrum disorder (ASD) diagnoses and the decrease in the number of children considered learning disabled?

2. List the characteristics associated with ASD.

3. How does ASD impact boys differently from girls?

4. Explain some of the evidence supporting biology's influence on ASD.

5. What are some of the myths or misconceptions that surround the disorder?

After You Read

Module 47 Review

Complete the questions below to see if you have mastered the basics.

Label the stage of cognitive development according to Jean Piaget. When noted, also identify the concept described.

> sensorimotor (S), preoperational (P), concrete operational (C), formal operational (F)

_____ 1. Seven-year-old Amal understands that when a cookie is broken into three smaller portions, it is still only one cookie, not three cookies. Concept described: _____

_____ 2. Thirteen-year-old Julie is contemplating the different ways humans express love and wondering if feeling love is innate. Concept described: _____

_____ 3. One-month-old Na He puts everything she can find into her mouth…her toes, the string on her clothing, even the stuffed elephant her grandmother gave her.

_____ 4. Three-year-old Matthew is talking with his aunt on the telephone and when she asks if he enjoyed preschool today, he excitedly nods his head up and down. Concept described: _____

_____ 5. Five-month-old Emma cries when you hide her play toy under the blanket in front of you, but smiles delightedly when you pull it back out again. Concept described: _____

Module 48

Infancy and Childhood: Social Development

Before You Read

Module Summary

Module 48 explains the numerous studies conducted on attachment and parent-child bonds. Differences in attachment styles due to temperament and culture are discussed, as well as the negative impact on attachment when children are neglected, abused, or raised in adverse conditions. The contradictory findings on day care's effect on children and the onset and development of a self-concept each receive ample treatment in this module. The module concludes with a review of Diana Baumrind's research on parenting styles and their correlation to children's personality traits.

Before beginning the module, take a moment to read each of the following terms and names you will encounter. You may wish to make vocabulary cards for each.

Key Terms		Key Names
stranger anxiety	basic trust	Konrad Lorenz
attachment	self-concept	Mary Ainsworth
critical period		Harry Harlow
imprinting		Margaret Harlow
temperament		Diana Baumrind

While You Read

Answer the following questions/prompts.

1. How does stranger anxiety play a role in forming parent-infant attachment bonds?

2. In what way did Margaret Harlow and Harry Harlow's experiments with wire and cloth monkeys overturn the previously held belief that attachment was based on satisfaction of nourishment needs? What were the implications of Harlow's finding?

3. How did the work of Konrad Lorenz add to the explanation of how attachment bonds are formed in children? Use key terms in your response.

4. Identify the significance of critical periods beyond the scope of Lorenz's work.

48-2

1. How did Mary Ainsworth's work with the strange situation design help answer the question of attachment differences?

2. List an example from the text and one from your own life of how temperament is persistent.

3. Discuss the studies conducted on fathers' presence and later development of the child. How are these studies significant?

4. Explain the ways in which early attachment styles predict later personality traits.

5. According to Erikson, what can parents do to help establish a sense of basic trust in their infants?

48-3

1. Explain the cognitive and physical effects of attachment deprivation as illustrated by Romanian children housed in orphanages.

2. List specific outcomes correlated with being raised in abusive homes.

48-4

1. Discuss the research on the impact of day care on children's cognitive, social and physical growth. What can we learn from this research?

48-5

1. How do the terms *attachment, self-concept, self-image,* and *self-esteem* differ from one another?

2. In what way is self-concept linked to personality traits? How does this inform and contribute to people moving closer to their "ideal self"?

48-6

1. A teenager wants to extend her curfew and stay out later with her friends. Using the information on Diana Baumrind's research on parenting styles, create an imagined dialog exchange between the teen and

   a. her authoritarian parent.

   b. her permissive parent.

   c. her authoritative parent.

2. What does research indicate is the correlation between parenting styles and future personality traits of children?

3. List two alternative explanations for the link between parenting and later competence.

4. Give two examples of how child-raising practices reflect cultural values.

After You Read

Module 48 Review

Select the best answer to see if you have mastered the basics.

1. The experiments conducted by Harry and Margaret Harlow showed that attachment derives from
   a. an association with nourishment.
   b. shared gender.
   c. time spent with caregiver.
   d. comfort and security.
   e. genetic imprinting.

2. The experiments conducted by Konrad Lorenz showed that
   a. comfort is a key component.
   b. instincts to attach vary widely in a species.
   c. species will often bond better with an animal of another species.
   d. attachment forms in a critical period.
   e. attachments to inanimate objects are easily reversed.

3. The experiments conducted by Mary Ainsworth showed that
   a. all infants who experience secure attachment handle their mother's departure in the same manner.
   b. attachment differs between children.
   c. all mothers who encourage independence.
   d. roughly one-third of infants display a secure attachment.
   e. infants with insecure attachments are more likely to explore their surroundings.

4. The research conducted by Diana Baumrind showed that
   a. parenting styles seem to be correlated with childhood social competence.
   b. parenting styles seem to have no impact on childhood social competence.
   c. children of authoritarian parents tend to have greater social skill and self-esteem.
   d. parents who use a permissive style raise children with high self-esteem and self-reliance.
   e. parenting styles cause certain childhood outcomes that can be predicted.

5. The studies on deprivation of attachment showed that
   a. babies raised in abusive or neglectful homes are more bold, verbal and stubborn.
   b. monkeys raised in isolation were more likely to mate frequently when with other monkeys.
   c. intelligence scores were lower and anxiety symptoms were higher.
   d. most children raised in abusive homes grow up to become violent criminals and abusive parents.
   e. children who have survived wartime atrocities or physical abuse are more likely to show physical resilience and resistance to substance abuse and other health problems.

Module 49

Gender Development

Before You Read

Module Summary

Module 49 reviews some of the data and research on gender similarities and differences. The importance in our culture of gender roles and gender typing and their impact on development is the primary focus of the module.

Before beginning the module, take a moment to read each of the following terms and the name you will encounter. You may wish to make vocabulary cards for each.

Key Terms

gender
aggression
gender role
role

gender identity
social learning theory
gender typing
transgender

Key Name

Carol Gilligan

While You Read

Answer the following questions/prompts.

1. What statistics does the author include to support his contention that men are more aggressive than women? From your experience, do you agree or disagree with these statistics?

2. What examples does the author cite to support his statement that social power is inequitably distributed? Why might these differences persist in our modern world?

3. What research does the author include that supports his view that women are more socially connected than are men? Based on your experience, do you agree or disagree with this view?

4. To what extent do you feel these or other differences are biological? Social?

49-2

1. Discuss how women's gender roles vary among cultures.

2. Discuss how men's gender roles vary among cultures.

3. How do the terms *biological sex* and *gender* differ from each other?

4. How do the terms *gender roles, gender typing, gender schema,* and *gender identity* relate and differ from one another?

5. How is gender identity different from sexual orientation?

After You Read

Module 49 Review

Complete the matching questions below to see if you have mastered the basics.

Terms

_____ 1. gender

_____ 2. gender role

_____ 3. gender identity

_____ 4. gender typing

_____ 5. gender schema

_____ 6. gender expression

Definitions

A. the communication of gender identity through behavior or appearance

B. the acquisition of a traditional masculine or feminine role

C. a person's sense of being male or female

D. the socially constructed roles and characteristics by which a culture defines male and female

E. a set of expected behaviors for males or females

F. a framework for organizing boy-girl characteristics

Module 50

Parents, Peers, and Early Experiences

Before You Read

Module Summary

Module 50 describes how early experiences can modify the brain and fleshes out the differing contributions to development made by peer groups and parents.

While You Read

Answer the following questions/prompts.

50-1

1. Briefly summarize Rosenzweig's work with rats and the implications of early experiences on brain development. How does this work address the intermingling between nature and nurture?

2. How can parenting impact one's behavior?

50-2

1. How does peer influence shape children's development?

2. In which areas do parents tend to have the greatest influence on their children's lives?

3. Summarize Howard Gardner's conclusions regarding the complementary nature of peer and parent influence on development.

After You Read

Module 50 Review

Complete the questions below to see if you have mastered the basics.

1. Using information from the module as evidence, support the claim that early experience affects brain development.

2. Using information from the module as evidence, compare and contrast the influence of peers versus parents on development.

3. How have your early experiences shaped who you are? How will they shape who you are 10 years from now?

Module 51

Adolescence: Physical and Cognitive Development

Before You Read

Module Summary

Module 51 reviews the major physical changes that occur during adolescence, as well as the cognitive and moral tasks involved in this changing time of life. The theories of Kohlberg are introduced briefly and a tie in to Piaget's work on cognitive development (discussed in Module 47) is included. The module concludes with a discussion of moral intuition and moral action.

Before beginning the module, take a moment to read the following term and name you will encounter. You may wish to make vocabulary cards for each.

Key Term	Key Name
adolescence	Lawrence Kohlberg

While You Read

Answer the following questions/prompts.

1. Discuss the two contradictory views of adolescence.

2. List the benefits and drawbacks to early physical maturation for boys.

3. List the benefits and drawbacks to early physical maturation for girls.

4. Describe the current trend and implications of research into the undeveloped prefrontal cortex of adolescents.

51-2

1. How might Kohlberg's stages of moral development be influenced by the work of Jean Piaget?

2. Explain how morality gradually changes from preconventional through conventional to postconventional stages, according to Lawrence Kohlberg.

3. Describe the decisions an individual might make when considering whether or not to cheat on an exam if they are in the

   a. preconventional stage:

   b. conventional stage:

   c. postconventional stage:

3. In what way does the concept of moral intuition differ from Kohlberg's theory?

4. How does *moral intuition* differ from *moral action*?

After You Read

Module 51 Review

Identify the Kohlberg stage of morality best illustrated by the following examples.

Preconventional (Pre), Conventional (C), Postconventional (Post)

_____ **1.** Justin, age 5, does as his kindergarten teacher asks because he is afraid to get into trouble.

_____ **2.** Omar, age 12, crosses at the crosswalk rather than jaywalking because he knows drivers will be more likely to yield if he is crossing in the approved section of the street.

_____ **3.** Although it was illegal, Susan, age 52, cast a vote and was arrested and jailed.

_____ **4.** Despite a law forbidding it, Mohandas led a group of people to the ocean to collect and process salt.

_____ **5.** Lorraine, age 6, promises her Stepmom to always tell the truth and be kind to others because Lorraine knows she will get big hugs and praise from her.

Module 52

Adolescence: Social Development and Emerging Adulthood

Before You Read

Module Summary

Module 52 describes the social tasks and challenges of adolescence, primary among them the forming of an identity. Erik Erikson's classic work on psychosocial development is presented and a section on parents and peers discusses the role each plays on development of self. The module concludes with an introduction to a novel idea in the field of development, the emerging adult, and provides solid history for the suggested phase as well as framing it in the context of culture.

Before beginning the module, take a moment to read each of the following terms and the name you will encounter. You may wish to make vocabulary cards for each.

Key Terms		Key Name
identity	intimacy	Erik Erikson
social identity	emerging adulthood	

While You Read

Answer the following questions/prompts.

52-1

1. Complete the chart below by filling in the issue for each stage and a real-life example that illustrates each stage.

Stage	Issue	Real-Life Example That Illustrates Stage
Infancy (to 1 year)		
Toddlerhood (1 to 3 years)		

Stage	Issue	Real-Life Example That Illustrates Stage
Preschool (3 to 6 years)		
Elementary school (6 years to puberty)		
Adolescence (teen years into 20ds)		
Young adulthood (20s to early 40s)		
Middle adulthood (40s to 60s)		
Late adulthood (late 60s and up)		

2. Discuss the findings of research on intimacy and discuss the link between intimacy and happiness.

52-2

1. List the ways research has shown peers influence your personal development.

2. List the ways research has shown parents influence your personal development.

52-3

1. Summarize and describe the characteristics of the phase of life some people call emerging adulthood.

After You Read

Module 52 Review

Complete the matching questions below to see if you have mastered the basics.

Stage

_____ 1. trust versus mistrust

_____ 2. autonomy versus shame and doubt

_____ 3. initiative versus guilt

_____ 4. competence versus inferiority

_____ 5. identity versus role confusion

_____ 6. intimacy versus isolation

_____ 7. generativity versus stagnation

_____ 8. integrity versus despair

Example

A. a mother of three coaches her daughter's lacrosse team

B. a teenager dyes her hair and tries out a new look

C. a toddler chooses his own clothes and dresses himself

D. a newborn infant cries and receives comfort and food from a caregiver

E. a retired professor reflects on the numerous books she published in her field

F. a third-grader independently completes a math worksheet in school

G. a preschooler grabs a broom and helps her father clean the kitchen floor

H. a 20-something joins an online dating service

Module 53

Sexual Development

Module Summary

Module 53 reviews the biological and social aspects of our sexuality. From a primer on X- and Y-chromosome conception through the primary and secondary sex characteristic development of puberty, the module presents the basic biological facts of development. Exceptions to traditional sex development are discussed, as well as the recent studies on AIDS prevalence and prevention. A thorough discussion of the factors both contributing to and deterring teen sexual activity precedes a Close-Up on the hypersexualization of girls in our culture. Lastly, the issue of sexual orientation is presented and research into the environmental and biological influences on heterosexuality and homosexuality are introduced.

Before beginning the module, take a moment to read each of the following terms you will encounter. You may wish to make vocabulary cards for each.

Key Terms

X chromosome

Y chromosome

testosterone

puberty

primary sex characteristics

secondary sex characteristics

menarche

AIDS (acquired immune deficiency syndrome)

sexual orientation

While You Read

Answer the following questions/prompts.

53-1

1. Explain how the father determines the sex of a baby.

2. Discuss the primary and secondary sex characteristics that develop during puberty for boys and girls. How are they alike? How are they different?

3. How do menarche and spermarche allow for eventual sexual reproduction?

53-2

1. What are some of the ways that sexual development varies?

2. What are some of the challenges intersex individuals face in today's society? What is your opinion of doctors deciding that many intersex individuals will be female?

53-3

1. What protections do condoms offer against sexually transmitted diseases? How was the increased use of condoms effectively instituted in Thailand?

2. Discuss the current statistics on the prevalence of AIDS worldwide.

3. Discuss why the statement "oral sex is safe sex" is not true.

53-4

1. How have the reported rates of adolescent sex changed since the 1900s?

2. Discuss and explain the impact of the four environmental factors that contribute to teen pregnancy.

a.

b.

c.

d.

3. Explain four factors that seem to predict sexual restraint in teens.

a.

b.

c.

d.

4. Discuss the forces that lead to the hypersexualization of girls in our culture.

5. What are the repercussions of this hypersexualization and how can parents and teachers combat them?

6. How do video games specifically impact males' image of females?

53-5

1. Discuss the different types of sexual orientation.

2. How has the view toward homosexuality changed over time? Why did the APA change their view of homosexuality in the 1970's?

3. List four environmental influences that have been shown not to impact homosexuality.

   a.

   b.

c.

d.

4. Discuss Simon LeVay's work on the brains of homosexual and heterosexual people.

5. Discuss in detail the three lines of evidence that suggest a genetic influence on sexual orientation.

6. What are two prenatal influences on sexual orientation?

After You Read

Module 53 Review

Answer the questions below to see if you have mastered the basics.

1. Using information from the module, explain how sexually transmitted diseases can be prevented.

2. Using information from the module, compare and contrast the effect of environmental influences on teen sexual behaviors.

3. Summarize the impact of nature and nurture as it relates to sexual orientation.

Module 54

Adulthood: Physical, Cognitive, and Social Development

Before You Read

Module Summary

Module 54 concludes the unit with an overview of aging and the physical, social, and cognitive changes that mark the later part of life. The specific impact of age on memory is reviewed and the trends in people's self-confidence and satisfaction with their life are presented. The various ways in which humans come to terms with death are discussed and the module draws to a close with a reminder of Erik Erikson's final stage of integrity versus despair.

Before beginning the module, take a moment to read each of the following terms and names you will encounter. You may wish to make vocabulary cards for each.

Key Terms

menopause   longitudinal study

cross-sectional study   social clock

Key Names

Albert Bandura

Sigmund Freud

While You Read

Answer the following questions/prompts.

1. Identify the physical changes that occur in men and in women in middle adulthood.

2. Identify the physical changes in men and women in later life.

54-2

1. Interpret the information in Figure 54.2 as it relates to recall in older adults.

2. Interpret the information in Figure 54.3 as it relates to the differing abilities of recall and recognition in older adults.

3. What have cross-sectional and longitudinal studies shown regarding cognitive abilities in older adults?

54-3

1. Discuss the evidence refuting the idea of a midlife crisis.

2. Define the social clock and explain how the 'ticking' changes during adulthood.

3. Discuss the tasks involved in the adult commitment of love.

4. How are work and happiness related?

54-4

1. In what way do confidence and life satisfaction vary across life stages? What common myths regarding happiness and age are refuted by these findings?

54-5

1. List three findings from studies on grief and coping.

   a.

   b.

   c.

2. How does Erik Erikson's final stage of 85 factor into the last years of life?

After You Read

Module 54 Review

Answer the questions below to see if you have mastered the basics.

1. Interpret and summarize the information in the graph below.

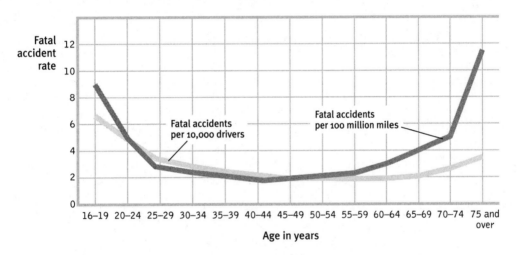

2. Your 70-year-old grandmother has complained of a poor memory and is worried that she will no longer be able to remember things like the events of her life or names of new people she meets. Using the information from the two graphs below, what can you tell your grandmother about her declining abilities? In what way does the information on the graphs confirm your grandmother's worries and in what way can the information give her comfort?

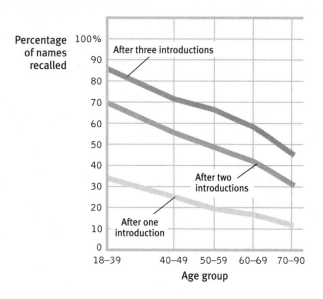

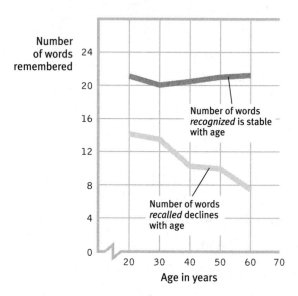

✓ **Check Yourself**   Now that you have mastered the basics, work through the problem below to see if you can *synthesize, evaluate,* and *analyze* what you have learned.

Danielle is an 11-year-old 5th grader who is the youngest of four children and comes from a stable and loving two-parent home. She lives in suburban Georgia and walks to school each day. She enjoys the piano and has been taking lessons for five years.

Stephen is an 11-year-old boy abandoned by his parents as a child and raised in a foster home system, bouncing from family to family for the past four years. He currently lives with a couple fostering two other children. He listens to alternative music on his headphones each day as he rides the public bus to the school he attends in the economically depressed town of Smallville.

Compare and contrast these two children in terms of the impact of the following::

- Erikson's theories of psychosocial development

- Maturation

- Influence of peers versus parents

- Gender roles of their culture

- Physiological changes of puberty

- Ainsworth's theories of attachment

- Diana Baumrind's research on parenting styles

Before You Move On

Use the checklist below to verify your understanding of the unit's main points.

☐ Do I know how nature and nurture interact to determine behavior (for instance, temperament, personality)?

☐ Can I explain the process of conception and the stages of prenatal development?

☐ Can I define *maturation* and provide examples of maturation in milestones of motor and physical development?

☐ Can I describe the various research and outcomes on the topic of attachment?

☐ Can I label and provide examples for each of Piaget's stages of cognitive development?

☐ Can I compare and contrast Kohlberg and Gilligan's theories of moral development?

☐ Can I explain how parenting styles influence development?

Can I compare and contrast the physical and cognitive changes that occur
  ☐ in childhood?
  ☐ in adolescence?
  ☐ in adulthood?
  ☐ in elderhood?

☐ Do I understand how sex and gender influence socialization and development?

Can I identify key contributors in developmental psychology?
  ☐ Mary Ainsworth
  ☐ Diana Baumrind
  ☐ Erik Erikson
  ☐ Harry Harlow
  ☐ Carol Gilligan
  ☐ Lawrence Kohlberg
  ☐ Konrad Lorenz
  ☐ Jean Piaget
  ☐ Lev Vygotsky

Unit X

Personality

Overview

Unit X explores the various approaches to identifying, quantifying, and explaining personality. The history of personality research is covered from Sigmund Freud's turn-of-the-century psychoanalytic theories of the unconscious, psychosexual stages, and defense mechanisms to the modern social-cognitive understanding of personality as being trait-based and environmentally influenced. The contributions of the humanists, neo-Freudians, and trait theorists to the discussion of personality are examined. The unit closes with an explanation of the self as an emerging focus of study.

Modules

Tip #10
Make a Study Space

Find a space in your home that can be uniquely dedicated to studying and claim it as your own. Make certain it is free of distractions, is quiet, and has good lighting. Make sure to put away any distractions such as your phone or computer in order to preserve your space just for studying. You will come to associate this space with the behavior you perform there and this will help make it easier to study each time you return.

Module 55

Freud's Psychoanalytic Perspective: Exploring the Unconscious

Before You Read

Module Summary

Module 55 introduces Sigmund Freud's view of personality with a description of the unconscious factors that drive and underlie individual traits. Freud's proposed psychosexual stages and defense mechanisms are presented. The module closes with a discussion on contemporary psychology's view of Freud's psychoanalytic perspective.

Before beginning the module, take a moment to read each of the following terms and name you will encounter. You may wish to make vocabulary cards for each.

Key Terms

personality	psychosexual stages
free association	Oedipus complex
psychoanalysis	identification
unconscious	fixation
id	defense mechanisms
ego	repression
superego	

Key Name

Sigmund Freud

While You Read

Answer the following questions/prompts.

55-1

1. How is *personality* defined?

2. Describe how free association is used as a tool in psychoanalysis.

3. Explain how the image of an iceberg illustrates the three components of Sigmund Freud's view of the mind.

4. The *New Yorker* cartoon on text page 558 features King Henry VIII of England and one of his six wives. King Henry called for the beheading of two of his wives for various reasons. Discuss how the cartoon describes Freud's idea that nothing is ever accidental and illustrates a "Freudian slip."

5. Jonathan dreams of a snake that enters a cave and tells his therapist about the dream. His therapist, a psychoanalyst, interprets the dream to be sexual and tells Jonathan that he is working through anxiety relating to the act of sex. First, define manifest and latent content. Then, label both the manifest and latent content of Jonathan's dream.

55-2

1. Complete the chart below.

	Function	Focus or Principle Upon Which It Operates	Personal Example
id			
ego			
superego			

55-3

1. Give a brief summary of each of Freud's psychosexual stages, and explain the conflicts that Freud believed were present during each.

2. How does identification help children cope with the threatening feelings present during the phallic stage, according to Freud?

3. Why is it important to study Freud's ideas, even though many of them are no longer relevant to contemporary psychology?

4. How might Sigmund Freud explain an adult's exaggerated sarcasm?

55-4

1. According to Freud, what role do defense mechanisms serve? Which part of the personality is responsible for controlling defense mechanisms?

2. Using Table 55.2, define each defense mechanism in your own words and come up with a new example to illustrate how each defense mechanism might manifest itself.

Defense Mechanism	Definition in Your Own Words	Example
Regression		
Reaction formation		
Projection		
Rationalization		
Displacement		
Sublimation		
Denial		

55-5

1. Discuss the problems and criticisms of Freud's theories.

2. List some of the aspects of Freud's theories that endure today.

3. In what ways has modern research challenged the idea of repression?

After You Read

Module 55 Review

Select the best answer to see if you have mastered the basics.

1. This aspect of the mind, according to Freud, operates on the pleasure principle and is chiefly concerned with gratification of needs and wants.
   a. ego
   b. superego
   c. the unconscious
   d. id
   e. free association

2. According to Freud, around the age of 4 or 5, the aspect of the mind that is the voice of our moral conscience develops. He called this the
   a. ego.
   b. superego.
   c. the unconscious.
   d. id.
   e. Oedipus complex.

3. Which of the following correctly lists, in order, the stages of psychosexual development according to Freud?
   a. oral, anal, phallic, latency, genital
   b. anal, oral, phallic, latency, genital
   c. phallic, latency, oral, anal, genital
   d. anal, latency, genital, oral, phallic
   e. latency, oral, phallic, anal, genital

4. Robert is 5 years of age. According to Freud, Robert is likely
   a. in the oral stage and focused on biting and sucking.
   b. in the phallic stage and attempting to identify with his father.
   c. in the anal stage and focusing on bladder control.
   d. in the latency stage and not interested in sexual feelings.
   e. in the genital stage and developing sexual interest.

5. Jeannette is an overweight adult who eats excessively and is often found chomping loudly on gum. Freud might propose that she is fixated in the
   a. anal stage.
   b. phallic stage.
   c. latency stage.
   d. oral stage.
   e. genital stage.

6. According to Freud, which of the following defense mechanisms underlies all the others?
   a. repression
   b. projection
   c. sublimation
   d. reaction formation
   e. denial

7. Luis was a violent child who frequently got into fights at school. This caused him a great deal of anxiety as he was always in the principal's office and frequently shunned by classmates and labeled a trouble maker. As an adult, he became a prize-winning boxer. Freud would explain this career choice in terms of which defense mechanism?
   a. projection
   b. denial
   c. rationalization
   d. reaction formation
   e. sublimation

8. Freud's use of free association was intended to
   a. bring out the thoughts of the superego.
   b. develop a relationship between the therapist and the patient.
   c. allow an exploration of the unconscious.
   d. release the patient's inhibitions.
   e. tap into the conscious control of the unconscious.

9. Anh recently immigrated to America and is generally scared and distrustful of her new environment. Among her friends she is known to criticize her American classmates for their standoffishness and rudeness toward her. Freud might explain that Anh is utilizing the defense mechanism of _____ to protect her mind from her anxiety about not being liked or accepted.
    a. reaction formation
    b. denial
    c. sublimation
    d. projection
    e. displacement

10. Nichole was raised in a physically and emotionally abusive home for over a decade before being removed to foster care. When speaking with her social worker, she professes great love for her birth parents and praises them for their care of her. Her social worker, being a great fan of Sigmund Freud, recognizes which of the following defense mechanisms at work?
    a. reaction formation
    b. sublimation
    c. displacement
    d. regression
    e. rationalization

11. Explain why the ego is considered the "executive" of personality.

12. What is considered the most serious problem with Freud's theory, and why?

Module 56

Psychodynamic Theories and Modern Views of the Unconscious

Before You Read

Module Summary

Module 56 discusses the contributions of the neo-Freudians and their acceptance and rejection of various aspects of Freud's theories. A description of the projective tests used in psychoanalytic therapy and an explanation of the modern view of the unconscious concludes this module.

Before beginning the module, take a moment to read each of the following terms and names you will encounter. You may wish to make vocabulary cards for each.

Key Terms		Key Names
psychodynamic theories	Rorschach Inkblot Test	Alfred Adlert
collective unconscious	false consensus effect	Karen Horney
projective test	terror-management theory	Carl Jung
Thematic Apperception Test (TAT)		

While You Read

Answer the following questions/prompts.

56-1

1. Briefly outline Karen Horney's beliefs about personality formation and discuss the ways in which her theories agreed and disagreed with Sigmund Freud's. Make sure to use the key terms associated with Horney's theory in your response.

2. Briefly describe Alfred Adler's beliefs about personality formation and discuss the ways in which his theories agreed and disagreed with Sigmund Freud's. What childhood conditions in Adler's life may have influenced his theories?

3. Briefly outline Carl Jung's beliefs about personality formation and discuss the ways in which his theories agreed and disagreed with Sigmund Freud's. Explain the concepts that add to Freud's levels of consciousness and the symbols which Jung believes tie all cultures together.

4. Which aspects of Freud's theories have been retained and which have been refuted by today's psychodynamic theorists? How do psychodynamic psychologists differ from traditional psychoanalytic psychologists?

56-2

1. What is the goal of projective tests?

2. Briefly describe the intent and usage of the Thematic Apperception Test.

3. Briefly describe the intent and usage of the Rorschach test. How do the responses that individuals provide differ on the TAT test from the Rorschach test?

4. Discuss the criticisms of projective tests such as the Rorschach and TAT.

56-3

1. How has the view of the unconscious changed into today's belief in dual processing?

2. Explain the research studies that have supported Freud's view of

   a. the defense mechanism of projection

   b. unconsciously defending ourselves against anxiety

After You Read

Module 56 Review

Answer the questions to see if you have mastered the basics.

1. What is the Thematic Apperception Test (TAT)?

2. What is the Rorschach Test?

3. Jerry regularly drives above the speed limit to and from work and claims that most other drivers speed. Freud might call this _____ , whereas modern research would refer to Jerry's belief as _____ .
    a. sublimation; the latency effect
    b. rationalization; the manifest effect
    c. projection; the false consensus effect
    d. reaction formation; the latency effect
    e. displacement; the false consensus effect

4. The terror-management theory is best defined as
    a. the terror resulting from our awareness of vulnerability and death.
    b. a method of combating the terror stemming from our childhood.
    c. the belief that we are in control of our terror.
    d. the terror that can be managed in the unconscious.
    e. the terror we feel when defense mechanisms fail.

5. According to Carl Jung, humans have a collection of archetypes or images derived from our species' universal experiences. He called this the
    a. manifest content.
    b. latent content.
    c. collective conscious.
    d. collective unconscious.
    e. inferiority complex.

6. Compare and contrast the theories of Carl Jung, Karen Horney, and Alfred Adler to those of Sigmund Freud. Discuss the aspects of Freud's theories on which they agreed and those on which they disagreed.

Module 57

Humanistic Theories

Before You Read

Module Summary

Module 57 introduces the humanistic view of personality and explains how humanistic psychologists assess a person's sense of self. Humanistic theories are described and a discussion on the criticisms of humanism concludes the module.

Before beginning the module, take a moment to read each of the following terms and names you will encounter. You may wish to make vocabulary cards for each.

Key Terms		Key Names
humanistic theories	unconditional positive regard	Abraham Maslow
self-actualization	self-concept	Carl Rogers

While You Read

Answer the following questions/prompts.

57-1

1. Explain the essential difference between the 1960s humanistic view on personality and the earlier emphasis on psychoanalytic and behaviorist views.

2. What characteristics did Maslow find were common among those who had achieved self-actualization?

3. Name and briefly discuss each of Carl Roger's three conditions for ideal growth:

   a.

   b.

   c.

4. Give an example of how a therapist might treat a client with unconditional positive regard.

5. How do Maslow and Rogers define "self-concept"? What happens if our self-concept is positive? Negative?

57-2

1. Describe the process humanistic psychologists use to assess a person's sense of self.

57-3

1. In what ways have the beliefs of humanistic psychologists influenced our modern perception of personality?

2. Explain the criticism of humanistic views.

After You Read

Module 57 Review

Complete the questions below to see if you have mastered the basics.

1. Elias is a seventeen-year-old high school student in a middle-class neighborhood. The crime rate in his neighborhood is the lowest in the state and his neighbors throw block parties and get-togethers monthly. Elias is popular in school and gets good grades. He participates in the drama program and is on the debate team. Elias has been dating a girl steadily for 6 months and they enjoy many of the same activities. All-in-all, Elias is a well-adjusted teenager and feels good about his achievements. According to the hierarchy of needs proposed by Abraham Maslow, what is Elias's next "task"?

2. Suzanne is a high school student who is well-liked by her peers. She is an open and transparent friend and can be counted on to tell the truth and share her feelings. She is praised by others for her understanding of friends' problems. She is the first person people go to when they need a good listener. According to Carl Rogers' person-centered perspective, which additional condition should be present in Suzanne's ideal growth climate?

3. Angelika is often unhappy with those around her and feels she misses out on much that life has to offer. She is dissatisfied with her job and her home life and is seeking help from a humanistic therapist. Most likely the therapist would begin by recognizing what about her self-concept? In what way might the therapist help Angelika?

Module 58

Trait Theories

Before You Read

Module Summary

Module 58 explains how psychologists use traits to describe personality. Personality inventories and their strengths and weaknesses as trait-assessment tools are explained. The question of whether personality traits are consistent over time and across situations is presented, and traits that seem to provide the most information about personality variation are identified.

Before beginning the module, take a moment to read each of the following terms and names you will encounter. You may wish to make vocabulary cards for each.

Key Terms

trait

personality inventory

Minnesota Multiphasic Personality Inventory (MMPI)

empirically derived test

Key Names

Robert McCrae

Paul Costa

While You Read

Answer the following questions/prompts.

58-1

1. Explain how Gordon Allport differed from Sigmund Freud in his description of personality.

2. Discuss the work of Isabel Briggs Myers and Katharine Briggs in sorting personality traits. How has their assessment tool been used? What are the criticisms of the Myers-Briggs Type Indicator (MBTI)?

3. How is factor analysis used to condense large lists of personality traits into a manageable number of basic traits?

4. What conclusion did Hans and Sybil Eysenck come to regarding personality traits?

5. Using Figure 58.1, describe four characteristics of unstable people. Briefly address why you believe these factors may lead to classification of instability.

6. Discuss the ways in which biology and autonomic nervous system arousal are connected with personality traits.

58-2

1. What is the purpose of the Minnesota Multiphasic Personality Inventory (MMPI)?

2. Define "empirically derived" and then apply the term to the items on the MMPI.

3. Explain how astrology and fortune telling utilize "stock" statements to produce the Barnum effect. How is this different from an empirically derived exam such as the MMPI?

58-3

1. According to trait theorists Costa and McCrae, what are the five basic dimensions of personality?

2. Using Table 58.1 describe the personality characteristics of someone you know who demonstrates high levels of conscientiousness and openness and low levels of neuroticism, extraversion and agreeableness.

3. Referring to Table 58.1, place yourself on the left (low), middle or right (high) of the scale for each of the "Big Five" personality factors.

4. Discuss the heritability of the "Big Five" personality characteristics.

5. Discuss the likelihood that the Big Five traits actually predict behavior.

58-4

1. Briefly summarize the evidence that suggests personality traits are consistent over time.

2. Summarize the person-situation controversy. What is your personal opinion on the consistency of traits over time and across situations?

After You Read

Module 58 Review

Answer the following questions to see if you have mastered the basics.

1. Which personality dimensions are most readily associated with the work and theories of Hans and Sybil Eysenck?

2. Which of the Big Five factors of personality is *best* exhibited in each of the following scenarios? (A few may seem similar—think carefully.)

   (C) for conscientiousness, (A) for agreeableness, (N) for neuroticism, (O) for openness and (E) for extraversion.

   _____ Katie is very down-to-earth and practical. She uses recycled grocery bags, shops every Tuesday afternoon to get the best discounts, and lines up her errands in the most efficient way possible. She eats pasta on Mondays and fish every Friday. She never misses any of her 8 P.M. TV shows.

   _____ Doug is a gullible, trusting man who will do almost anything for his friends as well as strangers. He is very helpful around the house and is readily counted on to be there when you need him. His teen daughters have him wrapped around their fingers and even though he tries to be firm with them, he usually gives them whatever they ask for.

   _____ Trevor is a fidgety, nervous bank teller. He frequently worries about a robbery and takes medication to control his anxiety. He sees himself as less capable than his fellow tellers and typically counts money multiple times before giving it to customers. Trevor often wonders if the bank cameras are watching him and if his manager thinks he is taking bank funds from his teller drawer.

   _____ Meghan is a high school student who participates on three athletic teams. She has tons of friends and has parties at her house at least once a month so she can see them all. Her parents are drawn to her vibrant spirit, great big bear hugs and infectious smile. Meghan is well-adjusted and really enjoys her life.

   _____ Cecilia is having a hard time in school. The work she produces for her courses is often riddled with errors and eraser marks but she rarely takes the time to rewrite her papers. Cecilia loses many important assignments because her backpack is filled to overflowing with individual papers crammed in sideways and backwards. Most agree… Cecilia is a mess!

3. A personality inventory that has hundreds of T/F questions grouped into 10 clinical scales is the

   _____ .

4. A characteristic pattern of behavior and conscious motive, such as stubbornness, is referred to as a

   _____ .

5. The two researchers recognized for their work on the five dimensions of personality are

   _____ and _____ .

6. How might knowledge of the Big Five personality traits affect the creation of something like an online dating profile?

Module 59

Social-Cognitive Theories and Exploring the Self

Module Summary

Module 59 presents the social-cognitive theories of personality and describes how social-cognitive researchers explore behavior. A discussion of the emphasis on the self in the field of psychology follows, and an explanation of the self-serving bias is introduced. The difference between individualistic and collectivist cultures closes out the module.

Before beginning the module, take a moment to read each of the following terms and names you will encounter. You may wish to make vocabulary cards for each.

Key Terms

		Key Names
social-cognitive perspective	self-esteem	Albert Bandura
behavioral approach	self-efficacy	Martin Seligman
reciprocal determinism	self-serving bias	
positive psychology	narcissism	
self	individualism	
spotlight effect	collectivism	

While You Read

Answer the following questions/prompts.

59-1

1. Explain the role of environment on personality development according to both a social-cognitivist and a behaviorist. In what ways are their explanations similar or different?

2. Provide an example from your own life of the three parts of the reciprocal-determinism model featured in Figure 59.1. How might reciprocal determinism impact one's feelings about taking exams?

3. Explain how we are both the "products and the architects of our environments."

4. Discuss the relationship between personal control and Martin Selgiman's idea of attributional style.

5. Discuss the downside to excessive optimism. How is this often tempered in real-life situations? How do we prepare ourselves to receive potential bad news?

6. Define positive psychology, and explain the work being done in this field. Who is the individual prominent in the movement?

7. Explain why blindness to one's own incompetence may skew one's self-perception. Why do we often fail to recognize those areas in which we are not particularly strong?

59-2

1. Explain how assessment centers look at past behavior to predict future behavior. Why is this currently a preferred strategy for assessing personality?

2. In what way have social-cognitive researchers been criticized? How have they responded to this criticism?

Use the information from Tables 59.1 and 59.2 to answer the following questions.

3. a. Jason is a therapist who is helping his clients focus on healthy behaviors and developing a positive self-concept. Jason is likely a _____ therapist.

   b. Suzanne is using the Rorschach and TAT to assess her patient's underlying unconscious conflicts. During therapy sessions, she asks her patients to reflect on their childhood experiences and dream content. Suzanne is likely a _____ therapist.

   c. Margarite is a therapist who believes the characteristics her patients show in therapy are probably similar to those they show at home or at work. Margarite is likely a _____ therapist.

4. a. Juan is investigating the link between caffeine consumption and energy levels. He asks his co-worker how many cups of coffee he drinks each day and then charts his co-worker's energy highs and lulls. Juan is conducting a _____ .

   b. Lakisha is curious to know how many of her classmates actually tune in to watch the Olympics. She develops a list of questions about the Olympics and circulates it in her classes throughout the day. Lakisha is conducting a _____ .

   c. Lamont is administering projective tests to his patients and is trying to get at their unconscious desires and urges. What advice can you give Lamont regarding the results of these tests?

59-3

1. What is the "self"?

2. Briefly explain Hazel Markus' work on possible selves. Explain why this process is important for one's development.

3. Explain Thomas Gilovich's research on the spotlight effect. Provide an example of when you felt like the spotlight effect was happening to you.

4. How does self-esteem differ from self-efficacy? Give an example of each.

5. Discuss what experiments reveal about the effect of low self-esteem.

59-4

1. Define the *self-serving bias,* and discuss research findings that support the phenomenon. Give an example from your own life.

2. Discuss the dangers of artificially inflated self-esteem.

3. Define *narcissism,* and explain what Jean Twenge's studies have shown about the increase in narcissism across the last several decades.

59-5

1. Explain, using examples, how an individualist culture differs from a collectivist culture.

2. Discuss how the data collected on newborn baby names supports Jean Twenge's assertion that Americans are experiencing increasing narcissism. How might these results simply be a reflection of a changing society?

3. Compare the costs and benefits of individualist and collectivist cultures in the chart below.

Type of Culture	Benefits	Costs
Individualist		
Collectivist		

4. Are there elements of collectivist cultures that you think should be more prevalent in America today?

After You Read

Module 59 Review

Answer the following questions to see if you have mastered the basics.

1. What are the three components of reciprocal determinism as explained by Albert Bandura? Briefly describe each.

2. Students who blame their poor grades on the teacher's dislike of them can be said to have a
_____ attributional style.

3. The leading proponent of positive psychology is _____ .

4. Sandra thinks everyone will notice the large pimple on her cheek and is very anxious about going to school. At the end of the day she is certain all of her classmates have been talking about her pimple when in reality not a single person noticed. Having studied psychology, you know that Sandra is falling victim to the
_____ .

5. Simon is asked to go skiing with friends and eagerly accepts. Although he has not skied before, he feels that he will do well because his skills as a skateboarder will transfer to skiing. Psychologists would say he has a high sense of _____ .

6. Last week, Clint scored two goals against the rival soccer team in the regional competition. When asked after the game about his goals, Clint told the school reporter that he was ranked #3 in the state and was just very skilled at the game. Last night, in the state competition, Clint was unable to score any goals. When the school reporter asked him about the game, Clint said the rain made the field too slick and the referee missed several calls. As a student of psychology, you know that Clint is affected by a _____ .

7. America is an example of a(n) _____ culture, while South Korea is an example of a(n) _____ culture.

8. Jean Twenge's research on common baby names supports the contention that Americans are
_____ .

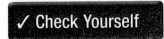 **Check Yourself**   Now that you have mastered the basics, work through the problems below to see if you can *synthesize*, *evaluate*, and *analyze* what you have learned.

Joshua is a junior vice president at MHH Enterprises, a high-paced advertising and marketing firm in New York. Josh is up for a promotion and is under a great deal of stress due to the timelines, heavy workload, and frantic pace of the firm. While taking one of his five-daily smoking breaks outside, he tells his assistants that he feels certain two other junior VPs are "plotting to keep him from being promoted" and Josh will resort to any means, even illegal means, to get the job. Josh thinks if he ran this company, it would be a better place. He is easily angered, quite sarcastic, and often moody. He is known in the office as being short-tempered. Recently, after losing a big account, Joshua lost control and yelled at his assistants for their incompetence. Today, in a hurry, he spilled his entire cup of coffee on his pants and is sure everyone at the office noticed. After leaving work at 7pm, he hits the gym for two hours to keep his body trim and buff. He arrives home at 9pm where he works to formulate more ideas and strategies for his new ad campaign.

Define each term below, identify the key researcher associated with the term, and describe with specific examples how each term is evident in Joshua's story above. You may want to use the chart below to organize your thoughts. Whether or not you use the chart to organize your thoughts, be sure to write your final answer as you would a regular AP®-style Free-Response Question.

Term/Concept	Definition	Researcher Associated With Term	Specific Evidence of Term in Scenario
Reciprocal determinism			
Oral stage of psychosexual development			
Displacement			
Agreeableness			
Narcissism			
Stable versus unstable			

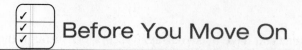

Before You Move On

Use the checklist below to verify your understanding of the unit's main points.

Can I compare and contrast the following major theories and approaches to explaining personality:

☐ Psychoanalytic

☐ Humanistic

☐ Cognitive

☐ Trait

☐ Social cognition

☐ Behavioral

☐ Can I describe and compare research methods (e.g., case studies and surveys) that psychologists use to investigate personality?

☐ Can I identify frequently used assessment strategies (for example, the Minnesota Multiphasic Personality Inventory, the Thematic Apperception Test) and evaluate relative test quality based on reliability and validity of the instruments?

☐ Can I speculate how cultural context can facilitate or constrain personality development, especially as it relates to self-concept?

Can I identify the following key contributors to personality theory?:

☐ Alfred Adler

☐ Albert Bandura

☐ Paul Costa and Robert McCrae

☐ Sigmund Freud

☐ Carl Jung

☐ Abraham Maslow

☐ Carl Rogers

Unit XI

Testing and Individual Differences

Overview

Unit XI tackles the enduring question and challenge of how to define and measure intelligence. The unit reviews the theories of Howard Gardner, Charles Spearman, and Robert Sternberg and the brain structures involved in activities requiring intelligence. Next follows an explanation of the origin and rise of intelligence testing and the methods researchers utilize to ensure reliability and validity of tests. The role genetics and environment play in intelligence and the traits of those who demonstrate extreme high or extreme low scores on intelligence assessments are also covered. The unit concludes by considering the roles gender, race, and ethnicity play in intelligence.

Modules

Tip #11
Visit the College Board® Website and Review

Take a moment to visit the AP® Psychology page of the College Board® website to look at the Course Description. There you will find a list of all of the AP® Psychology topics and learning objectives, along with the approximate percentage of the multiple choice portion of the test that will cover those topics. As you begin to review and prepare for the exam, group your vocabulary cards from previous units into topics and set up a schedule of review that takes into account the greater emphasis on certain topics. For instance, from the Course Description you can see that States of Consciousness, Unit V, makes up about 2–4% of the test while Social Psychology, Unit XIV, accounts for about 8–10% of the exam. Obviously you only have so many hours in the day, and perhaps other AP® courses you are preparing for, so it makes sense to allocate more vocabulary review time to the sections that make up more of the test.

Module 60

Introduction to Intelligence

Before You Read

Module Summary

Module 60 discusses the difficulty of defining intelligence and presents arguments for and against considering intelligence as one general mental ability, as Charles Spearman proposed. Various theories of intelligence, including those of Howard Gardner and Robert Sternberg are presented and compared. The four components of emotional intelligence are explained and the relationship between intelligence and brain structure and function is described.

Before beginning the module, take a moment to read each of the following terms and names you will encounter. You may wish to make vocabulary cards for each.

Key Terms		Key Names
intelligence	savant syndrome	Charles Spearman
intelligence test	grit	L. L. Thurstone
general intelligence (*g*)	emotional intelligence	Howard Gardner
factor analysis		Robert Sternberg

While You Read

Answer the following questions/prompts.

60-1

1. Why is it difficult to define intelligence? How would your definition differ from that given in the text? What would you add or delete from the text's definition?

60-2

1. Explain how L.L. Thurstone's studies on intelligence supported the results of Charles Spearman's work with g.

2. In what way did both Thurstone and Spearman use factor analysis in the development of their theories?

3. Describe how Satoshi Kanazawa's contentions about the evolution of intelligence complement the studies of Thurstone and Spearman.

60-3

1. List the common characteristics of someone with savant syndrome.

2. Discuss Howard Gardner's contribution to the discussion of intelligence. How do his critics refute his work?

3. Explain how the quote by Bill Gates below relates to the work of Thurstone, Spearman, and Gardner.

> "You have to be careful, if you're good at something, to make sure you don't think you're good at other things that you aren't necessarily so good at . . . Because I've been very successful at (software development) people come in and expect that I have wisdom about topics that I don't."—Bill Gates (1998)

Thurstone:

Spearman:

Gardner:

4. Summarize Sternberg's three intelligences.

5. Discuss how Robert Sternberg's triarchic theory of intelligence agrees with Gardner's theory. In what ways do Sternberg's and Gardner's theory differ?

60-4

1. List and elaborate on the four components of emotional intelligence.

   a.

   b.

   c.

   d.

2. How might each of the components listed above help or hinder someone involved in an unwanted break up of a relationship?

60-5

1. Summarize the statistical information on the connection between brain size and intelligence.

60-6

1. Summarize the research findings on the connection between neural processing speed and intelligence.

After You Read

Module 60 Review

Complete the chart to see if you have mastered the basics.

Theory	Brief Summary of the Theory	An Example of Someone Demonstrating This Proposed Intelligence
Spearman's general intelligence (*g*)		
Thurstone's primary abilities		
Gardner's multiple intelligences		
Sternberg's triarchic theory		

Module 61

Assessing Intelligence

Before You Read

Module Summary

Module 61 discusses the history of intelligence testing and distinguishes between aptitude and achievement tests. The meaning of standardization is explained, and validity and reliability in relation to testing is covered. The normal curve is also described.

Before beginning the module, take a moment to read each of the following terms and names you will encounter. You may wish to make vocabulary cards for each.

Key Terms

mental age

Stanford-Binet

intelligence quotient (IQ)

achievement test

aptitude test

Wechsler Adult Intelligence
  Scale (WAIS)

standardization

normal curve

reliability

validity

content validity

predictive validity

Key Names

Francis Galton

Alfred Binet

Louis Terman

David Wechsler

While You Read

Answer the following questions/prompts.

1. Explain how Francis Galton attempted to measure intelligence. Discuss which of his assertions were disproved and which have shown a lasting impact on the study of intelligence.

2. Discuss the events leading up to Alfred Binet's commission to develop intelligence tests for French children.

3. What components did Binet emphasize in his assessment of intelligence?

4. Explain the relationship between mental age and chronological age.

5. What were Binet's hopes and fears regarding the implementation of his test?

6. How did Binet believe that children could improve their intelligence scores?

7. How did Lewis Terman revise Binet's original tests for use with American children?

8. Compare and contrast Binet's and Terman's ideas on the importance of intelligence test results.

9. Practice using William Stern's IQ formula in the scenarios below. Begin by writing out his formula for calculating IQ in the space below.

> IQ =

Without using a calculator, show your work when calculating the IQ of

a. a 10-year-old boy who answers questions at an 8-year-old level

b. a 6-year-old boy who answers questions at a 10-year-old level

c. a 7-year-old girl who answers questions at the 7-year-old level

10. Discuss how the use and calculation of IQ scores has changed since Stern's formula was used.

11. Explain the misuses and abuses of intelligence testing in our culture through the early 1900s.

61-2

1. Give an example of a test you have taken that was

   a. an achievement test:

   b. an aptitude test:

2. Discuss the components and subsets of David Wechsler's intelligence test. How does it differ from the Stanford-Binet?

61-3

1. What population should be used in order to standardize the AP® Psychology exam you will be taking? After determining your population, explain how the exam can be standardized.

2. Draw and label a normal curve of intelligence scores in the space below. Include three standard deviations above and below the mean and the percentages that fall within one, two and three standard deviations. Refer to Figure 61.2. when finished to check your work.

3. Why is the normal curve important to standardized testing?

4. Define the *Flynn effect* and describe the explanations that have been suggested for its occurrence.

61-4

1. Why is reliability a key consideration in test development? What are two specific methods researchers utilize to measure the reliability of a test?

2. In what way is validity different from reliability?

3. How can a test be reliable and yet invalid?

4. How does the content validity differ from predictive validity of a test? Give a real-life example of a test that demonstrates both content and predictive validity.

5. Explain how a test can lose its predictive validity.

After You Read

Module 61 Review

Answer the following questions to see if you have mastered the basics.

1. When and why were intelligence tests created?

2. Alfred Binet referred to children's actual age in years as their _____ age and their performance ability level as their _____ age.

3. The rising average intelligence test score over the last century is referred to as the

_____ .

4. The Advanced Placement® exam you will take this year is an example of an _____ test.

5. The researcher credited with adapting and revising Binet's original test for use with American children is
   a. Francis Galton.
   b. Charles Darwin.
   c. Louis Terman.
   d. William Stern.
   e. David Wechsler.

6. A test-taker is asked to use four white and red shaded geometric blocks to make patterns. The tester is most likely taking the
   a. Stanford-Binet.
   b. MMPI.
   c. Stern-Terman.
   d. WAIS.
   e. Achievement Test.

7. A researcher who wishes to be sure her personality test for teen introversion is accepted in the field initially gives it to a representative sample of teens to establish a base line performance score. This researcher is in the process of
   a. making the test reliable.
   b. establishing the aptitude quotient.
   c. validating the test.
   d. establishing the achievement quotient.
   e. standardizing the test.

8. Draw and label the normal curve of intelligence scores in the space below. Once finished, use it to answer questions 9 and 10.

9. According to your normal curve from #8, a score of 115 is higher than what percentage of scores?
   a. 68%
   b. 95%
   c. 2%
   d. 84%
   e. 81.5%

10. According to your normal curve from #8, approximately 99% of scores fall between which two scores on an intelligence test?
   a. 55-70
   b. 70-130
   c. 55-145
   d. 145 and beyond
   e. 115-145

11. Gwen is attempting to produce a solid intelligence test that will give dependable and consistent results each time it is taken. She gives her prototype test to one group then retests them one week later. Gwen is attempting to prove the test's
   a. reliability.
   b. validity.
   c. standardization.
   d. Flynn effect.
   e. normality.

12. Cynthia is preparing for her semester exam in biology. Her instructor has covered 7 units and Cynthia expects to see material from all 7 units on the exam. When over one-half of the exam deals with the life cycle of the Amazon tree frog, Cynthia is upset. Her dissatisfaction with the exam comes primarily due the exam's lack of
   a. predictive validity.
   b. aptitude validity.
   c. content validity.
   d. split-half reliability.
   e. test-retest reliability.

Module 62

The Dynamics of Intelligence

Before You Read

Module Summary

Module 62 discusses the changes in crystallized and fluid intelligence that occur with age. Studies comparing intelligence over the decades are presented to prove that intelligence is stable over time. The traits of those at the low and high extremes of intelligence are discussed.

Before beginning the module, take a moment to read each of the following terms you will encounter. You may wish to make vocabulary cards for each.

Key Terms

cohort

crystallized intelligence

fluid intelligence

intellectual disability

Down syndrome

While You Read

Answer the following questions/prompts.

62-1

1. Summarize the cross-sectional evidence for intellectual decline.

2. How did the longitudinal studies begun in the 1920s challenge the findings of cross-sectional evidence discussed earlier?

3. Explain how our crystallized and fluid intelligence differ as we age.

4. List several tasks and skills which older people perform better than younger individuals.

5. Explain the evidence that supports the claim that intelligence remains stable over the life span.

62-2

1. Discuss the two components required before a label of intellectual disability can be applied to a child.

2. What is one of the challenges of creating strict cutoffs for labeling an individual as intellectually disabled?

3. Explain how the Flynn effect may be correlated with changes in independent living for those with an intellectual disability.

4. Discuss Lewis Terman's work with his "Termites." What were his findings?

5. Explain how recent studies of math and verbal "whiz kids" support Terman's findings.

After You Read

Module 62 Review

Select the best answer to see if you have mastered the basics.

1. In an experiment to test the cognitive abilities of various age groups, a researcher forms four groups of equal numbers of participants. Those aged 15–25 are in Group 1, 26–35 in Group 2, 36–45 in Group 3, and 46–55 in Group 4. The researcher is utilizing which method to test his hypothesis?
   a. naturalistic observation
   b. cross-sectional
   c. case study
   d. longitudinal
   e. survey

2. If Roger is in his late 70s, which task is he likely to have difficulty with?
   a. Recalling mnemonic devices for the names of the five Great Lakes.
   b. Naming the original thirteen colonies.
   c. Reading the Sunday newspaper and understanding what he read.
   d. Playing Scrabble with his grandchildren.
   e. Coming up with as many uses for a brick as he can think of.

3. Roger is a retired math professor in his 70s and is curious about the cognitive changes he might experience in this stage of life. Advise Roger on the changes he can expect in his

   a. fluid intelligence:

   b. crystallized intelligence:

4. How might longitudinal versus cross sectional studies provide a different picture of Roger's aging?

5. How might socioeconomic status impact Roger's aging?

Module 63

Studying Genetic and Environmental Influences on Intelligence

Before You Read

Module Summary

Module 63 discusses the evidence for a genetic influence on intelligence and explains what is meant by heritability. The module also discusses the evidence for environmental influences on intelligence.

Before beginning the module, take a moment to read each of the following term and name you will encounter. You may wish to make vocabulary cards for each.

Key Term	Key Name
heritability	Carol Dweck

While You Read

Answer the following questions/prompts.

63-1

1. In Module 14 (Unit III), the concept of heritability was discussed. Refresh your memory by defining heritability in your own words.

2. Explain why the heritability of intelligence can range from 50 percent to 80 percent.

3. How do you account for heritability in your own levels of intelligence?

4. Using the data presented in Figure 63.1, explain why siblings raised together would have a lower correlation of intelligence scores than fraternal twins raised together.

5. Discuss the findings of behavior geneticists with regard to the heritability of intelligence in adoptive children and their families.

63-2

1. Compare the varying effects of early enrichment on the development of intelligence. In what instances does early intervention contribute to intelligence and in what instances do we see little or no impact?

2. How does epigenetics (which you learned about in Module 14) explain the weaving together of genes and experience in intelligence?

3. Explain how schooling influences the development of intelligence.

4. Discuss Carol Dweck's contention that believing intelligence is biologically set and unchanging can lead to a "fixed mindset".

5. Do you think intelligence is a fixed mindset or a growth mindset? Explain.

After You Read

Module 63 Review

Answer the following questions to see if you have mastered the basics.

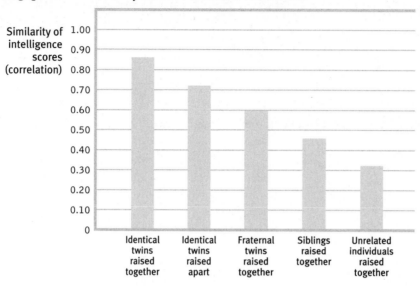

Use the graph above to answer questions 1 and 2.

1. Janelle and Chantelle are identical twins but grew up in different homes. Janelle's score on an intelligence test is 134. What can you predict about Chantelle's intelligence test score? Provide a rational explanation based on your reading.

2. Timothy and Kristen are both adopted children living in the Murphy's home. They are unrelated. Kristen has an intelligence test score of 101. What can you predict about Timothy's intelligence test score?

3. Your father tells you he will not pay for you to take additional classes in college although you are hoping to double-major and pursue as many courses as possible in your time there. Use the findings of Carol Dweck to formulate an argument to convince your father that his money will be well-spent.

Module 64

Group Differences and the Question of Bias

Before You Read

Module Summary

Module 64 describes research of gender and racial differences in mental ability scores. The question of bias in intelligence tests is discussed.

Before beginning the module, take a moment to read each of the following term you will encounter. You may wish to make vocabulary cards for each.

Key Term

stereotype threat

While You Read

Answer the following questions/prompts.

64-1

1. Summarize the findings of various researchers regarding differing intellectual abilities of girls versus boys.

2. How do biological and sociological (nature and nurture) factors play a role in these differing abilities?

64-2

1. Summarize the findings of various researchers regarding differing intellectual abilities in racial and ethnic groups.

2. Using the following figure, explain why the flowers in the garden box to the right have grown larger than the flowers in the left garden box. Describe the heritability of height in this example.

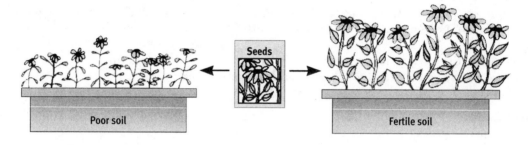

3. Using the figure above, explain why certain flowers in the left garden box are taller than other flowers in that same box. Describe the heritability of height in this example.

64-3

1. Explain and compare the two meanings of bias in a test. Use examples to illustrate your comparison.

2. If you suspect that a test is biased against a given group of individuals, how can you test this belief?

3. Using examples from the text, explain how the stereotype threat hijacks mental performance for minority groups.

4. Suggest two ways that stereotype threat could be reduced in testing situations.

After You Read

Module 64 Review

Answer the following questions to see if you have mastered the basics.

1. You are good friends with a girl in your class who believes that girls are much smarter than boys. Since you are studying psychology and intelligence, what can you tell her?

2. A teacher in your school tells you that boys are evolutionarily built for hunting and girls are evolutionarily built for gathering. What evidence can you provide to support that statement? What evidence can you provide to refute this statement?

3. Your friend believes that all intelligence tests are biased as they only reflect the environment and experiences you have been exposed to. Another friend responds that intelligence tests are not biased. Since you are taking psychology, how can you respond to your friends?

4. Explain why heredity may contribute to individual differences in intelligence but not necessarily contribute to group differences.

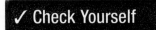 **Check Yourself**   Now that you have mastered the basics, work through the problems below to see if you can *synthesize*, *evaluate*, and *analyze* what you have learned.

Justin is an unusually bright seventh grade student who is being tested for acceptance into a school for gifted children. He has taken one intelligence test three times and received the scores of 150, 149, and 150. Justin is an accomplished and recognized violist, and has been invited to perform with the National Symphony Orchestra. He has many friends and is so well-liked in his school that he won the election for class president. As president, Justin has presented some cool new ideas for homework help, class service projects and an innovative way to move the lunch trays through the cafeteria. However, he is also known to be a silly kid who forgets his lunch quite frequently, gets lost in the halls of the school and often does not have his assignments or materials for class. His parents worry that despite his IQ, his distracted habits may inhibit his future success.

Answer the following questions with specific information from the scenario above to support your response.

1. What is the relationship of Justin's intelligence test scores to other scores on the normal curve?

2. Which two of Gardner's multiple intelligences does Justin seem to possess?

3. How would you assess Justin's three components of intelligence as Robert Sternberg would identify them?

4. How reliable are the intelligence tests Justin has taken?

Before You Move On

Use the checklist below to verify your understanding of the unit's main points.

Can I define intelligence and lists characteristics of how psychologists measure intelligence using

☐ Abstract versus verbal measures

☐ Speed of processing

☐ Can I discuss how culture influences the definition of intelligence?

Can I compare and contrast the historic and contemporary theories of intelligence of:

☐ Charles Spearman

☐ Howard Gardner

☐ Robert Sternberg

☐ Can I explain how psychologists design tests, including standardization strategies and other techniques to establish reliability and validity?

☐ How do I interpret the meaning of scores in terms of the normal curve?

Can I describe relevant labels related to intelligence testing such as:

☐ Gifted

☐ Intellectually disabled

☐ Can I debate the appropriate testing practices, particularly in relation to culture-fair test uses?

Can I identify key contributors in intelligence research and testing such as:

☐ Alfred Binet

☐ Francis Galton

☐ Howard Gardner

☐ Charles Spearman

☐ Robert Sternberg

☐ Louis Terman

☐ David Wechsler

Unit XII

Abnormal Behavior

Overview

Unit XII introduces psychological disorders with a discussion of the difficulty and limitations of defining normality. The controversy over the diagnosis of ADHD is used as a case in point. The biomedical, learning, and social-cognitive models that are used to help us understand disorders are reviewed. The benefits and drawbacks to labeling and diagnosing disorders are discussed along with how sociological factors, such as poverty, impact diagnosis and prevalence. Modules 66 through 69 each focus on one of the main categories of disorders as identified by the DSM-5: anxiety disorders, OCD, PTSD, and mood disorders. You'll also learn about schizophrenia's symptoms, potential causes, and the evidence for genetic and environmental impacts on its development in an individual. The unit closes with a review of dissociative and somatic disorders as well as sections on eating and personality disorders.

Modules

65 Introduction to Psychological Disorders

66 Anxiety Disorders, Obsessive-Compulsive Disorder, and Posttraumatic Stress Disorder

67 Mood Disorders

68 Schizophrenia

69 Other Disorders

Tip #12
Cumulative Review

The end of each unit has included a Before You Move On checklist that allows you to indicate which concepts, terms, and material you understand and which you still need to review. As you progress in the course, the amount of material you need to review increases. If your instructor has been using cumulative tests in the classroom, you will likely have been tested and retested on the material several times. If not, you'll want to keep track of the material from previous units that you did not master and allow yourself 15–20 minutes on top of your normal homework and reading schedule to review old material. In March and April, several weeks before the AP® exam, you should start going back over the old test and quiz questions, rereading small sections on the harder-to-understand material, and finally adding that checkmark to your mastered material checklist!

Module 65

Introduction to Psychological Disorders

Before You Read

Module Summary

Module 65 introduces psychological disorders through examining the difficulty of determining the line between normality and disorder. Attention is given to the debate over ADHD and the various models of understanding disorders are reviewed. The use of diagnostic labels and the argument against labeling are explored. The module concludes with an overview of the prevalence of psychological disorders and the link between disorders and poverty.

Before beginning the module, take a moment to read each of the following terms you will encounter. You may wish to make vocabulary cards for each.

Key Terms

psychological disorder

attention-deficit/hyperactivity disorder (ADHD)

medical model

DSM-5

While You Read

Answer the following questions/prompts.

65-1

1.

> **Psychological disorder:** a syndrome marked by a clinically significant disturbance in an individual's cognition, emotion regulation, or behavior.

Considering the definition above, explain what is meant by clinically significant. Break the definition into smaller parts for your explanation:

disturbance:

cognition:

emotion regulation:

behavior:

2. Discuss why a fear of spiders may not be a psychological disorder, but routinely dusting books on a shelf might be considered a disorder. What is required for something to be diagnosed as a disorder?

3. How has our understanding of psychological disorders changed over time? Give an example of a behavior or belief that was considered abnormal or normal in the past but considered otherwise today.

65-2

1. List three arguments or research findings that support the existence of attention-deficit/hyperactivity disorder (ADHD) as a legitimate diagnosis.

   a.

b.

c.

2. List three arguments skeptics of ADHD cite to refute the legitimacy of the diagnosis.

a.

b.

c.

3. What key component needs to be present to differentiate ADHD from normal high energy or rambunctious-ness? Why is this distinction important?

65-3

1. Define the *medical model,* and discuss how it explains psychological disorders. How has this model changed the way that patients are treated?

2. Define the *biopsychosocial model*, and discuss how the biopsychosocial model explains psychological disorders.

65-4

1. Explain what clinicians seek to accomplish by classifying a disorder. How does the DSM-5 help clinicians with these diagnoses?

2. List three diagnostic changes that occurred with the release of the newest DSM.

3. If you were a parent of a child with what was formerly diagnosed as Asperger's syndrome, how might you feel about these changes?

4. Explain why the DSM is often criticized for "casting too wide a net." What are the advantages and disadvantages of this approach?

5. Discuss why properly diagnosing symptoms of depression or hyperactivity, for example, is so important to mental health.

65-5

1. Explain what David Rosenhan means by saying a label has "a life and an influence of its own."

2. Discuss the research findings on the stigmatizing power of labels.

3. What role do Hollywood movies play in further stigmatizing mental disorders?

4. In what way can labels be beneficial in diagnosing, treating and curing mental disorders?

5. Discuss the uses and misuses of the insanity plea.

65-6

1. According to Table 65.1 and Figure 65.2 (page 657), which country is reported to have the greatest prevalence of disorders and which disorders are most frequently reported? What are potential explanations for these results?

2. In what way can the research on collectivist and individualist cultures be applied to the information reported in Table 65.1 and Figure 65.2?

3. Explain the poverty-pathology link as it relates to the chicken-egg question.

4. Using Table 65.2, select two risk factors and two protective factors for mental disorders and discuss how these can either accelerate or protect against the development of a mental illness.

After You Read

Module 65 Review

Use the following scenario to answer questions 1 and 2.

> Janine is a high-school senior suffering from symptoms of depression. She is overeating, sleeping more hours than normal, and has no interest in going out with her friends. Her parents are very worried about Janine because they fear her grades will slip and she won't get into college.

1. How might the medical model explain Janine's depressive symptoms?

2. How might the biopsychosocial model offer an explanation for Janine's depressive symptoms?

3. Which of the following is an argument in support of the diagnosis of attention-deficit/hyperactivity disorder (ADHD)?
   a. Teachers inconsistently refer children for ADHD assessment.
   b. The proportion of American children being treated for ADHD has quadrupled in the decade after 1987.
   c. In neuroimaging studies, ADHD has associations with abnormal brain activity.
   d. Boys are more frequently diagnosed with the disorder.
   e. African-American youth do not receive an ADHD diagnosis as often as Caucasian children.

4. Which of the following is not an aim of the DSM-5?
   a. To guide medical diagnoses
   b. To estimate the prevalence of a disorder
   c. To describe a disorder
   d. To classify and order symptoms
   e. To stigmatize patients by labeling them

5. In 1973, eight people went to hospital admissions offices complaining of "hearing voices" saying *empty, hollow, and thud*. The researcher who conducted this study of the biasing power of labels was
   a. Philippe Pinel.
   b. David Rosenhan.
   c. Charles Singleton.
   d. Martin Seligman.
   e. Lawrence Langer.

6. Consider the photos in this module, particularly on page 651. Explain how what is considered "abnormal" can differ by culture. Give additional examples of behaviors from your culture that may be viewed as abnormal by someone of another culture.

Module 66

Anxiety Disorders, Obsessive-Compulsive Disorder, and Posttraumatic Stress Disorder

Before You Read

Module Summary

Module 66 discusses the symptoms and prevalence of anxiety disorders, obsessive-compulsive disorder, and posttraumatic stress disorder. The way in which the learning and biological perspectives attempt to explain these disorders is described.

Before beginning the module, take a moment to read each of the following terms you will encounter. You may wish to make vocabulary cards for each.

Key Terms

anxiety disoroders

generalized anxiety disorder

panic disorder

phobia

social anxiety disorder

agoraphobia

obsessive-compulsive disorder (OCD)

posttraumatic stress disorder (PTSD)

posttraumatic growth

While You Read

Answer the following questions/prompts.

66-1

1. Explain what differentiates *anxiety* from an *anxiety disorder*.

2. Discuss the common symptoms of generalized anxiety disorder.

3. Explain why free-floating anxiety can be disabling.

4. Describe the common symptoms of panic disorder. How does panic disorder differ from generalized anxiety disorder?

5. Which category of people is at greater risk for panic disorder? Why?

6. Describe the symptoms of phobias. Give an example of two specific phobias.

7. How does having social anxiety disorder differ from having a specific phobia?

8. According to Figure 66.1, what is the most common specific phobia? What differentiates a strong fear from a phobia?

9. Describe agoraphobia. Hypothesize about why agoraphobia is often one of the most frequently diagnosed types of phobias but may not actually be the most frequently occurring.

10. How can suffering from agoraphobia impact someone's life?

66-2

1. Explain how obsessive-compulsive disorder (OCD) differs from normal obsessions or tendencies toward perfectionism.

2. Approximately what percent of the population suffers from OCD? At what age do the symptoms typically appear?

3. Discuss why the sufferer's knowledge that the obsessions are irrational actually adds to the suffering.

66-3

1. Discuss the origins and symptoms of posttraumatic stress disorder (PTSD).

2. List the factors that determine whether a person is more likely to suffer from PTSD after a traumatic event.

3. Explain what the author means when he says that "suffering can lead to benefit finding."

66-4

1. Discuss how classical conditioning and operant conditioning principles can be used to explain the development of anxiety disorders, OCD, and PTSD.

2. Discuss how observational learning principles can be used to explain the development of phobias.

3. In what way does the biological perspective help us understand the development of phobias and anxiety? Consider both natural selection and genetics in your response.

4. What brain structures are activated in someone who suffers from OCD?

After You Read

Module 66 Review

Answer the following questions to see if you have mastered the basics.

1. Michelle is riding in an elevator to the 17th floor of her office building and is experiencing intense fear that the elevator is going to break. She finds it hard to breathe and cannot swallow. Michelle's heart rate has accelerated and she is dizzy. She has never been afraid of elevators before and has ridden them easily all of her life. Most likely, Michelle is suffering from
   a. panic disorder.
   b. posttraumatic stress disorder.
   c. generalized anxiety disorder.
   d. obsessive-compulsive disorder.
   e. social anxiety disorder.

2. John, one of Michelle's co-workers, finds that he experiences many of Michelle's symptoms every time he rides in an elevator. Because of this, he always takes the stairs the 17 floors up to his office. Most likely John is suffering from
   a. posttraumatic stress disorder.
   b. generalized anxiety disorder.
   c. a specific phobia.
   d. social anxiety disorder.
   e. obsessive-compulsive disorder.

3. One of the concerns regarding panic attacks and specific phobias is that, if intense enough, the fears can lead to avoiding places where the attack or stimulus may occur and may eventually keep a person trapped in the home. This subsequent disorder is called
   a. generalized anxiety disorder.
   b. social anxiety disorder.
   c. obsessive-compulsive disorder.
   d. posttraumatic stress disorder.
   e. agoraphobia.

4. Your friend Rachel is fond of saying "I'm so OCD" when people comment on her color-organized pens or neatly labeled school folders. Offer an explanation to Rachel as to why this statement is (a) offensive and insensitive, and (b) inaccurate.

   a.

   b.

5. Roberto leaves his home for the office each morning at 5:30 a.m. to allow time to check to see if his front door is locked. After locking the door, he gets into his car, but on the way to work he wonders if he actually locked the door. He returns home to make certain he has locked the front door. He confirms that it is locked and gets back into his car. As he turns the ignition in the car, preparing to head back toward work, he wonders once again if he fully engaged the lock and leaving the engine running, he returns to check the front door. Roberto will check and recheck his front door an additional 27 times before finally arriving to work at 8:00. It is likely that Roberto suffers from
   a. obsessive-compulsive disorder.
   b. posttraumatic stress disorder.
   c. generalized anxiety disorder.
   d. phobias.
   e. agoraphobia.

6. Malcolm experiences severe anxiety when he visits his aunt at her home. The anxiety has increased to the point that Malcolm limits his visits to his aunt to once per year and as the visit date approaches, finds his level of unease increases each day. In a session with his therapist, Malcolm reveals that as a child, his aunt used to lock him in a closet when he was "acting up" and this caused Malcolm great distress. His therapist points out that Malcolm has associated the feelings of being locked in the closet with his aunt and her home. The therapist's assessment most clearly reflects the
   a. biological perspective.
   b. learning perspective.
   c. psychoanalytic perspective.
   d. humanist perspective.
   e. psychodynamic perspective.

7. Malcolm's cousin, Gerry, also experienced being locked in a closet at his aunt's when he was young. Gerry, however, used his time in the closet to imagine himself in a deep cave that he explored looking for creatures and treasure. Gerry visits his aunt monthly and has none of the anxiety about the visit that his cousin Malcolm experiences. The biological perspective would help explain the difference in Malcolm and Gerry's anxiety by
   a. identifying Gerry's cognitions as more healthy than Malcolm's.
   b. stressing the impact Gerry's imagination had on his experience.
   c. emphasizing the reinforcement Gerry experienced as a result of his imagination.
   d. pointing out that Malcolm may be genetically more anxious than Gerry.
   e. associating Malcolm's fear with his aunt's discipline method.

8. In those with OCD, what area of the brain seems to be hyperactive?
   a. occipital lobe
   b. anterior cingulate cortex
   c. temporal lobe
   d. hypothalamus
   e. cerebellum

9. Describe how Freud assumed anxiety developed in an individual, and contrast that with how today's psychologists believe anxiety develops.

Module 67

Mood Disorders

Before You Read

Module Summary

Module 67 defines and describes mood disorders such as major depressive disorder and bipolar disorder. Biological and social-cognitive perspectives are presented to help explain mood disorders. The factors that affect suicide and self-injuring are presented along with the early warning signs for suicide.

Before beginning the module, take a moment to read each of the following terms you will encounter. You may wish to make vocabulary cards for each.

Key Terms

mood disorders

major depressive disorder

mania

bipolar disorder

rumination

While You Read

Answer the following questions/prompts.

67-1

1. Discuss the prevalence of depression in Canada and the United States.

2. In what way does depression serve as a "warning light" for us? What sense can be found in suffering?

3. List the symptoms of major depressive disorder.

4. Compare the characteristics of a state of mania to the state of depression.

5. Discuss the diagnostic trend for bipolar disorder.

1. In your own words, list and elaborate on the six facts about depression.

   a.

   b.

c.

d.

e.

f.

2. Explain the genetic influences on depression.

3. Discuss the changes in brain function that occur in major depressive disorder and bipolar disorder.

4. What are the research findings regarding the role neurotransmitters play in depression and mania?

5. Discuss the cognitive characteristics of someone impacted by major depressive disorder.

6. What is meant by rumination? In what ways do negative thoughts and negative moods interact?

7. What role does explanatory style play in depression? Give an example.

8. Assume you recently failed a big test, missed a big score in the game, or your sweetheart broke up with you. Create an explanation for your situation within each of the three contexts:

   a. stable or temporary:

b. global or specific:

c. internal or external:

9. Explain how depression is thought to be a vicious cycle.

67-3

1. List and explain the research findings on suicide as it relates to:

   a. national differences

   b. racial differences

   c. gender differences

d. age differences and trends

e. other group differences

f. day of the week differences

2. What are the triggers or factors that affect suicide?

3. Why do people engage in nonsuicidal self-injury (NSSI)?

4. Discuss the connection between self-injury and suicide.

After You Read

Module 67 Review

Answer the following questions to see if you have mastered the basics.

1. Rebecca is a high school student who is president of the National Honor Society, a gifted athlete and co-captain of the field hockey team, and takes numerous AP® courses. Over the last few weeks she has not felt hungry and is sleeping for only two hours a night. Rebecca knows she is low on energy and is making mistakes on the playing field and on her course exams. She feels guilty for not being a better co-captain and for letting down her parents in her studies. Most likely Rebecca is dealing with
   a. bipolar disorder.
   b. major depressive disorder.
   c. generalized anxiety disorder.
   d. mania.
   e. manic-depressive disorder.

2. Terrance often worries. He is worried he won't pass the rigorous swim tests to become a lifeguard. He is thinking so deeply about this that he cannot think clearly in class and keeps missing the conversations his friends are having around him. This compulsive fretting is referred to as
   a. obsessive-compulsive disorder.
   b. bipolar disorder.
   c. major depressive disorder.
   d. rumination.
   e. panic disorder.

3. The neurotransmitter thought to increase arousal and boost mood is _____ . It is _____ during depression and _____ during mania.
   a. serotonin; overabundant; overabundant
   b. norepinephrine; overabundant; reduced
   c. dopamine; reduced; overabundant
   d. norepinephrine; reduced; overabundant
   e. acetylcholine; overabundant; reduced

4. Two brain structures that seem implicated in depression are
   a. the amygdala and temporal lobes.
   b. the occipital lobes and amygdala.
   c. the frontal lobes and hippocampus.
   d. the hippocampus and hypothalamus.
   e. the cerebellum and hypothalamus.

5. Selena suffers from bipolar disorder. List three common behaviors you might expect to see when Selena is in the manic phase.

  a.

  b.

  c.

6. Describe how depressed people differ from others in their explanations of failure and how such explanations tend to feed depression.

Module 68

Schizophrenia

Module Summary

Module 68 presents the patterns of thinking, perceiving, and feeling that character-ize schizophrenia. A contrast between chronic and acute schizophrenia with attention to both onset and recovery of the disorder is made, and the role brain abnormalities and viral infections play in the disorder is explained. The role of genetic influences on schizophrenia and some factors that may be early warning signs of schizophrenia are also discussed.

Before beginning the module, take a moment to read each of the following terms you will encounter. You may wish to make vocabulary cards for each.

Key Terms

schizophrenia   delusions

psychosis   hallucination

While You Read

Answer the following questions/prompts.

68-1

1. Discuss the disorganized thinking and speaking that are symptoms of schizophrenia.

2. Describe and contrast a typical schizophrenic hallucination with a delusion.

3. Explain the way in which selective attention is impacted by schizophrenia.

4. Describe the diminished and inappropriate emotions characteristic of schizophrenia. What is meant by "flat affect"?

5. In what way is motor behavior impacted by schizophrenia?

68-2

1. Discuss the prevalence of schizophrenia.

2. What are two ways in which schizophrenia develops?

3. List and contrast positive symptoms with the negative symptoms of schizophrenia.

4. How might the terms "positive" and "negative" used in #3 be similar to the use in reinforcement and punishment, which you studied in Unit VI?

5. Explain the relationship between the likelihood of recovery and the speed of onset of schizophrenia. How does this differ in acute schizophrenia as compared to chronic schizophrenia?

68-3

1. Explain the role dopamine plays in schizophrenia.

2. Describe the findings of brain scans on people with chronic schizophrenia. Which brain structures are impacted or implicated in the disorder?

3. How have PET scans been used to determine how the brain of those suffering from schizophrenia differs from those who are not?

4. Discuss the evidence for prenatal viral infections as a cause for schizophrenia.

68-4

1. What does the evidence suggest regarding a genetic link to schizophrenia? How can sets of twins be tested to be sure that the differences are not due to environmental factors?

2. Explain what is meant by a predisposition.

3. Discuss the psychological and environmental factors that may trigger schizophrenia.

After You Read

Module 68 Review

Answer the following questions to see if you have mastered the basics.

1. The literal translation of schizophrenia is
   a. "multiple personality."
   b. "split personality."
   c. "split mind."
   d. "psychotic mind."
   e. "divided person."

2. Which of the following is not offered as a potential factor in the development of schizophrenia?
   a. overabundance of dopamine
   b. a viral infection during the middle of fetal development
   c. fluid-filled ventricles of the brain
   d. a family history of schizophrenia
   e. heavy birth weight

3. Which of the following is true regarding schizophrenia?
   a. It affects women more than men.
   b. It affects approximately 1% of the population worldwide.
   c. It tends to develop in the late 40s.
   d. It is more prevalent in western European countries.
   e. Overweight young women are more vulnerable.

4. List three characteristic symptoms of schizophrenia.
   a.

   b.

   c.

5. Label the symptoms of schizophrenia below as either positive (P) or negative (N).

   _____ a. auditory hallucinations

   _____ b. voice lacking in tone

   _____ c. expressionless face

   _____ d. inappropriate laughter

   _____ e. rigid body

   _____ f. disorganized speech

Module 69

Other Disorders

Before You Read

Module Summary

Module 69 ends Unit XII with a review of somatic, dissociative, eating, and personality disorders. The symptoms and behaviors of specific disorders within each category are addressed.

Before beginning the module, take a moment to read each of the following terms you will encounter. You may wish to make vocabulary cards for each.

Key Terms

somatic symptom disorder

conversion disorder

illness anxiety disorder

dissociative disorders

dissociative identity disorder (DID)

anorexia nervosa

bulimia nervosa

binge-eating disorder

personality disorders

antisocial personality disorder

While You Read

Answer the following questions/prompts.

 69-1

1. Describe the general characteristics of somatic symptom disorders.

2. How does culture influence people's expression of physical complaints?

3. Compare the symptoms of conversion disorder to those of illness anxiety disorder.

69-2

1. Describe the phenomenon of dissociation and explain how it differs from a dissociative disorder.

2. Explain what happens to an individual in a fugue state.

3. Describe the characteristics of dissociative identity disorder.

4. Dissociative identity disorder is often misportrayed in movies and is frequently confused with schizophrenia by the general public. Explain the differences between the two disorders.

5. Explain the arguments against DID as a genuine disorder.

6. How do other researchers support the view that DID is a genuine disorder?

69-3

1. Describe the symptoms and prevalence of anorexia nervosa.

2. Describe the symptoms and prevalence of bulimia nervosa.

3. Describe the symptoms and prevalence of binge-eating disorder.

4. Discuss the general findings of characteristics of families with a child suffering from an eating disorder.

5. Explain the impact of genetics and environment on the development of an eating disorder. What factors would make a person vulnerable to an eating disorder?

69-4

1. Complete the chart below for personality disorders.

Behaviors or Emotions Expressed in This Cluster	Example of Personality Disorder

2. Describe the symptoms of antisocial personality disorder.

3. Discuss the research findings that have helped us to understand antisocial personality disorder.

4. Discuss the impact genetics and brain structures may have on antisocial personality disorder.

5. Explain how environmental factors influence the development of antisocial personality disorder.

After You Read

Module 69 Review

Select the best answer to see if you have mastered the basics.

1. Deborah is an underweight teenager who has dropped 15 pounds in the last year yet is constantly on a weight-loss diet. She obsesses about her image in the mirror and points to magazine covers and celebrity models as ideals of how thin she thinks she should be. Deborah runs 3 miles every day, even in bad weather, and signs up to run 5K races each month. Her parents take her to a psychologist who considers a diagnosis of
   a. binge-eating disorder.
   b. avoidant personality disorder.
   c. anorexia nervosa.
   d. histrionic personality disorder.
   e. bulimia nervosa.

2. Cynthia has been experiencing blurred vision, headaches, dizziness and aches in her muscles. She has seen her doctor who ran a series of tests but cannot identify a physical cause to her pain. Finally she is referred to a therapist who diagnoses her symptoms as
   a. schizophrenia.
   b. a somatic disorder.
   c. depression.
   d. a dissociative disorder.
   e. bipolar disorder.

3. A controversial disorder in which a person exhibits two or more distinct personalities is called
   a. bipolar disorder.
   b. obsessive-compulsive disorder.
   c. schizophrenia.
   d. dissociative identity disorder.
   e. panic disorder.

4. Vince is a 35-year-old mechanic who moves from town to town in search of work. When he finds a job, he is often unable to keep it due to his irresponsible and aggressive manner. He has been arrested several times for thefts and fights and reports that this behavior began in his teens. He has been divorced twice and both of his ex-spouses report that he was verbally and physically abusive and has never shown any remorse for the pain he caused. A psychologist studying Vince's case would consider a diagnosis of
   a. histrionic personality disorder.
   b. antisocial personality disorder.
   c. narcissistic personality disorder.
   d. avoidant personality disorder.
   e. schizoid personality disorder.

5. Bethany has various illness, aches and pains on a rather regular basis. She searches online medical sites to see if her symptoms are a sign of a larger disease. Bethany has had to switch doctors quite a few times as none of them are able to diagnose any serious illness, yet she is sure she has one. She eventually consults a psychologist who is able to diagnose her symptoms as
   a. illness anxiety disorder.
   b. depression.
   c. dissociative disorder.
   d. bipolar disorder.
   e. schizophrenia.

 Now that you have mastered the basics, work through the problems below to see if you can *synthesize*, *evaluate*, and *analyze* what you have learned.

1. Use your understanding of psychology to answer the following questions about Darya.

> Darya has been experiencing low moods and feelings of worthlessness over the past few weeks. Her grades in her core classes are slipping and Darya doesn't feel she can do anything to change that. She doesn't see an end in sight and thinks she cannot do anything right. Her friends are beginning to worry because she is turning down their invitations to go to the movies and to hang out. Darya is sleeping much more than she used to and doesn't have much of an appetite. She finds that she is constantly worrying about her mood and blames herself for bringing it about.

Potential diagnosis:

How would the biopsychosocial approach offer an explanation?

How would the learning perspective offer an explanation?

How would the social-cognitive perspective view this disorder?

How will diagnosing/labeling this individual with a specific disorder impact perceptions of this person's behavior?

Additional symptoms or behaviors to watch for:

How could Darya change her explanatory style to alleviate the depressive symptoms?

Identify the following disorders and support your reasoning with evidence from the unit.

2. Celeste is a middle-aged woman who finds that she is plagued by constant worry. For the past 8 months, she has been having difficulty sleeping and is jittery and agitated at work. Celeste has begun to develop twitches in her eyelids and is worried that something serious is wrong. She can't pinpoint any particular issue that is causing these feelings and decides to seek a therapist's opinion.

3. Jarrod is a 21-year-old college student who is beginning to notice changes in his personality and sensations. He is certain he is hearing voices directing him to hurt himself and he is finding it increasingly difficult to ignore them. His friends are finding him increasingly distracted and report that he seems to lose interest in their conversations. More disturbingly, when Jarrod does contribute to his friends' conversations, he says odd things. Last week he told his friend Jerry that his car "had a tension the shade of libraries." Jarrod's worried friends have told him to consult a psychiatrist for help.

4. Walter was a soldier in World War II and was involved in several hand-to-hand combat incidents. Using his army-issued rifle, he was directly responsible for the killing of 12 enemy combatants. Walter did not enjoy killing other humans and found that he was greatly troubled by his actions. When Walter returned to the United States in 1945, he found that he could not move his right arm. He experienced paralysis in this arm for over two decades and although he consulted several medical doctors, they could locate no organic cause for the problem. His wife suggests he see a psychologist.

5. Sal has just been arrested for domestic abuse and is in the county jail awaiting a visit from the court-appointed psychologist. Sal has been in jail several times in his life, beginning with his first arrest at age 12 for stealing a car from the grocery store parking lot. He has had a very spotty job record, being unable to re-main employed for longer than 4 or so months at a time. Although he has been in and out of jail many times, he shows no remorse or regret for the actions that landed him there.

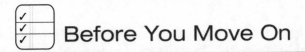 Before You Move On

Use the checklist below to verify your understanding of the unit's main points.

☐ Can I describe contemporary and historical conceptions of what constitutes psychological disorders?

☐ Can I recognize the use of the *Diagnostic and Statistical Manual of Mental Disorders* (DSM) published by the American Psychiatric Association as the primary reference for making diagnostic judgments

Can I discuss the following major diagnostic categories and their corresponding symptoms:

☐ Anxiety and somatoform disorders

☐ Mood disorders

☐ Schizophrenia

☐ Personality disorders

☐ Dissociative disorders

Can I evaluate the strengths and limitations of various approaches to explaining psychological disorders, namely:

☐ Medical model

☐ Psychoanalytic

☐ Humanistic

☐ Cognitive

☐ Biological

☐ Biopsychosocial

☐ Can I identify the positive and negative consequences of diagnostic labels (e.g., the Rosenhan study)?

☐ Can I discuss the intersection between psychology and the legal system (e.g., confidentiality, insanity defense)?

Unit XIII

Treatment of Abnormal Behavior

Overview

Unit XIII introduces, compares, and reviews psychotherapy, biomedical interventions, and treatments of psychological disorders. A detailed comparison of the techniques and methods of psychoanalytic, humanistic, cognitive, behavioral, and group therapies makes up the bulk of the unit. The final module discusses the biomedical treatments available both historically and today to treat depressive disorders, anxiety, and schizophrenia. It also compares medications to the use of psychosurgery or brain-stimulation techniques.

Modules

70 Introduction to Therapy, and Psychodynamic and Humanistic Therapies

71 Behavior, Cognitive, and Group Therapies

72 Evaluating Psychotherapies and Prevention Strategies

73 The Biomedical Therapies

Tip #13
Get to Know the Exam

As you get closer to the AP® exam in May, it pays to make a visit to the College Board® website where actual previous AP® exams are available and come complete with answer keys for you to check yourself. Set aside a quiet time on a weekend a few months before the exam to take a released exam from beginning to end. The current time the College Board® allows for the multiple choice portion of the psychology exam is 70 minutes, so set your clock and give it a try! When you are finished, check your answers and create a short study guide of the content of all the questions and concepts you missed. Take some time to review that material and then take another released exam a week or two later to see if you have improved!

Module 70

Introduction to Therapy, and Psychodynamic and Humanistic Therapies

Before You Read

Module Summary

Module 70 is an introduction to three different kinds of therapy: psychotherapy, biomedical therapy, and an eclectic approach. The psychodynamic and humanistic therapies are compared and contrasted. The goals, techniques, and themes of psychoanalysis and humanistic psychology are compared side-by-side and an explanation of Carl Rogers' client-centered approach closes the module.

Before beginning the module, take a moment to read each of the following terms and names you will encounter. You may wish to make vocabulary cards for each.

Key Terms

psychotherapy

biomedical therapy

eclectic approach

psychoanalysis

resistance

interpretation

transference

psychodynamic therapy

insight therapies

client-centered therapy

active listening

unconditional positive regard

Key Names

Sigmund Freud

Carl Rogers

While You Read

Answer the following questions/prompts.

70-1

1. Compare the methods of psychotherapy, biomedical therapy, and the eclectic approach in how they are used to treat psychological disorders.

70-2

1. Explain the assumption that psychoanalytic theory relies on to explain disorders.

2. What was Freud's goal with psychoanalytic therapy?

3. What is one of the main techniques utilized in psychoanalytic therapy? Describe its process.

4. According to psychoanalytic theory, what role does resistance play in therapy?

5. How does the psychoanalyst's interpretation of your resistance offer insight into the cause of your disorder or conflicts?

6. Explain transference in psychoanalytic therapy.

7. Briefly address why many modern day therapists have moved away from this treatment approach.

8. Describe how psychodynamic therapy differs from traditional psychoanalysis.

9. Explain how interpersonal psychotherapy attempts to help clients and what types of illnesses it might be helpful in treating.

70-3

1. In what way are psychodynamic and humanistic therapies similar?

2. List the ways in which humanistic therapy differs from psychoanalytic therapy.

3. Which three traits do humanistic therapists use in therapy? Describe how they are used.

4. Why does Rogers believe that active listening would be helpful in treating clients?

5. Create a hypothetical dialogue between yourself and a close friend based on the following prompt in which you demonstrate Rogers' technique of active listening.

Friend: "I feel worthless and like I'll never amount to anything."

You:

Friend:

You:

Friend:

You:

Friend:

6. How can changing the word "patient" to "client," as Carl Rogers did, impact therapy?

7. Explain how unconditional positive regard is used as a tool in therapy by humanistic psychologists.

After You Read

Module 70 Review

Complete the Matching Questions below to see if you have mastered the basics.

Terms or Names

_____ **1.** psychotherapy

_____ **2.** biomedical therapy

_____ **3.** eclectic approach

_____ **4.** psychoanalysis

_____ **5.** resistance

_____ **6.** interpretation

_____ **7.** transference

_____ **8.** client-centered therapy

_____ **9.** active listening

_____ **10.** unconditional positive regard

Definitions or Associations

A. an approach to psychotherapy that uses techniques from various forms of therapy

B. the analyst's noting supposed dream meanings, resistances and other significant behaviors to promote insight

C. Sigmund Freud's therapeutic technique

D. a humanistic therapy, developed by Carl Rogers, in which the therapist uses techniques such as active listening

E. a caring, accepting, nonjudgmental attitude, which Rogers believed, would help clients to develop self-awareness and self-acceptance

F. treatment involving psychological techniques and interactions between a trained therapist and a patient

G. empathic listening in which the listener echoes, restates, and clarifies

H. the blocking from consciousness of anxiety-laden material

I. feeling emotions for the analyst that are actually linked with other relationships

J. prescribed medications or procedures that act directly on the person's physiology

Module 71

Behavior, Cognitive, and Group Therapies

Before You Read

Module Summary

Module 71 explains how the basic assumption of behavior therapy differs from human-istic and psychodynamic therapies. The techniques and methods of exposure therapy, aversive conditioning, and operant conditioning (all behavior therapies) are reviewed and compared. The goals and techniques of cognitive, cognitive-behavioral, group, and family therapies are presented in the last portion of the module.

Before beginning the module, take a moment to read each of the following terms and names you will encounter. You may wish to make vocabulary cards for each.

Key Terms

behavior therapy

counterconditioning

exposure therapies

systematic desensitization

virtual reality exposure therapy

aversive conditioning

token economy

cognitive therapy

rational-emotive behavior therapy (REBT)

cognitive-behavioral therapy (CBT)

group therapy

family therapy

Key Names

Mary Cover Jones

Joseph Wolpe

B. F. Skinner

Albert Ellis

Aaron Beck

While You Read

Answer the following questions/prompts.

71-1

1. Explain one key manner in which behavioral therapies differ from insight/Freudian therapies. Use the cartoon on page 716 for help if needed.

2. Correctly label the conditioning components of the bed-wetting scenario on page 716.

US:

UR:

NS:

CS:

CR:

3. Briefly address how a behavioral psychologist would treat bed-wetting.

4. Define *counterconditioning*. Then, explain how a behavior therapist might use counterconditioning to replace a fear response to spiders.

5. Briefly summarize Mary Cover Jones' 1924 work with counterconditioning.

6. Reflecting on the story of Little Albert in Module 26, how might Cover Jones' counterconditioning be used to replace Albert's fear of small, white furry objects?

7. Discuss Joseph Wolpe's work with exposure therapies and explain how they are used to treat anxiety or phobias.

8. How does Joseph Wolpe's assumption that you cannot be simultaneously anxious and relaxed explain systematic desensitization?

9. Detail the steps in which systematic desensitization would be used by a behavior therapist to treat a phobia of flying in aircraft?

10. How does progressive relaxation help those going through exposure therapy?

11. Describe how virtual reality exposure therapy is being used to treat anxiety.

12. How does aversive conditioning differ from systematic desensitization? Provide your own example of an illness that might be treated with aversive conditioning.

71-2

1. Explain the way in which therapy based on operant conditioning principles works.

2. Explain how operant conditioning could be used by a behavior therapist to treat ADHD.

3. Explain how a token economy can be utilized to impact and change behavior. What are the concerns with using this method?

71-3

1. Discuss the assumptions that cognitive theory relies on to explain disorders.

2. Using Figure 71.2 as a guide, fill in the thoughts a person might have as a result of the event in the first box that would produce the emotional reaction in the third box. Use specific original thoughts that would apply in a breakup situation.

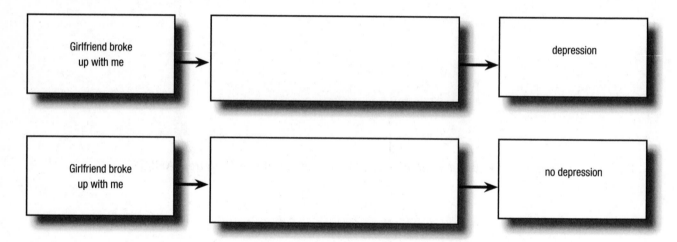

| Girlfriend broke up with me | | depression |

| Girlfriend broke up with me | | no depression |

3. How does Albert Ellis' rational-emotive behavior therapy (REBT) address illogical thinking?

4. Explain how Aaron Beck's therapy differs from Albert Ellis'.

5. Explain the goals and methods of cognitive-behavioral therapy (CBT).

71-4

1. What are the benefits to group therapy?

2. Why is group therapy often more accessible for those seeking treatment?

3. Discuss the reasons a therapist would suggest family therapy for someone suffering from a disorder.

4. Discuss the benefits of joining a self-help group.

After You Read

Module 71 Review

1. Complete the chart below to see if you have mastered the basics. Some have been filled in for you to get started.

> Samantha is a high school senior who is struggling in her courses. This is a shock to her, because she has always been a strong student. Samantha has been overeating, sleeping longer hours than usual, and has been having troubling thoughts of suicide. She is overcome with negativity and feels that maybe she just isn't smart enough to do well in school. Her mother, Andrea, suffers from depression and wants to take Samantha to a therapist but doesn't understand how therapists differ and what to expect. Use the chart below to explain the differences between the treatment options, methods and techniques available to Samantha.

	How They Would View Cause	How They Would Treat	Techniques Unique to Method
Psychoanalysis			*free association, interpretation, dream analysis*
Client-centered therapy			
Behavior therapy			
Cognitive therapy	*Samantha's self-blaming and overgeneralizing bad events, ruminating and thoughts*		

	How They Would View Cause	How They Would Treat	Techniques Unique to Method
Cognitive-behavioral therapy			
Group therapy	*would not focus on cause— support and feeedback from others*		
Family therapy			
Self-help groups		*bond with others who suffer similar disorders provides emotional support*	

2. Fill in the blanks in the diagram below to reflect two alternative thoughts that will result in two very different reactions to the same event.

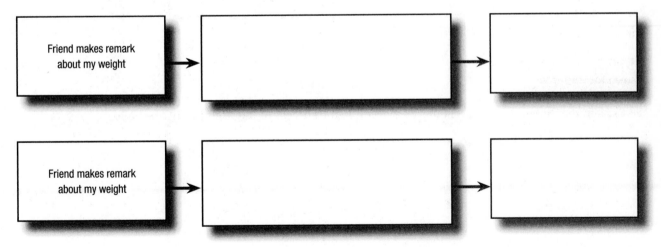

Friend makes remark about my weight →

Friend makes remark about my weight →

Module 72

Evaluating Psychotherapies and Prevention Strategies

Before You Read

Module Summary

Module 72 evaluates the various psychotherapies and describes the elements shared by all forms of psychotherapy. The impact of culture, gender, and values on the therapist-client relationship is explored. Finally, the author offers guidelines for selecting a therapist.

Before beginning the module, take a moment to read each of the following terms you will encounter. You may wish to make vocabulary cards for each.

Key Terms

regression toward the mean   therapeutic alliance

meta-analysis   resilience

evidence-based practice

While You Read

Answer the following questions/prompts.

72-1

1. Explain the three reasons the client's perception of the success of therapy may not be valid.

   a.

   b.

   c.

2. Describe the findings of the Massachusetts experiment that support the unreliability of a client's perceptions of treatment.

3. In what way are the clinician's perspectives on the success of treatment equally unreliable?

4. How are studies being conducted today to attempt to address the question "Is psychotherapy effective?" What statistical procedure is used in the studies?

5. Explain how regression toward the mean can describe two friends who have a fight then later go to the movies together.

6. Summarize the answer to the question "Is psychotherapy effective?" taking into account client perceptions, clinician perceptions, and outcome research.

7. What are the dangers to not seeking treatment?

72-2

1. Are some psychotherapies more effective than others for specific disorders? Explain.

2. Explain what is meant by *evidence-based practice*.

72-3

1. Discuss the supporting arguments and evidence in favor of EMDR therapy.

2. Present the case against EMDR therapy.

3. Discuss the supporting arguments and evidence in favor of light exposure therapy.

72-4

1. In your own words, summarize the benefits of therapy.

2. Explain how the therapeutic alliance is a key aspect of effective therapy.

72-5

1. Discuss the impact of culture, gender, and values on the success of therapy.

72-6

1. What are some signs that indicate a person should seek the help of a mental health professional?

2. Discuss the responsibilities of clinical psychologists, psychiatrists, clinical social workers and counselors.

72-7

1. Discuss the role resilience plays in preventing psychological disorders.

2. In what way can psychologists, therapists, and society in general use the concept of resilience to decrease the number of cases of disorders?

After You Read

Module 72 Review

Answer the questions below to see if you have mastered the basics.

1. Your friend is having difficulties in school and seems to be showing signs of depression. Since you are taking psychology, you suggest that she seek out a therapist and try to find help. She replies to your suggestion with " Therapy? HA! That mumbo-jumbo doesn't work!" Use your understanding of client's perspectives, therapists' perspectives, and outcome research to convince your friend that she is incorrect in her assertion.

2. After convincing your friend that therapy is not a bunch of junk, she asks you about alternative therapies such as EMDR and light exposure therapy. How do you address her question about the effectiveness of these two therapies?

3. If your friend does agree to see a therapist, explain her options when selecting between different types of mental health professionals.

Module 73

The Biomedical Therapies

Module Summary

Module 73 reviews the various biomedical therapies and identifies the use and outcomes of drugs, brain stimulation, and psychosurgery techniques. A discussion of self-care through a healthy lifestyle and the importance of recognizing our biopsychosocial systems completes the module.

Before beginning the module, take a moment to read each of the following terms you will encounter. You may wish to make vocabulary cards for each.

Key Terms

psychopharmacology	electroconvulsive therapy (ECT)
antipsychotic drugs	repetitive transcranial magnetic stimulation (rTMS)
antianxiety drugs	psychosurgery
antidepressant drugs	lobotomy

While You Read

Answer the following questions/prompts.

73-1

1. How has psychopharmacology revolutionized the field of psychological treatment?

2. Describe how double-blind procedures are used in experimentation (you learned this in Unit II).

3. Discuss the findings of double-blind studies on the effectiveness of drug therapies in treating psychological disorders.

4. Complete the following chart.

	Drug Names	Method of Operation—Neurotransmitter Activity	Side Effects and Drawbacks	How Successful Are These Drugs?
Antipsychotic drugs				
Antianxiety drugs				
Antidepressant drugs				
Mood stabilizers				

73-2

1. Complete the following chart.

Technique	Procedures	Outcomes
Electroconvulsive therapy (ECT)		
Repetitive transcranial magnetic stimulation (rTMS)		
Deep-brain stimulation		

2. Describe the controversial lobotomy surgery and compare the outcomes to today's modern psychosurgery. How prevalent is psychosurgery as a treatment today?

73-3

1. Explain how changing lifestyle habits can have an impact on depression.

2. List the lifestyle factors that seem to promote healthy, well-adjusted minds and bodies. Which of these lifestyle factors do you embrace? Which can you improve upon?

After You Read

Module 73 Review

Answer the following questions to see if you have mastered the basics.

1. A patient suffering from schizophrenia would likely be prescribed
    a. an antidepressant drug.
    b. an antianxiety drug.
    c. an antipsychotic drug.
    d. lithium.
    e. an SSRI.

2. An antianxiety drug such as Xanax
    a. is not addicting.
    b. produces no withdrawal symptoms upon ceasing the medication.
    c. works more efficiently when combined with alcohol.
    d. should be used alone without additional therapy.
    e. depresses the central nervous system.

3. Which of the following is not treated with the use of an antidepressant?
    a. depression
    b. somatoform disorders
    c. obsessive-compulsive disorder
    d. posttraumatic stress disorder
    e. anxiety

4. Which of the following accurately describes how Prozac works in the nervous system to relieve depression?
   a. It prevents the release of dopamine into the synapse.
   b. It allows for the increased reuptake of dopamine from the synapse.
   c. Prozac partially blocks the reuptake of serotonin from the synapse.
   d. Prozac increased the speed of reuptake of serotonin and norepinephrine from the synapse.
   e. It blocks acetylcholine from entering the synapse.

5. A patient undergoing _____ would experience a brief electrical current sent through their brain.
   a. ECT
   b. rTMS
   c. deep-brain stimulation
   d. psychosurgery
   e. a lobotomy

✓ Check Yourself

Now that you have mastered the basics, work through the problems below to see if you can *synthesize, evaluate,* and *analyze* what you have learned.

Frank has been diagnosed with depression and an anxiety disorder and is considering the best treatment options. Explain the goals and specific techniques of each of the following so Frank can evaluate his options.

• Psychoanalytic therapy:

• Behavioral therapy:

• Humanistic therapy

• Cognitive therapy

• Group therapy

• Use of drugs

• ECT

Before You Move On

Use the checklist below to verify your understanding of the unit's main points.

☐ Can I describe the central characteristics of psychotherapeutic intervention?

Can I describe the major following treatment orientations used in therapy and how those orientations influence therapeutic planning?

☐ Behavior

☐ Cognitive

☐ Humanistic

☐ Can I compare and contrast the different treatment formats (e.g., individual, group)

☐ Can I summarize the effectiveness of specific treatments used to address specific problems?

☐ Can I discuss how cultural and ethnic context influence choice and success of treatment (factors that lead to premature termination of treatment)

☐ Can I describe prevention strategies that build resilience and promote competence?

Can I identify major figures in psychological treatment?

☐ Aaron Beck

☐ Albert Ellis

☐ Sigmund Freud

☐ Mary Cover Jones

☐ Carl Rogers

☐ B. F. Skinner

☐ Joseph Wolpe

Unit XIV

Social Psychology

Overview

Unit XIV considers the factors that impact the individual within a group as well as the role of culture and norms on both group and individual behavior. The unit explains the formation of attitudes and prejudices, and the actions that stem from these attitudes, including pro-social helping behavior and antisocial discrimination. The factors and triggers of aggression are covered, followed by a critical examination of the role violent media and video games play in increasing aggression. The classic studies of Zimbardo, Milgram and Asch are presented along with a review of the factors that influence attraction. The unit concludes with a discussion of conflict and peacemaking.

Modules

Tip #14
Get to Know the Free-Response Question

As you get closer to the time of the AP® Exam in May, visit the College Board® website and attempt some of the free-response questions posted on the site. Actual essay questions from previous administrations of the AP® Exam are available with student samples and detailed rubrics to verify your answers. Set aside a quiet time before the exam to answer two FRQs in a 50-minute time period. When you are finished, read the rubrics and use them to score one or two of the sample essays provided to make sure you understand how it works. Then score your two essays. Practice rewriting your essays with the rubric in mind. Take some time to review any missed terms on the essay and then answer another two FRQs to see if you have improved

Module 74

Attribution, Attitudes, and Action

Before You Read

Module Summary

Module 74 describes the issues and behaviors social psychologists study and discusses how we tend to explain behavior. The relationship between thoughts and actions is presented.

Before beginning the module, take a moment to read each of the following terms and names you will encounter. You may wish to make vocabulary cards for each.

Key Terms

social psychology

attribution theory

fundamental attribution error

attitude

peripheral route persuasion

central route persuasion

foot-in-the-door phenomenon

role

cognitive dissonance theory

Key Names

Philip Zimbardo

Leon Festinger

While You Read

Answer the following questions/prompts.

74-1

1. Give an example of a particular behavior or situation that a social psychologist might study.

2. Explain the difference between a dispositional (internal) and a situational (external) attribution. Give an example of each.

3. Janine recently received an F on her history essay. What might be a situational attribution Janine could make to explain the F? How about a dispositional attribution?

4. Describe the fundamental attribution error. How do cultural influences impact the prevalence of the fundamental attribution error?

5. Based on research findings on attribution styles, complete each sentence with:

- "situational" or "dispositional" to describe the most likely attribution, and
- an example of what that attribution might be.

The first one has been done for you.

a. I give $100 to charity every year.
- *Dispositional: According to the self-serving bias, I attribute my own admirable actions to my own good reasons.*
- *I give $100 because I am generous and look out for others.*

b. The CEO of a company gives $100 to charity every year.

c. My mom yelled at my nephew.

d. That man over there just yelled at that child.

e. I cheated on my history test in school.

f. That kid in my 3rd period class cheated on the test.

6. Module 74-1 ends with this point to remember:

> Our attributions--to a person's disposition or to the situation--have real consequences.

Think of a time when you have made an incorrect attribution. What was the consequence of that error?

74-2

1. Give an original example of how our attitudes and behaviors/actions affect each other.

2. Explain how an advertising agency would convince you to buy a new product using the following:

   a. peripheral route persuasion

   b. central route persuasion

3. Describe how the foot-in-the-door phenomenon is utilized to get people to comply with a large request. What three components are necessary to realize the foot-in-the-door phenomena?

4. Describe how you would use the foot-in-the-door technique to convince your parents to let you go to the beach for a week with 15 of your classmates.

5. Explain what is meant by the quote "Fake it until you make it" as it relates to role playing.

6. Summarize what Philip Zimbardo's research showed regarding the roles people are asked to play.

7. Explain Leon Festinger's cognitive dissonance theory.

8. What are the components necessary to create cognitive dissonance?

9. Describe a time that you have experienced cognitive dissonance.

After You Read

Module 74 Review

Answer the following questions to see if you have mastered the basics.

1. As John walks down the hallway between classes, he says "hi" to classmates as they walk by. One classmate does not return his greeting and John assumes he is standoffish and cold. In reality, the classmate who did not return John's greeting had just received a bad grade in Geometry and was disappointed and deep in thought. He didn't even notice John. John's mistaken explanation for his classmate's behavior is best explained by
   a. the peripheral attitude.
   b. the self-serving bias.
   c. the fundamental attribution error.
   d. the central attitude error.
   e. the foot-in-the-door phenomenon.

2. Serena is a marketing major and is tasked with developing an ad campaign to promote vaccinations in children. A strong believer in vaccinations, Serena researches the statistics on disease prevention as a result of the shots and prepares a fact-based campaign intending to convince her audience. The method Serena is employing for her campaign is called the
   a. self-serving bias.
   b. fundamental attribution technique.
   c. attitude adjustment.
   d. peripheral route persuasion.
   e. central route persuasion.

3. Which psychologist, in his classic prison study, was able to show that the role someone plays has a clear impact on attitudes and behaviors?
   a. Stanley Milgram
   b. Solomon Asch
   c. Philip Zimbardo
   d. Leon Festinger
   e. Martin Seligman

4. Reynaldo is heading up a school-wide fundraising event. Since he knows it will be difficult to get people involved, he first asks the teachers if he can have 2 minutes in their classrooms to announce the event. The teachers agree to this. Instead of asking his classmates for money right away, he asks if they will sign a poster in the cafeteria pledging to help spread the word and most of his classmates come to sign the poster. The next month he invites a group of friends over to his house to eat pizza and make posters for the halls. Over time Reynaldo is able to build his support base, and eventually raises a record amount of money for the event. It is apparent that Reynaldo was well-versed in the
   a. peripheral route persuasion.
   b. central route persuasion.
   c. cognitive dissonance theory.
   d. foot-in-the-door phenomenon.
   e. fundamental attribution theory.

5. Ashton participated in anti-smoking education classes from elementary through high school and had always rejected smoking. Recently, however, Ashton has begun smoking. Ashton feels bad about going against his beliefs and when asked by his peers why he is smoking when he knows it is dangerous to his health, he tries to rationalize his actions by telling them "I might die sooner, but at least I'll have fun." Ashton's conflicting actions and beliefs are evidence of

   a. cognitive dissonance.
   b. role playing.
   c. peripheral attitudes.
   d. attitude change.
   e. attribution theory.

Module 75

Conformity and Obedience

Before You Read

Module Summary

Module 75 introduces the research on conformity. Automatic mimicry and the power of the situation in determining behavior are also discussed. The studies conducted by Solomon Asch and Stanley Milgram are presented as illustrations of the power of social influence.

Before beginning the module, take a moment to read each of the following terms and names you will encounter. You may wish to make vocabulary cards for each.

Key Terms		Key Names
conformity	informational social influence	Solomon Asch
normative social influence		Stanley Milgram

While You Read

Answer the following questions/prompts.

1. Define *conformity* and provide real-life examples from your school.

2. Define the *chameleon effect* and briefly summarize the work of Chartrand and Bargh.

3. Where have you seen the chameleon effect in your classrooms or social events?

4. How does automatic mimicry help us to empathize?

5. What can be a downside to mimicry?

6. Summarize the methodology and findings of Solomon Asch's experiment on conformity.

7. Discuss the factors that make us more likely to conform.

8. Define and describe the two kinds of social influence and explain the difference between the two.

75-2

1. Summarize Stanley Milgram's work on obedience.

2. Milgram noted several instances in which obedience to authority was higher. List those below.

a.

b.

c.

d.

3. Looking at the list from #2, apply the instances to four events in your own life, or the world in general.

   a.

   b.

   c.

   d.

4. How might conformity be useful in society? How might it at times be harmful?

After You Read

Module 75 Review

Answer the following questions to see if you have mastered the basics.

1. When Samantha travels south from her hometown in Philadelphia, she often takes on a Southern accent and uses words and phrases unique to the south when speaking with others. This is an example of the

   _____ .

2. Solomon Asch showed that when in a group of participants giving an incorrect answer to a question, one-third of the subjects gave the incorrect answer as well. With these experiments, Asch was demonstrating the occurrence of _____ .

3. All of Grace's peers are wearing jeans tucked into boots and furry jackets to school these days. Grace does not really like that look but is eager to be accepted by her classmates. Grace asks her parents to buy her the same boots as her friends and goes to school dressed like them. According to social psychologists, Grace is responding to _____ .

4. Stanley Milgram showed that when subjects were asked by a researcher to deliver electric "shocks" to participants in an experiment, two-thirds of the subjects went along with the request. Milgram was demonstrating the power of _____ to authority.

5. What is the difference between conformity and obedience? Give an example of each.

Module 76

Group Behavior

Module Summary

Module 76 explains how group behavior differs from individual behavior. The role of the group in influencing and allowing behavior is explored, and the concepts of groupthink and group polarization are presented. The role of norms and culture on group behavior are also discussed.

Before beginning the module, take a moment to read each of the following terms you will encounter. You may wish to make vocabulary cards for each.

Key Terms

social facilitation	groupthink
social loafing	culture
deindividuation	norm
group polarization	

While You Read

Answer the following questions/prompts.

76-1

1. How does the example of Norman Triplett's work with adolescents demonstrate social facilitation? Give a personal example of a time when social facilitation occurred in your life.

2. Explain the phenomenon of social loafing. Give an original example of social loafing.

3. Explain how deindividuation might make a shy teenager cheer loudly at a pep rally.

76-2

1. Briefly explain how group polarization works and provide a real-life example.

2. Discuss how group polarization might impact a jury deliberating on a death-penalty case.

3. What are factors that are likely to contribute to groupthink?

4. Explain how groupthink differs from group polarization.

5. Describe how minority influence can impact majority beliefs.

76-3

1. Explain how the word *norm* relates to the word *culture*.

2. Describe two personal cultural norms not mentioned in the text.

3. Give an actual or hypothetical example of a time when your own cultural norms conflicted with the norms of someone you encountered from another culture.

After You Read

Module 76 Review

Complete the Matching Questions below to see if you have mastered the basics.

Terms

_____ 1. groupthink

_____ 2. norm

_____ 3. culture

_____ 4. deindividuation

_____ 5. group polarization

_____ 6. social loafing

_____ 7. social facilitation

Examples

A. Ethan joins an online group that discusses how to promote liberal ideas. The group's ideas become more liberal as they all trade ideas online.

B. Bethany and Brandon are dressing for the prom. Brandon puts on a tuxedo; Bethany puts on a formal dress.

C. Stephen puts on his black tee shirt and joins the thousands of black tee-shirted protesters in front of the courthouse. He soon chants, screams and hurls rocks along with the group.

D. The President's cabinet does not speak up about the dangers of the President's plan to invade another country because the President seems determined to invade and everyone in the cabinet just wants to get along.

E. The Roosevelt HS Rockets win their home game in front of their cheering classmates.

F. Manuel loves group projects at school and tries to pick a group with kids who will do the work so he can chill out.

G. Chandi studies Indian dance forms with her sisters and mother.

Module 77

Prejudice and Discrimination

Before You Read

Module Summary

Module 77 defines prejudice and describes the relationship between prejudice, stereotypes, and discrimination. The cognitive roots of prejudice are explored and distinct phenomena that impact group stereotypes are presented.

Before beginning the module, take a moment to read each of the following terms you will encounter. You may wish to make vocabulary cards for each.

Key Terms

prejudice

stereotype

discrimination

just-world phenomenon

ingroup

outgroup

ingroup bias

scapegoat theory

other-race effect

While You Read

Answer the following questions/prompts.

77-1

1. Complete the chart.

Term	Definition	Example	Is It a Belief (B), Feeling (F), or Action (A)?
Stereotype			

Term	Definition	Example	Is It a Belief (B), Feeling (F), or Action (A)?
Prejudice			
Discrimination			

2. How is ethnocentrism related to prejudice?

3. Explain the difference between overt and subtle prejudice. Give an original example of each in your explanation.

4. Explain the just-world phenomenon.

5. How does the just-world phenomenon relate to the statement "stereotypes rationalize inequalities"? How might it be used today to explain why residents of high-crime areas may find themselves victims of crime?

6. In the circles below, fill in characteristics of the members of your ingroup (perhaps a club or class at school) and those in the outgroup.

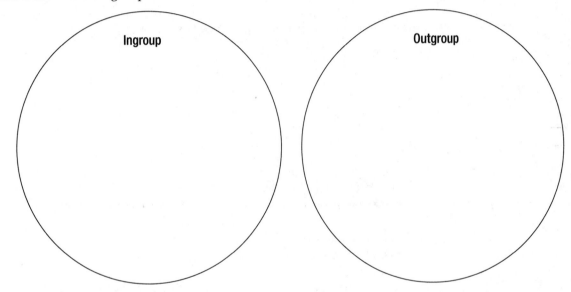

Ingroup

Outgroup

7. Explain how ingroup bias is present in high school cliques, rival sports teams and politics. How might this bias lead to prejudice and discrimination?

8. Discuss how the scapegoat theory might be used to explain bullying.

77-2

1. Explain how the other-race effect can lead to discrimination.

2. How does the tendency to remember vivid cases increase the presence of stereotypes?

After You Read

Module 77 Review

Answer the following questions to see if you have mastered the basics.

For questions 1–5, indicate if the situation describes a prejudice (P), a stereotype (S) or discrimination (D).

_____ 1. Nathaniel is not hired for a job because he is gay.

_____ 2. Robert is not pleased that the teacher has seated him next to two Hispanic kids since he doesn't really like Hispanics.

_____ 3. Ari and Tasha are forming a group for their science fair project and need three additional members. Three cheerleaders ask to join them, but Ari and Tasha turn them away because they assume cheerleaders are not good at science.

_____ 4. Ariel needs help sewing a project for class and doesn't think to ask Wyatt since he is a boy and she can't imagine him knowing how to sew.

_____ 5. Cindy hopes to work with Quan for her school project since he is Asian and she believes all Asians are smart.

6. Claudia is heading to Harvard in the fall and believes all of her hard work in school and volunteering in the community have been rewarded with acceptance into this prestigious university. Her belief is an example of

_____ .

7. Dylan is a jock at your school and believes that jocks really ROCK! He always wears school jerseys and hangs with other jocks at lunch. He doesn't hold the band and orchestra kids in very high regard. Dylan would consider himself and the other jocks to be the _____ and the band and orchestra kids to be the _____ . His favoring of jocks in general would be an _____ .

Module 78

Aggression

Before You Read

Module Summary

Module 78 defines *aggression* and identifies the biological factors and psychological and social-cultural triggers of aggression.

Before beginning the module, take a moment to read each of the following terms you will encounter. You may wish to make vocabulary cards for each.

Key Terms

aggression
frustration-aggression principle
social script

While You Read

Answer the following questions/prompts.

78-1

1. How is the definition of *aggression* presented in the opening paragraph of the module different from the definition of aggression commonly used? Do you agree or disagree with the definition in the text? How would you define *aggression*?

2. What are the genetic influences of aggression?

3. Explain how neural systems and biochemistry can influence aggression.

78-2

1. Describe how the frustration-aggression principle explains increased amounts of aggression in certain cases.

2. In what way do reinforcement and modeling trigger aggressive behavior?

3. Describe how a social script is created and how it can lead to aggressive behavior. How could social scripts be changed to make society more peaceful?

4. Explain what current research suggests about the link between watching television or movie violence and real-life aggression. Based on your experiences, do you agree with these findings?

5. Summarize the research findings on the link between video game violence and aggression. How could your knowledge of Albert Bandura's "Bobo doll" study help you to create a hypothesis regarding this link?

After You Read

Module 78 Review

Answer the following question to see if you have mastered the basics.

> You often babysit two boys; Bart, age 7 and Scott, age 10. Bart is rather shy and quiet and enjoys reading books but Scott is very active and tends to invent war games to play. Bart and Scott's parents have been thinking of buying them a new video game system that comes with games that involve destroying buildings, war, and using guns to kill people. Since they know you are taking psychology, Bart and Scott's parents ask you for your opinion on whether they should buy the game for the boys.

Using your knowledge of aggression, social scripts, the frustration-aggression principle, and research into the effects of violent video games on children, discuss what advice you would give the parents about the purchase of the game.

Module 79

Attraction

Module Summary

Module 79 discusses the research on attraction and love and explains why we fall in love with some people but not with others. The characteristics of a strong marriage and the typical phases of love in a committed relationship are also covered.

Before beginning the module, take a moment to read each of the following terms you will encounter. You may wish to make vocabulary cards for each.

Key Terms

mere exposure effect   equity

passionate love   self-disclosure

companionate love

While You Read

Answer the following questions/prompts.

79-1

1. How does proximity influence how much we like something or someone? Give an example of how this might work in your high school.

2. How does the mere exposure effect increase odds that we will like someone or something?

3. How might advertisers use this knowledge to persuade you to buy certain products?

4. How has online dating changed dating relationships?

5. In what way does physical attractiveness impact liking?

6. How have various cultures defined attractiveness? How do norms and culture influence what we tend to find attractive in others?

7. What does your culture consider "attractive"?

8. Discuss the role similarity plays in attraction.

79-2

1. Describe how passionate love differs from companionate love.

2. Explain how the "Rickety bridge" study relates to passionate love.

3. How does the expectation of passionate love in a marriage sometimes lead to frustration?

4. Explain how equity can have a positive impact on a relationship.

5. How does self-disclosure lead to a successful relationship?

After You Read

Module 79 Review

Answer the following question to see if you have mastered the basics.

> Chantal and Jermaine have been dating awhile and are considering marriage as the next step in their relationship. You are a marriage counselor who understands the factors that influence attraction.

Prepare a brief overview for Chantal and Jermaine of how they can expect their love to change over time, and the factors that can increase the odds of them having a successful marriage. Use key psychological concepts in your response that demonstrate an understanding of the factors involved in attraction.

Module 80

Altruism, Conflict, and Peacemaking

Before You Read

Module Summary

Module 80 deals with altruism, conflict, and peacemaking. This module explores social exchange theory and considers the way in which social norms explain why people help one another. Conflict fueled by social traps and mirror-image perceptions is discussed. The module concludes by suggesting how we can transform feelings of prejudice, aggression, and conflict into peace.

Before beginning the module, take a moment to read each of the following terms you will encounter. You may wish to make vocabulary cards for each.

Key Terms

altruism	social trap
bystander effect	mirror-image perceptions
social exchange theory	self-fulfilling prophecy
reciprocity norm	superordinate goals
social-responsibility norm	GRIT
conflict	

While You Read

Answer the following questions/prompts.

80-1

1. Define *altruism* and explain how it impacts an individual's likelihood of helping others in need.

2. Briefly explain how the Kitty Genovese story illustrates the bystander effect.

3. What factors are important when determining whether or not we will intervene when someone needs help?

80-2

1. Describe the social exchange theory and explain how it impacts helping behavior.

2. Describe the reciprocity norm and discuss how it differs from a social-responsibility norm. How might the reciprocity norm impact relationships?

80-3

1. Describe how a social trap can create conflict.

2. Give an example of a social trap in your high school or personal life.

3. Explain how mirror-image perceptions can lead to self-fulfilling prophecies.

4. Explain how the self-fulfilling prophecy may help or hinder a student's performance in school.

80-4

1. Summarize the research that demonstrates the role that contact can play in promoting peace.

2. In what way are superordinate goals used to achieve cooperation?

3. Explain specifically how superordinate goals were used by Muzafer Sherif at the boys camp in Oklahoma.

4. Discuss the importance of communication in reducing conflict.

5. Explain how you might use the components of GRIT to alleviate conflict in a friendship or between a teacher and student.

After You Read

Module 80 Review

Choose the term from the box that is best exemplified by each situation below.

altruism	bystander effect	social exchange theory
social trap	reciprocity norm	social-responsibility norm
conflict	GRIT	superordinate goals
self-fulfilling prophecy		

1. Although they were competing for first chair in the violin section, Adele and Sean knew they needed to work together if this concert was to be a success.

   _____

2. Denise wants to go to prom next month, but her boyfriend wants to go to the NBA finals game in town instead.

   _____

3. Although it put his family in jeopardy, Hans, a German civilian, sheltered three Jewish children in his home during the Holocaust.

   _____

4. The Rodriguez family drives a gas-guzzling SUV because they like the space it gives them.

   _____

5. Mr. Johanssen believes the new student in his class is going to be a troublemaker and as such, treats him with strict discipline from the first day of class. The student, responding to Mr. Johanssen's behavior, begins to act out and confirms Mr. Johanssen's belief about him.

   _____

6. Fiona is deciding whether or not to help her classmate with Geometry. Although it will take up her time, she will feel good about helping and may earn the respect of her teacher, so she decides to help.

   _____

7. Jan knew she could count on her classmates to donate blankets for the homeless this winter.

   _____

8. Having donated money to her neighbor's son's track fundraiser, Ms. Callahan expected her neighbor to buy cookies from her daughter for the choral fundraiser.

   _____

9. The new players on the basketball team are resentful that the veteran players get more playing time. Chris, the captain of the team, recognizes the guys on the team all need to get along and offers to sit out a game in order to let the newer players have time on the court.

   _____

10. Leticia dropped her textbooks in the crowded hall and only one person stopped to help her pick them up.

   _____

✓ Check Yourself   Now that you have mastered the basics, work through the problems below to see if you can *synthesize*, *evaluate*, and *analyze* what you have learned.

Shanice, an African-American junior in high school, is transferring midyear from a predominantly African-American student population to a new high school that is predominantly Caucasian. Discuss the effect the following will have on her ability to adjust to this change in a healthy manner.

Fundamental attribution error:

Ingroup bias:

Conformity:

Social facilitation:

Deindividuation:

Norms:

Stereotypes:

Mere-exposure effect:

Before You Move On

Use the checklist below to verify your understanding of the unit's main points.

Can I apply attribution theory to explain motives?

- [ ] Fundamental attribution error
- [ ] Self-serving bias

Can I describe the structure and function of different kinds of group behavior?

- [ ] Deindividuation
- [ ] Group polarization

Can I explain how individuals respond to expectations of others?

- [ ] Groupthink
- [ ] Conformity
- [ ] Obedience to authority

- [ ] Can I discuss attitudes and how they change (e.g., central route persuasion)?

Can I predict the impact of the presence of others on individual behavior?

- [ ] Bystander effect
- [ ] Social facilitation

Can I describe processes that contribute to different treatment of group members, such as:

- [ ] Ingroup/outgroup social dynamics
- [ ] Ethnocentrism
- [ ] Prejudice

Can I articulate the impact of the following social and cultural categories on self-concept and relations with others?

- [ ] Gender
- [ ] Race
- [ ] Ethnicity

- [ ] Can I anticipate the impact of behavior on a self-fulfilling prophecy?

- [ ] Can I describe the variables that contribute to altruism, aggression, and attraction?

- [ ] Can I discuss attitude formation and change, including persuasion strategies and cognitive dissonance?

Can I identify the following important figures in social psychology?

- [ ] Solomon Asch
- [ ] Leon Festinger
- [ ] Stanley Milgram
- [ ] Philip Zimbardo

Preparing for the AP® Psychology Examination

I. Overview

After studying and working on psychology all year, you will take the AP® Psychology exam in early May. Not only will you be able to apply all that you have learned, but you will have an opportunity to earn college credit for your efforts! If you earn a "passing score" on the exam, you may be eligible to receive credit at a college or university. This means you will have demonstrated a level of knowledge equivalent to that of students completing an introductory psychology course. You may gain credit hours, advanced placement in a course sequence, and possibly a savings in tuition!

For these reasons, it is to your advantage that you do your best on the exam. Doing your best requires that you have a plan to prepare and review for the exam in addition to having a strong conceptual understanding of the content you've learned all year. The material that follows is designed to help you as you prepare for and take the AP® Psychology exam.

Every year the number of students attempting the AP® Psychology exam grows. Since 1992, 1,804,801 bright students have taken the AP® Psychology exam. In 2013, 67% of test-takers earned a 3 or higher and have a good chance of earning college credit. And just think, many students taking the exam probably didn't prepare as well as you have! After working through this Strive Guide along with your textbook, you will be well poised to earn a high score on the exam!

According to the College Board®, AP® test scores carry the following recommendations:

AP® Score	Qualification	Our Translation
5	Extremely well qualified	Extremely well-qualified psychology rock star!
4	Well qualified	Likely to earn college credit
3	Qualified	Possibly earn college credit
2	Possibly qualified	Will probably not earn college credit
1	No recommendation	No credit, but you're still better off for having taken the course!

Maximizing your performance on any AP® exam requires a well thought out preparation and review plan. The next section suggests a schedule for preparing for your AP® Psychology exam. Keep in mind that this suggested schedule will need to be modified to fit your individual circumstances. In particular, you will need to adjust the schedule based on any other AP® exams and activities that you will also have during this very busy time of year!

II. Sample Schedule

What follows is a general guide for creating a plan to prepare and review for the AP® Psychology exam. While each student's routine and method of studying will differ, consider these suggestions for creating your own plan to maximize your performance on the exam!

1. At the start of your AP® Psychology course

During the first few weeks of your class, familiarize yourself with the course outline and AP® exam information, both of which are presented in the next few sections. It has been said that any student can hit a target that is clear and holds still for them. If you know where you are going, it is far easier to get there. The course outline clearly indicates the topics you will study and the exam format is the same from year to year. Additional information on the exam is available on the College Board's® AP® Central website.

2. During your AP® Psychology course

As you work through each unit, be sure to read the textbook and do all assigned practice questions. Use this guide to help you organize your notes, define key terms, and practice important concepts. Be sure to complete all the problems in this guide and note any concepts that give you difficulty, and be sure to spend time with those difficult concepts. It is important to understand the level at which the material will be tested and to see how questions testing that material are typically written. You can find sample exam questions in the practice exam section of this Strive Guide and on the College Board's® AP® Central website.

3. Six weeks before the exam

About six weeks before the exam, you should begin planning for your exam preparation and review. If you are currently taking more than one AP® course, be sure you know when each exam will be given and plan accordingly. Remember that all AP® exams are given over a two-week period in May, so check when your AP® Psychology exam will be in relation to other AP® exams you will be taking.

4. Four weeks before the exam

In early April, you should be wrapping up your studies in the course. This is a good time to attempt a practice test. Your teacher may provide one and you should take one of the practice exams in this section. Be sure to note any concepts that give you difficulty to determine how much additional studying you will need and what specific areas you should emphasize as you allocate your additional study time There are still several weeks of class left at this point and plenty of time for you to review, practice, and solidify your understanding of the key concepts in the course.

5. The week before the exam

The week before the exam, you should be done with your studies and should practice, practice, practice. Take this time to refresh your memory on the key concepts and review the topics that gave you the most trouble during the year. Use another practice test to help you get used to the exam format. Be sure to allow 70 minutes for the multiple-choice section and 50 minutes for the free-response section.

6. One or two nights before the exam

Schedule time for one last review of the course material to make sure it is fresh in your mind. You can take one last practice exam, take time for a flash card review, or meet with a study group. Your final review session should not be too long or intense. Make sure you arrange to get a good night's sleep the night before the exam!

7. The day of the exam

You have prepared and reviewed as much as possible and are ready for the exam! Make sure you eat a good breakfast, have everything you need to take to the exam with you, and get to your exam site early on the day of your exam. Good luck!

III. The AP® Psychology Course Outline

The course outline for AP® Psychology is provided below. This outline lists the topics covered in the course and the percentage of the exam devoted to that material. Additional information on the course outline can be found at the College Board's® AP® Central website.

Course Content Overview

The topics for AP® Psychology are divided into fourteen major themes, outlined below.

Topic Outline

I. History and Approaches (2–4%)
 A. History of Psychology
 B. Approaches
  1. Biological
  2. Behavioral
  3. Cognitive
  4. Humanistic
  5. Psychodynamic
  6. Sociocultural
  7. Evolutionary
  8. Biopsychosocial
 C. Subfields in Psychology

II. Research Methods (8–10%)
 A. Experimental, Correlational, and Clinical Research
 B. Statistics
  1. Descriptive
  2. Inferential
 C. Ethics in Research

III. Biological Bases of Behavior (8–10%)
 A. Physiological Techniques (e.g., imaging, surgical)
 B. Neuroanatomy
 C. Functional Organization of Nervous System
 D. Neural Transmission
 E. Neuroplasticity
 F. Endocrine System
 G. Genetics
 H. Evolutionary Psychology

IV. Sensation and Perception (6–8%)
   A. Thresholds and Signal Detection Theory
   B. Sensory Mechanisms
   C. Attention
   D. Perceptual Processes

V. States of Consciousness (2–4%)
   A. Sleep and Dreaming
   B. Hypnosis
   C. Psychoactive Drug Effects

VI. Learning (7–9%)
   A. Classical Conditioning
   B. Operant Conditioning
   C. Cognitive Processes
   D. Biological Factors
   E. Social Learning

VII. Cognition (8–10%)
   A. Memory
   B. Language
   C. Thinking
   D. Problem Solving and Creativity

VIII. Motivation and Emotion (6–8%)
   A. Biological Bases
   B. Theories of Motivation
   C. Hunger, Thirst, Sex, and Pain
   D. Social Motives
   E. Theories of Emotion
   F. Stress

IX. Developmental Psychology (7–9%)
   A. Life-Span Approach
   B. Research Methods (e.g., longitudinal, cross-sectional)
   C. Heredity–Environment Issues
   D. Developmental Theories
   E. Dimensions of Development
      1. Physical
      2. Cognitive
      3. Social
      4. Moral
   F. Sex and Gender Development

X. Personality (5–7%)
   A. Personality Theories and Approaches
   B. Assessment Techniques
   C. Growth and Adjustment

XI. Testing and Individual Differences (5–7%)
   A. Standardization and Norms
   B. Reliability and Validity
   C. Types of Tests
   D. Ethics and Standards in Testing
   E. Intelligence

XII. Abnormal Behavior (7–9%)
   A. Definitions of Abnormality
   B. Theories of Psychopathology
   C. Diagnosis of Psychopathology
   D. Types of Disorders
      1. Anxiety
      2. Somatoform
      3. Mood
      4. Schizophrenic
      5. Organic
      6. Personality
      7. Dissociative

XIII. Treatment of Abnormal Behavior (5–7%)
   A. Treatment Approaches
      1. Psychodynamic
      2. Humanistic
      3. Behavioral
      4. Cognitive
      5. Biological
   B. Modes of Therapy (i.e., individual, group)
   C. Community and Preventive Approaches

XIV. Social Psychology (8–10%)
   A. Group Dynamics
   B. Attribution Processes
   C. Interpersonal Perception
   D. Conformity, Compliance, Obedience
   E. Attitudes and Attitude Change
   F. Organizational Behavior
   G. Aggression/Antisocial Behavior
   H. Cultural Influence

IV. Exam Format

The AP® Psychology test is divided into two sections. The first section consists of 100 multiple-choice questions, which counts for two-thirds of the exam grade. The second section is composed of two free-response questions, which count for one-third of the exam grade. The number of questions you will be asked from each section of the course outline corresponds to the percentages provided in the course outline. For example, "I. History and Approaches: 2-4%" means that anywhere from two to four questions on this topic will be asked on the multiple-choice section.

Multiple-Choice Section

You will have 70 minutes to complete the 100 questions on the multiple-choice section of the exam. This time translates to roughly 42 seconds per question. Each multiple-choice question has five answer choices (A-E), only one of which is correct. Each correct answer earns you one point, while each question answered incorrectly (or left blank) earns you no points. This means it is in your best interest to answer every question, even if you need to make an educated guess! You are trying to rack up as many points as possible. So when in doubt, give it your best shot and guess; you just might get lucky. The worst thing that can happen is that no point will be earned. It is also worth noting that AP® exams do not include "all of the above," "none of the above" or "true/false" questions.

Free-Response Section

The second section of the exam is made up of two free-response questions. This section is meant to evaluate your mastery of scientific research principles and the ability to synthesize and apply information across different psychological domains to a novel situation or prompt. Once you turn to the free-response section, take a few minutes to read over the questions and map out your responses.

Plan to give each question about 25 minutes' time. Spend the first 3-5 minutes planning your answer for each question and then write away for the remaining time!

V. Planning Your Exam Preparation and Review

This book has been designed to help you identify your areas of strength and areas in which you need improvement. If you have been working through all the questions in both the book and this Strive Guide, you should have a good idea of which topics are in need of additional study or review. The practice tests that are included in the last section of the book are designed to help you get familiar with the format of the exam as well as check your understanding of the key concepts in the course. Plan on taking both of these tests as part of your preparation and review. Allow yourself 70 minutes for the first section and 50 minutes for the second section of the test and coordinate with your teacher to access the full answer keys. For each question you missed, determine whether it was a simple mistake or whether you need to go back and study that topic again. After you complete the tests, continue reviewing before the exam date. The best preparation for the exam (other than having a solid understanding of psychology) is to practice as many multiple-choice and free-response questions as possible. Ask your teacher or refer to the College Board's® AP® Central website for additional resources to help you with this!

VI. Test-Taking Tips

Once you have mastered all of the concepts and have built up your psychological science skills, you are ready to begin reviewing for the actual exam.

General Advice

Relax and breathe deep! Remember that everyone else taking the exam is in a situation identical to yours. You've spent a lot of time preparing for the exam, and you will most likely do just fine.

Read each question carefully before you begin working. This is especially important for problems with multiple parts or lengthy introductions. Underline key words, phrases, and information as you read the questions.

Multiple-Choice Questions:

- Examine the question carefully. What topic is being tested? What is the purpose of the question? After deciding on an answer, make sure you haven't made a careless mistake or an incorrect assumption.
- If an answer choice seems "too obvious," think about it. If it's so obvious to you, it's probably obvious to others, and chances are good that it is not the correct response.
- Since there is no penalty for a wrong answer, it is to your advantage to attempt every question or make an educated guess, if necessary.
- Be sure to keep your eye on the clock and don't spend too much time on any one question.

Free-Response Questions:

- Read each question carefully, sentence by sentence, and underline key words or phrases. Look for action verbs, as they will help you identify what you need to include in your answer.
- Be sure to address all parts of the question and tie in all portions of your response back to the prompt.
- Always answer each question in context.
- Respond to the prompt in the order that the question is asked.
- Do not write an introduction or conclusion, and do not repeat the question. This is not the time for flowery language and style; be as clear, concise, and correct as possible.
- Remember to write your answer in paragraph form using complete sentences. It's important to not use outlines for your answer. Even if a response is correct, it will not be scored if it is presented in an incomplete sentence.
- Use psychological terms in your answers.
- Even if the question does not ask for a definition, it is good to include one because it can serve to bolster your example or application.

Communicate Your Thinking Clearly.

- Organize your thoughts before you write, just as you would for an English paper.
- Write neatly. The AP® Exam Readers cannot score your response if they can't read your writing!
- Write efficiently. Say what needs to be said, and move on. Don't ramble.
- The burden of communication is on you. Don't leave it to the Reader to make inferences, because the point will not be rewarded.
- When you finish writing your answer, look back. Does the answer make sense? Did you address the context of the question?

Follow Directions.

- Read your psychology textbook! Most exam questions start with a paragraph that describes the context of the problem. You need to be able to pick out important psychology cues. The only way you will learn to do that is through hands-on experience.
- Practice writing. Your success on the AP® Psychology exam depends on how well you explain your reasoning.
- Practice with as many questions as you can in the weeks leading up to the exam.

Practice Exam 1

This full-length practice exam contains two parts. Part I consists of 100 multiple-choice questions and Part II consists of two free-response questions.

You will have 70 minutes to complete the multiple-choice section of the exam. This section counts for 66% of the exam grade. As you will not be penalized for incorrect answers, you should answer every question on the test. If you do not know an answer to a question, try to eliminate any incorrect answer choices and take your best guess. Do not spend too much time on any one question.

You will have 50 minutes to complete the free-response section of the exam. This section counts for 33% of the overall exam grade. Be sure to answer each part of the question and to provide thorough explanations using the terms and themes you have learned in the course.

Directions: Each of the questions or incomplete statements below is followed by five suggested answers or completions. Select the one that is best in each case and then fill in the corresponding circle on the answer sheet.

1. Alex observes his neighbor yell at her daughter. He knows the neighbor to be warm and friendly and has never seen her behave this way before. Alex concludes that the neighbor must have had a stressful day. What type of attribution has Alex made about his neighbor?

   (A) The fundamental attribution error
   (B) A dispositional attribution
   (C) A situational attribution
   (D) The actor-observer effect
   (E) The self-fulfilling prophecy

2. Sigmund Freud emphasized the role of childhood events and the unconscious in one's life. Which of the following theoretical approaches does Freud represent?

   (A) Cognitive
   (B) Structuralism
   (C) Behavioral
   (D) Humanistic
   (E) Psychoanalytic

3. Katherine and her classmates volunteered to paint houses in their neighborhood. Because there were many volunteers, some of the students did not work very hard, assuming others would do the work. What phenomenon best explains this behavior?

   (A) Groupthink
   (B) Social Loafing
   (C) Social Facilitation
   (D) Social Inhibition
   (E) Group Polarization

4. Joseph feels that his life is stagnating; he has been dating the same woman for a number of years, but does not see a future with her. He feels as if he is stuck in a "dead end" job, but lacks the motivation to look for a new position. Which theoretical perspective would focus on Joseph's future and emphasize his ability to grow in both his professional and interpersonal relationships?

   (A) Cognitive
   (B) Psychoanalytic
   (C) Behavioral
   (D) Functionalism
   (E) Humanistic

5. Johann is 83 years old and has recently experienced a stroke, which left the right side of his body paralyzed. In addition, he is having trouble understanding direct questions or requests. Johann has no trouble speaking. Which of the following brain areas is likely to have been damaged by Johann's stroke?

   (A) The somatosensory cortex
   (B) Wernicke's area
   (C) The hypothalamus
   (D) Broca's area
   (E) The reticular activating system

6. Lisa wants to assess the intelligence of students in her kindergarten class. She tests thirty-students over the course of the year to determine how their cognitive abilities change. She uses validated IQ tests and reports each student's IQ at the start and end of the school year. She informs all parents of the results at the conclusion of the study and uses numerical codes to keep the students identities confidential. Which of the following ethical guidelines has Lisa overlooked?

   (A) Informed consent from parents
   (B) No clear dependent variable
   (C) Debriefing
   (D) Confidentiality
   (E) The emotional toll of the research on the children.

7. Jayla spent most of her free time playing lacrosse because she loved the strategy of the game and enjoyed spending time with her teammates. She earned a college scholarship for lacrosse and must continue playing in order to keep her scholarship. She appreciates the financial incentive this opportunity has provided, but now finds herself playing only to keep her scholarship rather than for the love of the game. Which of the following best explains her feeling towards lacrosse when she is in college?

   (A) Positive punishment
   (B) The drive reduction theory of motivation
   (C) The overjustification effect
   (D) Maslow's hierarchy of needs
   (E) Negative reinforcement

8. Mary is a high school senior who is nervous about her AP® exams because she wants to earn as many college credits as possible. As her exams draw near, Mary begins to feel tired and worn down, but she perseveres in her studies. Which stage of Hans Seyle's general adaptation syndrome would best explain Mary's ability to fight through her flu-like symptoms?

   (A) Fight or flight
   (B) A low level of conscientiousness
   (C) Alarm
   (D) Exhaustion
   (E) Resistance

9. William James believed that one's stream of consciousness would allow the individual to be properly evaluated by sharing his collective life experiences. James posed this as an alternative to Wundt's process of introspection. James's theory is known as

   (A) the structuralist approach.
   (B) Gestalt psychology.
   (C) the functionalist approach.
   (D) the psychoanalytic theory.
   (E) the James-Lange theory.

10. A visual message moves from the visual receptors located in the retina (rods and cones) towards the occipital lobe. Choose the correct route of the message as it is processed by the respective components of the visual system.

   (A) Optic nerve; bipolar cells; ganglion cells
   (B) Fovea; ganglion cells; bipolar cells
   (C) Bipolar cells; fovea; ganglion cells
   (D) Bipolar cells; ganglion cells; optic nerve
   (E) Ganglion cells; bipolar cells; optic nerve

11. Henry has great anxiety before any exam. If he performs a ritual to organize exam materials before he begins, his anxiety temporarily goes away. Because this ritual provides relief for Henry, he has increased this habit. This is an example of
    (A) negative reinforcement.
    (B) positive punishment.
    (C) aversive conditioning.
    (D) negative punishment.
    (E) positive reinforcement.

12. Janet is studying for her final exam in Biology. She is trying to recall the correct order for the classification of living things. She creates the saying Ken Puts Candy On Fred's Good Suit to remember Kingdom, Phylum, Class, Order, Family, Genus, and Species. This technique for remembering is known as
    (A) functional fixedness.
    (B) insight.
    (C) breaking set.
    (D) a mnemonic device.
    (E) method of loci.

13. According to Carl Rogers, the key component of creating an empathetic relationship between client and therapist was to demonstrate _____ toward the client.
    (A) reciprocal determinism
    (B) internal locus of control
    (C) unconditional positive regard
    (D) belief in the client's potential for self-actualization
    (E) behavioral therapy

14. Elaine is no longer interested in the activities she previously enjoyed and feels a general lack of energy. She has been feeling this way for about two months. Elaine has also started having thoughts of suicide. Which of the following best describes the condition Elaine is likely to be experiencing?
    (A) Manic disorder
    (B) Dissociative disorder
    (C) Major depressive disorder
    (D) Bipolar disorder
    (E) Somatoform disorder

15. Jonathan has been seeing his therapist for three years. Typically, Jonathan sits on a couch and talks about his week. He may discuss his dreams or conflicts with his wife and parents. Jonathan's therapist will then make a connection between what Jonathan is discussing and what is occurring in his unconscious. What type of treatment is Jonathan's therapist employing?
    (A) Client-centered therapy
    (B) Free association
    (C) Rational-emotive therapy
    (D) Counterconditioning
    (E) Psychopharmacology

16. Josiah took his ACT four times. Each time he received the same score. Josiah is frustrated because he wanted to score a few points higher to be accepted to his preferred university. The results of the exams indicate that the tests are high in
    (A) content validity.
    (B) split-half reliability.
    (C) content reliability.
    (D) test-retest reliability.
    (E) face validity.

17. Kaitlin found out where her favorite pop star attended college and let that drive her decision to attend the same school. Kaitlin used which of the following methods of persuasion when making her college decision?
    (A) Mere exposure effect
    (B) Central route persuasion
    (C) Reciprocity
    (D) Foot-in-the-door
    (E) Peripheral route persuasion

18. Gwendolyn believes that because she has failed a test she will not be able to pass her chemistry class or get into the college of her choice and therefore will not be able to major in chemistry. Which of the following psychologists would be most likely to help change Gwendolyn's negative thoughts?
    (A) Sigmund Freud
    (B) Carl Rogers
    (C) Abraham Maslow
    (D) Aaron Beck
    (E) Albert Bandura

19. Maria conducted a survey regarding the amount of sleep individuals in her study had each night for one month. She then tested them in a virtual driving machine to see how many errors they made while driving . She wanted to determine if sleep deprivation impacted driving accuracy. She found that the less sleep people received, the more errors they made while driving. What kind of study did Maria create and what type of relationship can be identified?
    (A) Experiment; negative
    (B) Correlational study; negative
    (C) Correlational study; illusory
    (D) Correlational study; positive
    (E) Experiment; positive

20. Which branch of the nervous system controls digestion, breathing, and heart rate?
    (A) Autonomic
    (B) Central
    (C) Somatic
    (D) Limbic
    (E) Endocrine

21. Nadia has been suffering from a major depressive episode. If her therapist has prescribed her an SSRI to help her overcome her depression, what impact would the SSRI have on Nadia's neurotransmitters?
    (A) Act as an agonist for serotonin.
    (B) Act as an agonist for dopamine.
    (C) Act as an agonist for acetylcholine.
    (D) Act as an antagonist for serotonin.
    (E) Act as an antagonist for dopamine.

22. Researchers at the Big City University are studying the impact of weight lifting on the speed of student athletes on the track and field team. One group will weightlift for one hour per day and the other group will not weightlift at all during the trial period. The independent variable is _____ and the dependent variable is _____ .
    (A) speed; weight lifting
    (B) studying; weightlifting
    (C) weightlifting; studying
    (D) weightlifting; speed
    (E) studying; speed

23. Edwin is experiencing problems forming new memories. He recently suffered a stroke and can remember episodic and semantic memories prior to the stroke, but nothing after the incident. Which of the following brain regions may have been damaged in the stroke?

(A) Hypothalamus
(B) Thalamus
(C) Hippocampus
(D) Amygdala
(E) Wernicke's area

For Question 24, please refer to the chart below.

Problem #	Number 1	Number 2	Answer
1	6	8	7
2	3	9	6
3	12	2	7
4	10	6	8
5	4	6	5
6	6	6	6
7	6	2	4

24. Sarah has been presented with the problems in the chart above. For the first six problems, Sarah added the two numbers and then divided to find the mean. For the seventh problem the same strategy will work but she can also simply subtract from the first number to arrive at the correct answer. Which of the following best explains why she does not attempt to try a different and simpler approach when attempting to solve problem 7?

(A) Prototypes
(B) The representative heuristic
(C) A mental set
(D) The availability heuristic
(E) Algorithms

25. Before discussing the French Revolution, a teacher gives her class a pre-test to assess their prior knowledge. After examining the results, she determines that most of her students do not have much knowledge of the time period. However, a few students seem to know quite a bit about the topic. Which of the following best represents the distribution of scores on the instructor's pre-test?

(A) A positively skewed distribution
(B) An illusory correlation
(C) A normal distribution
(D) A negatively skewed distribution
(E) A bimodal distribution

26. Three-year old Arjun does not realize that if he stands in front of his mother as she watches television, she cannot see what is displayed. He thinks that because he can see the television that she will be able to as well. What Piagetian stage and concept are demonstrated by Arjun's behavior?

(A) Preoperational; object permanence
(B) Concrete operational; egocentrism
(C) Preoperational; egocentrism
(D) Preoperational; conservation
(E) Preconventional; conservation

27. In the Montessori model of education, students do not receive grades and are allowed to explore independently. Even though students are not "rewarded" by receiving grades, they often learn much information. Which of the following concepts is exemplified by this situation?
(A) Negative reinforcement
(B) Positive punishment
(C) Modeling
(D) Intrinsic motivation
(E) Classical conditioning

28. Jerry becomes ill after eating a Caesar salad. Now, whenever Jerry even smells Caesar salad he begins to feel nauseous. Which component of classical conditioning explains Jerry's reaction to the smell of Caesar salad?
(A) A neutral stimulus
(B) An unconditioned stimulus
(C) An unconditioned response
(D) A conditioned stimulus
(E) A conditioned response

29. Alana has been playing roulette for the past hour. Red has come up as the winning bet eight times in a row. Alana is convinced that it is time for black to win and places her bet accordingly. Which of the following is driving Alana's decision to place her money on black?
(A) An algorithm
(B) A representative heuristic
(C) Insight
(D) An availability heuristic
(E) The conjunction fallacy

30. Edith just returned from a three week "trip" to Orlando in which she took on a new identity. She suddenly realized who she was and returned home to her "normal" life in Cleveland, but has no recollection of her time spent in Orlando and seems to have simply "blacked out." Edith's experience is most consistent with which of the following category of disorders?
(A) Somatic
(B) Psychotic
(C) Anxiety
(D) Dissociative
(E) Mood

31. Ralph is a clinical psychologist diagnosing a new client. He wants to be sure to take into account any neurological, stress/trauma or cultural influences that may be impacting the client's behavior. From which of the following approaches is Ralph conducting his diagnosis?
(A) Medical model
(B) Biopsychosocial approach
(C) Humanistic approach
(D) Psychodynamic approach
(D) Behavioral approach

32. Which of the following concepts best illustrates the behavioral component of stereotypical beliefs?
(A) Self-serving bias
(B) Discrimination
(C) Stereotype threat
(D) Prejudice
(E) Scapegoating

33. Although Sasha sees her AP® Psychology teacher every day, she didn't recognize the teacher when she ran into her at the movie theatre. This best illustrates
   (A) monocular cues.
   (B) context effects.
   (C) perceptual set.
   (D) perceptual adaptation.
   (E) proximity.

34. As Maylin looks at the desks in her classroom, she is able to distinguish between the horizontal and vertical lines that make up the desks. What part of the visual system allows Maylin to distinguish these different types of inputs?
   (A) Ganglion cells
   (B) Feature detectors
   (C) Rods
   (D) Bipolar cells
   (E) The optic nerve

35. As Emily transitions from an alert to a sleeping state, her brain waves begin to slow down but she has bursts of small rapid brain waves. What are these small bursts of activity called which occur in NREM-2?
   (A) Sleep spindles
   (B) Beta waves
   (C) Delta waves
   (D) Theta waves
   (E) NREM waves

36. As an action potential moves through an axon, which of the following occurs?
   (A) Sodium ions rush in as potassium ions are pushed out.
   (B) All potassium and chloride ions remain in the axon.
   (C) Potassium ions rush in as sodium ions are pushed out.
   (D) Chloride ions rush in as sodium ions are pushed out.
   (E) Potassium ions rush in as chloride ions are pushed out.

37. If a rabbit were frightened by a German shepherd, which area of the brain would allow the rabbit to experience fear?
   (A) Wernicke's area
   (B) Amygdala
   (C) Thalamus
   (D) Medulla
   (E) Pituitary gland

38. Professor Kempt finds out that the results of her study on visual stimuli and activity in the right hemisphere are statistically significant. What does it mean when a study is statistically significant?
   (A) The results are important.
   (B) There is a clear operational definition.
   (C) The outcome is not likely due to chance.
   (D) The independent variable is the only reason for the outcome.
   (E) The result has been replicated.

39. Brad is thinking about settling down with his girlfriend. They met in college and have been dating for three years; they share their inner thoughts and feelings with one another and feel a special bond. Which stage of Erikson's psychosocial development is Brad experiencing?

(A) Competence vs. inferiority
(B) Identity vs. role confusion
(C) Generativity vs. stagnation
(D) Intimacy vs. isolation
(E) Ego Integrity vs. despair

40. Kari does not like her math instructor because she does not understand his style of teaching and finds him to be abrasive with students. However, she is convinced that he does not like her and does not admit her own feelings of dislike towards him. According to Sigmund Freud, which of the following defense mechanisms is Kari demonstrating?

(A) Repression
(B) Projection
(C) Regression
(D) Sublimation
(E) Displacement

41. Debbie needs to change a flat tire by herself, which she has never done before. She has all the necessary tools, but at first cannot make any sense of how to use them to change the tire. All of a sudden she understands what she needs to be done. This sudden understanding is referred to by psychologists as

(A) insight.
(B) functional fixedness.
(C) a mental set.
(D) a cognitive map.
(E) associative learning.

42. Each time baby Adlelade says "ba" she is given a soft, cuddly lamb which she likes to squeeze and bite. Because she is given the lamb for making this specific utterance, she says, "ba" more frequently. Which of the following psychologists would support this method of language acquisition?

(A) Noam Chomsky
(B) Benjamin Lee Whorf
(C) Jean Piaget
(D) B. F. Skinner
(E) Mary Ainsworth

43. Darren feels that he is entitled to special treatment because he is smarter and better looking than anyone he has met. When people comment on his behavior, he reasons that they are "just jealous" of his special talents. Which of the following personality disorders is most consistent with Darren's behavior?

(A) Schizoid
(B) Paranoid
(C) Narcissistic
(D) Histrionic
(E) Borderline

44. Selma is an interior designer who recently created a "new look" in a living room for a client. She thought through a number of options, all of which would create a beautiful effect. Creating a workable design in which many solutions could be considered correct is an example of
    (A) an availability heuristic.
    (B) an algorithm.
    (C) divergent thinking.
    (D) insight.
    (E) functional fixedness.

45. Compared with identical twins, fraternal twins are
    (A) less likely to be the same sex and more likely to be similar in extraversion.
    (B) more likely to be the same sex and more likely to be similar in extraversion.
    (C) less likely to be the same sex and less likely to be similar in extraversion.
    (D) more likely to be the same sex and less likely to be similar in extraversion.
    (E) less likely to be the same sex and equally likely to be similar in extraversion..

46. Karen Horney believed that childhood anxiety is caused by
    (A) an Electra complex.
    (B) a sense of helplessness.
    (C) penis envy.
    (D) regression.
    (E) sexual tension.

47. A group of politically active high school students listen to a radical speaker. Rather than being persuaded by his extreme message, the audience collectively moves towards the argument opposing the speaker's perspective. Which social psychology phenomenon is demonstrated in this example?
    (A) Group polarization
    (B) Fundamental attribution error
    (C) Social facilitation
    (D) Groupthink
    (E) Social loafing

48. Even though John does not have much money and needs a new pair of shoes, he does not steal a pair because he is afraid his name will appear in the paper and he will be embarrassed in front of his friends and family. Which level of Lawrence Kohlberg's moral development is John demonstrating?
    (A) Preoperational
    (B) Post conventional
    (C) Concrete Operational
    (D) Conventional
    (E) Preconventional

49. Janice creates training programs to develop the emotional intelligence of her company's sales force. This is done to increase sales and to help the climate of her workplace. Which of the following best describes the field in which Janice works?
    (A) Human factors psychology
    (B) Industrial-organizational psychology
    (C) Psychometric psychology
    (D) Cognitive psychology
    (E) Educational psychology

50. Nanuk enjoys when his friend Riley joins him for an afternoon jog. Nanuk runs each day at 4:00p.m., but he does not know which days Riley will accompany him on his run. Riley's attendance is based on which of the following schedules of reinforcement?
    (A) Variable-ratio
    (B) Variable-interval
    (C) Continuous
    (D) Fixed-ratio
    (E) Fixed-interval

51. Robert Rescorla indicated that rewards and punishments are not the only explanations for behavior as radical behaviorists proposed. Rescorla added that individuals will be more likely to exhibit a behavior if
    (A) they have the expectation of receiving a reward.
    (B) they are predisposed for certain behaviors.
    (C) they fear punishment.
    (D) they are reinforced on a continuous schedule.
    (E) they have been classically conditioned.

Use the following scenario to answer questions 52 and 53:

> Professor Randolph is conducting research on the impact of chewing gum on weight loss. She randomly places her 200 participants into either the group that gets sugar-free chewing gum or the group that gets regular chewing gum. After two weeks, she measures how much weight each of the participants has lost.

52. During which part of the experimental process has Professor Randolph placed the individuals into one of the two groups?
    (A) Population selection
    (B) Cohort grouping
    (C) Random assignment
    (D) Random selection
    (E) Stratified sampling

53. Professor Randolph wants to clarify the operational definition of the dependent variable. For the study described above, the operational definition of the dependent variable is
    (A) the amount of regular gum eaten.
    (B) the amount on sugar free gum eaten.
    (C) pounds of lost weight.
    (D) two weeks.
    (E) amount of gum distributed in the study.

54. A high school teacher wants to study the seating habits of students in the cafeteria. She wants to determine if students sit in the same seats or change seats from day to day. She sits in the cafeteria and without interacting with the students, records where they sit each day. A potential benefit to this type of research is
    (A) there is a clear independent variable.
    (B) there is a clear dependent variable.
    (C) this can be beneficial for gaining much information about a specific individual.
    (D) that the participants should act normally.
    (E) it can be beneficial for gaining information over and extended period of time.

55. Penelope used to have an intense fear of the dentist. After finding a highly skilled dentist with a warm personality, the fear faded and eventually went away completely. Suddenly, when visiting her dentist for a routine check-up, her fear returns. This phenomeno9n is known as

(A) extinction.
(B) acquisition.
(C) insight.
(D) stimulus generalization.
(E) spontaneous recovery.

56. Carl Rogers believed that one is mentally healthy when

(A) the real self and ideal self have a fairly good match.
(B) one resolves their basic anxiety.
(C) one overcomes their inferiority complex.
(D) one becomes self-actualized.
(E) one examines their collective unconscious.

57. A young pregnant woman drinks during her pregnancy. This is dangerous because the alcohol may act as _____ to the unborn child.

(A) an agonist
(B) a stimulant
(C) a hallucinogen
(D) a teratogen
(E) an antagonist

58. Diana Baumrind classified parents with extremely rigid, inflexible rules who seek little input from their children as which of the following?

(A) Permissive
(B) Rejecting-Neglecting
(C) Authoritative
(D) Authoritarian
(E) Uninvolved

59. Which of the following correctly identifies the "Big Five" personality characteristics?

(A) Extraversion, Impulsiveness, Openness, Neuroticism, Agreeableness
(B) Agreeableness, Impulsiveness, Extraversion, Intelligence, Openness
(C) Agreeableness, Extraversion, Openness, Neuroticism, Conscientiousness
(D) Conscientiousness, Openness, Intelligence, Agreeableness, Extraversion
(E) Openness, Intelligence, Agreeableness, Extraversion, Neuroticism

60. Danita has just learned to ride her bike. What type of memory is formed from learning this new skill?

(A) Iconic
(B) Echoic
(C) Semantic
(D) Episodic
(E) Procedural

61. Rhonda was shown an ambiguous picture and was asked to tell a story about what was happening before, during and after the event in the picture. What type of test has Rhonda been given?

(A) TAT
(B) MMPI
(C) NEO-PI-R
(D) Rorschach
(E) IQ

62. E. L. Thorndike placed kittens in puzzle boxes to see if they could figure out how to escape. Once the kittens solved the problem, they could easily replicate the procedure and escape over and over again. This led Thorndike to create which of the following concepts?
    (A) Classical conditioning
    (B) Negative punishment
    (C) Behaviorism
    (D) The law of effect
    (E) Positive punishment

63. Cassie believes that she should do her part to save the environment. However, she does not take the time to sort through the different remnants of her lunch to place some items in the recycling bin and others in the garbage. Later, she feels tense and guilty about not behaving in a fashion consistent with her beliefs. Cassie is experiencing which of the following phenomenon?
    (A) Cognitive dissonance
    (B) Social inhibition
    (C) Scapegoating
    (D) Social loafing
    (E) Groupthink

64. In Stanley Milgram's landmark study regarding obedience, which of the following factors most limited the amount of obedience to the experimenter?
    (A) The "learner" was moved closer to the "teacher."
    (B) The "teacher" witnessed another "teacher" refuse to continue with the shocks.
    (C) The experimenter was physically close to the "teacher."
    (D) The "teacher" had to physically place the "learner's" hand onto a shock plate.
    (E) The experiment was moved from an anonymous office building to the campus of Yale University.

65. If a child was afraid of a dog, one could play pleasant music playing in the background each time he was presented with the dog. If the child learned to associate the pleasant music with the dog, Mary Cover Jones suggested he could overcome his fear of dogs. This type of treatment is known as
    (A) implosive therapy.
    (B) aversive conditioning.
    (C) cognitive therapy.
    (D) counterconditioning.
    (E) client-centered therapy.

66. Which of the following is a negative symptom of schizophrenia?
    (A) Hallucinations
    (B) Delusions
    (C) Flat effect
    (D) Word salad
    (E) Increased emotional responses

67. Anytime Jared walks through a doorway, he must pass through exactly in the center. If he does not, he goes back and tries again until it is perfect. This exercise often consumes hours of his days. From what disorder does Jared likely suffer?
    (A) Conversion
    (B) PTSD
    (C) Obsessive-compulsive
    (D) Phobia
    (E) Dissociative fugue

68. After Kimberly completed a woodworking class, she took an exam to determine the best type of wood for certain projects and the tools typically used for specific woodworking techniques. The test intended to measure what Kimberly had learned from the course. What type of test did Kimberly take?

    (A) Intelligence
    (B) Achievement
    (C) Aptitude
    (D) Personality
    (E) Projective

69. Charles Spearman believed that one's overall intelligence was a combination of specific talents. The overall intelligence Spearman identified is known as

    (A) the g factor.
    (B) multiple intelligences.
    (C) practical intelligence.
    (D) emotional intelligence.
    (E) creative intelligence.

70. Dustin believes government officials are taking secret pictures of him. He is suspicious that his family members are reporting his every movement to government agencies. Dustin is experiencing which of the following symptoms of schizophrenia?

    (A) Delusions
    (B) Flat effect
    (C) Compulsions
    (D) Hallucinations
    (E) Somatic symptoms

71. Which Neo-Freudian discussed the significance of overcoming an inferiority complex and "striving for superiority"?

    (A) Carl Jung
    (B) Alfred Adler
    (C) Karen Horney
    (D) Erik Erikson
    (E) Carl Rogers

72. Edie just celebrated her 97th birthday. She lives independently and has many social interactions. Edie walks two miles each day and makes an effort to eat right and take care of her health. Until recently she had also remained cognitively alert. In the last few months, she has experienced a sharp decline in her cognition. This sudden decline of cognition in extreme old age in known as

    (A) multiple intelligence.
    (B) fluid intelligence.
    (C) terminal decline.
    (D) Alzheimer's disease.
    (E) Parkinson's disease.

73. A criticism of Lawrence Kohlberg's theory of moral development was that

    (A) it only examined civil disobedience and parenting.
    (B) the postconventional level was based primarily on masculine behaviors found in western cultures.
    (C) it looked at disobedient response rates.
    (D) it emphasized care and relationships.
    (E) it placed too much emphasis on personal identity.

74. A type of therapy wthat has been beneficial for individuals to recognize that they are not alone in their suffering and that others are experiencing similar issues is known as
    (A) family therapy.
    (B) systematic desensitization.
    (C) rational emotive therapy.
    (D) client-centered therapy.
    (E) group therapy.

75. What area of the brain is responsible for the production of one's growth hormone and often referred to as the "master gland" of the endocrine system?
    (A) Adrenal gland
    (B) Thyroid gland
    (C) Pancreas
    (D) Thalamus
    (E) Pituitary gland

76. Ernest Hilgard found that hypnotized participants tend to withstand higher levels of pain than participants who were not hypnotized. Hilgard attributed this resistance to pain to which of the following?
    (A) Dissociation
    (B) Meditation
    (C) Endorphins
    (D) Hormones
    (E) Latent tolerance for pain

77. Which of the following is not considered one of Paul Ekman's universal facial expressions?
    (A) Disgust
    (B) Jealousy
    (C) Anger
    (D) Happiness
    (E) Surprise

78. Miguel has been an avid runner for many years. He has always been competitive and is training to run a marathon in under three hours. Miguel has finally broken this barrier and feels that he has reached his full potential as a runner. According to Maslow, in regard to his running, Miguel
    (A) is satisfying his physiological needs.
    (B) is fulfilling his safety needs.
    (C) is fulfilling his belonging and love needs.
    (D) is fulfilling his self-esteem needs.
    (E) is self-actualized.

79. Alicia is in a yoga class. She is very thirsty and finds herself preoccupied with thoughts of quenching her thirst as she attempts to hold different yoga poses. Which theory of motivation best explains her preoccupation with her thirst?
    (A) The incentive theory
    (B) The drive-reduction theory
    (C) Maslow's hierarchy
    (D) Schachter's theory
    (E) James-Lange theory

80. John Garcia found that some types of associative learning occurred more quickly than others. He proposed that this learning seemed to be a mechanism by which an organism protects oneself. His research focused primarily on

(A) latent learning.
(B) positive punishment.
(C) taste aversion.
(D) cognitive learning.
(E) insight.

81. Jacob complains of many body aches and pains that occur when he is under a great deal of stress. This has been happening for several years. Doctors can find no physical cause for the complaint. Jacob is likely suffering from which of the following types of disorders?

(A) PTSD
(B) Mood
(C) Anxiety
(D) Somatic symptom
(E) Psychotic

82. In the Robber's Cave experiment Muzafer Sherif pitted the "The Rattlers" and "The Eagles" against one another in many tasks. Eventually, Sherif combined the teams and found that they would work collaboratively if they were presented with which of the following?

(A) Superordinate goals that needed collaboration to be successful.
(B) Rewards for achieving a given task.
(C) They did not work together regardless of the task provided.
(D) Verbal recognition of their accomplishments.
(E) A competitive atmosphere in which to work.

83. Kara is afraid of social encounters. She is working with a therapist to become more comfortable around others. Her therapist first exposes her to photographs of individuals she would like to converse with. Next, they work through a role playing exercise in which she asks friends to join her for a movie night. Eventually, Kara is able to interact more comfortably with others. What type of therapy is Kara's therapist using?

(A) Rational-emotive therapy
(B) Psychoanalytic therapy
(C) Client-centered therapy
(D) Systematic desensitization
(E) Group therapy

84. Jonathan has two older sisters who often leave the house in disarray and blame him. Because he is younger and serves as a good target, Jonathan's sisters are engaging in _____ towards Jonathan.

(A) the just world phenomenon
(B) social loafing
(C) scapegoating
(D) social interference
(E) discrimination

85. Before a national examination is proctored, all students are read the same instructions. Testing conditions must be the same in all testing centers and include the same amount of time for students to complete the exam. These measures are efforts to be sure that the test has

(A) been normed.
(B) test-retest reliability.
(C) construct validity.
(D) been standardized.
(E) a normal bell curve.

86. After France mandated public school for children in the early 1900s, an IQ test was developed. This test attempted to assess those students who needed extra help to catch up to their classmates before starting school. Which of the following individuals is responsible for creating these initial IQ tests?
(A) Charles Spearman
(B) Alfred Binet
(C) Sir Francis Galton
(D) Lewis Terman
(E) William Stern

87. As we look at an image, we follow the direction of an established pattern rather than seeing it as different components. This Gestalt principle is known as
(A) closure.
(B) similarity.
(C) proximity.
(D) figure-ground.
(E) continuity.

88. Stanley Schachter and Jerome Singer modified earlier theories of emotion by adding which of the following components?
(A) Physiological arousal
(B) The role of the thalamus in directing emotional responses.
(C) Cognitive appraisal
(D) An empathetic understanding of others.
(E) The movement between opposing emotions.

89. _____ believed that IQ was genetic and that those with "dull" parents would be destined to have a low IQ. He believed in testing IQ through physical measurements of the brain and body.
(A) Sir Francis Galton
(B) Alfred Binet
(C) Lewis Terman
(D) Charles Spearman
(E) William Stern

90. The second stage of prenatal development in which the heart and limbs develop is known as the _____ stage.
(A) fetal
(B) embryonic
(C) sensorimotor
(D) germinal
(E) preconventional

91. Josie is a baby who cries often and seeks constant attention from her parents. She is often fussy and irritable. According to Thomas and Chess, Josie has which of the following types of temperament?
(A) Difficult
(B) Easy
(C) Slow-to-warm-up
(D) Anxious
(E) Ambivalent

92. The release of stored serotonin and the eventual damage of serotonin-producing neurons is most closely associated with the long-term use of
    (A) alcohol.
    (B) Ecstasy.
    (C) morphine.
    (D) barbiturates.
    (E) amphetamines.

93. Individuals who suffer from diabetes often have low levels of which of the following hormones?
    (A) Glycogen
    (B) Free-fatty acids
    (C) Insulin
    (D) Adrenaline
    (E) Ghrelin

94. Which of the following scanning techniques is used on the brain to best discern the difference between normal soft tissue and pathologic tissues?
    (A) PET
    (B) CT
    (C) EEG
    (D) Electrodes
    (E) MRI

95. As a ballerina, Betty has a sense of when she needs to move a part of her body to get a position just right. This sense of one's bodily position in space is known as
    (A) gustation.
    (B) olfaction.
    (C) nociception.
    (D) kinesthesis.
    (E) depolarization.

96. The process by which information is changed from physical information to neural information that can be processed by the brain is known as
    (A) resting potential.
    (B) transformation.
    (C) transduction.
    (D) action potential.
    (E) depolarization.

97. When Andrew lifts a 10-pound weight, he has to add one pound to notice that it is heavier. Based on Weber's law, how much weight would Andrew have to add to a 50-pound weight to notice the same difference?
    (A) 10 pounds
    (B) 5 pounds
    (C) 8 pounds
    (D) 2 pounds
    (E) 1 pound

98. The area of the cortex that controls incoming messages such as temperature and pain and the lobe that holds this particular area are, respectively, the _____ and _____ .
    (A) somatosensory cortex; temporal lobe
    (B) somatosensory cortex; parietal lobe
    (C) Wernicke's area; temporal lobe
    (D) motor cortex; frontal lobe
    (E) motor cortex; parietal lobe

99. Elizabeth Loftus interviewed college students about their childhood experiences. After students reported specific events from childhood, Loftus inserted the memory of being lost at a shopping mall. Weeks later when the students were presented with a list of memories they accepted the shopping mall experience as their own. What term does Loftus give to "adopting" these new memories?

    (A) Flashbulb memories
    (B) Misinformation effect
    (C) Availability heuristic
    (D) Source amnesia
    (E) Framing effect

100. A distribution in which the three measures of central tendency are the same is known as a

    (A) positive skew.
    (B) negative skew.
    (C) normal bell curve.
    (D) positively correlated.
    (E) negatively correlated.

SECTION II
Time- 50 minutes

DIRECTIONS: Answer the following questions in essay form. It is not enough to answer a question by merely listing facts. You should present a cogent argument based on your critical analysis of the questions posed, using appropriate psychological terminology.

1. Alexis recently attended an amusement park for the first time with her family. The park had many rides and attractions that Alexis had never experienced before.

   A. Explain how the following terms might help or hinder Alexis' experience at the amusement park.
- Openness to experience
- Yerkes-Dodson law
- Selective attention
- Reticular formation
- Confirmation bias

   B. Explain how the following concepts may impact her memory of the experience.
- Retroactive interference
- Misinformation effect

2. Professor Brody is interested in the impact of diet on athletic performance. He is examining students enrolled at his university. He provides one group of participants with a high protein, low-fat diet and asks the other group of participants to continue eating their normal diet.

   A. Identify the following factors in Professor Brody's experiment.
- Independent variable
- Dependent variable
- Operational definition
- Control group
- Experimental group

   B. Consider how Professor Brody might complete each of the following components in his experiment.
- An ethical consideration
- Debriefing
- Selection of participants
- Assignment participants

Practice Exam 2

This full-length practice exam contains two parts. Part I consists of 100 multiple-choice questions and Part II consists of two free-response questions.

You will have 70 minutes to complete the multiple-choice section of the exam. This section counts for 66% of the exam grade. As you will not be penalized for incorrect answers, you should answer every question on the test. If you do not know an answer to a question, try to eliminate any incorrect answer choices and take your best guess. Do not spend too much time on any one question.

You will have 50 minutes to complete the free-response section of the exam. This section counts for 33% of the overall exam grade. Be sure to answer each part of the question and to provide thorough explanations using the terms and themes you have learned in the course.

PSYCHOLOGY
SECTION I
Time—1 hour and 10 minutes
100 Questions

Directions: Each of the questions or incomplete statements below is followed by five suggested answers or completions. Select the one that is best in each case and then fill in the corresponding circle on the answer sheet.

1. Social facilitation theory suggests that
   (A) the presence of others diminishes performance on tasks at which we are well practiced.
   (B) the presence of others increases performance on tasks at which we are well practiced.
   (C) the presence of others increases performance on tasks we struggle with.
   (D) the presence of others causes us to lose our sense of self in a group setting.
   (E) the presence of more than 3 people causes us to change our opinions to fit in with the group.

2. James and Elena are fraternal twins. Although they are the same age, their mother is more lenient with James' curfew and allows him more freedom because she believes boys are more independent than girls. Their mother's belief is an example of a
   (A) theory of mind.
   (B) schema.
   (C) gender schema.
   (D) gender assimilation.
   (E) gender identity.

3. Julia got 6 "A's" on her report card because her mom promised her $10 for each "A" she earned. Her mom is evidently using which of the following to help her earn higher grades?
   (A) Negative reinforcement
   (B) Just noticeable difference
   (C) Extrinsic motivation
   (D) Mnemonics
   (E) Shaping

4. Which of the following sets of scores would have the greatest standard deviation?
   (A) 2, 4, 6, 8, 10
   (B) 1, 10, 20, 30, 40
   (C) 1, 2, 3, 4, 5
   (D) 99, 100, 101, 103, 104
   (E) 1000, 1002, 1004, 1006, 1008

5. Which of the following is not one of the basic Gestalt organizational principles?
   (A) Closure
   (B) Proximity
   (C) Connectedness
   (D) Retinal disparity
   (E) Similarity

6. When asked, "Is it more dangerous to fly or drive across country?" many Americans answer "fly." This is most likely due to
   (A) a norm.
   (B) the availability heuristic.
   (C) intuition.
   (D) the representativeness heuristic.
   (E) the misinformation effect.

7. When asked to think of a bird, most Americans first think of a robin. This is because a robin best fits their _____ for a bird.
    (A) prototype
    (B) heuristic
    (C) gestalt
    (D) hierarchy
    (E) syllogism

8. In 1848, Phineas Gage suffered severe damage to his frontal lobes in a horrible accident. Which of the following tasks would be most affected by this injury?
    (A) Feeling pain
    (B) Seeing his sister
    (C) Hearing someone call his name
    (D) Making the decision about whether to trust someone
    (E) Counting to ten

9. Which section of the brain is most involved in our sense of touch?
    (A) Parietal lobe
    (B) Frontal lobe
    (C) Amygdala
    (D) Hypothalamus
    (E) Hippocampus

Questions 10 and 11 refer to the situation below:

> Mr. Alexander believes that students who study in rooms with dim lighting will score better on his exams. His third period class studies in a dimly lit room and the fourth period class studies in their usual brightly lit classroom. The next day, each class takes the same Psychology exam and Mr. Alexander compares their scores. He finds that the fourth period class actually scores better than the third period class on the exam.

10. The independent variable in his study is
    (A) the scores on the psychology exam.
    (B) the dimly lit room.
    (C) the fact that the students are enrolled in Mr. Alexander's course.
    (D) the students in the third period class.
    (E) whether or not the students study while in the assigned room.

11. The control group in Mr. Alexander's study is
    (A) the students who studied in the dimly lit room.
    (B) the students in Mr. Alexander's fifth period class.
    (C) the students enrolled in Ms. Munroe's psychology course.
    (D) the students who studied in the brightly lit room.
    (E) all of the students enrolled in the school where Mr. Alexander teaches.

12. Ten years after returning from the Middle East, Morgan still has flashbacks of the war and wakes up from vivid nightmares several times a week. After a visit to a psychologist Morgan receives a diagnosis of
    (A) bipolar disorder.
    (B) generalized anxiety disorder.
    (C) agoraphobia.
    (D) fugue.
    (E) posttraumatic stress disorder (PTSD).

13. Traci is terrified of spiders. Her therapist has been gradually exposing her to spiders by first looking at pictures and, once she is comfortable with that step, working up to Traci actually touching a spider. This type of therapy is called

    (A) dual processing.
    (B) aversive conditioning.
    (C) systematic desensitization.
    (D) factor analysis.
    (E) resistance.

14. Talya has always been very impulsive. When she wants something she is unable to wait for it and must have it immediately. Which of the following would Freud say is the strongest part of her personality?

    (A) Id
    (B) Attachment
    (C) Ego
    (D) Superego
    (E) Industry

15. On a test in which the scores are normally distributed, approximately what percentage of the scores are within 2 standard deviations of the mean?

    (A) 20%
    (B) 33%
    (C) 50%
    (D) 68%
    (E) 95%

16. Casinos know that gamblers are likely to keep playing slot machines in the hopes that the next time will be the time they win. This is because gambling is reinforced on which schedule?

    (A) Continuous
    (B) Fixed-ratio
    (C) Fixed-interval
    (D) Variable-interval
    (E) Variable-ratio

17. Approximately 25 minutes after falling asleep, Juanita's EEG displays sleep spindles. Which stage of sleep is she most likely entering?

    (A) NREM-1
    (B) NREM-2
    (C) Somnambulism
    (D) REM
    (E) NREM-3

18. Which of the following depth cues requires two eyes to be successful?

    (A) Linear perspective
    (B) Interposition
    (C) Light and shadow
    (D) Retinal disparity
    (E) Texture gradient

19. The zipper tab on Colleen's sweatshirt has broken and she cannot get the zipper down. She has a paperclip with her but does not realize that she could use it in place of the tab to help pull her zipper down. Colleen is unable to solve her problem because of
    (A) the confirmation bias.
    (B) belief perseverance.
    (C) the Premack principle.
    (D) functional fixedness.
    (E) displacement.

20. Gio thinks that he has less pizza than Chandra because his mom cut his slice of pizza into four pieces and his sister's into five. He does not, however, take one of her slices because he is afraid he will get a time out if he is caught. Piaget would say that Gio is in the _____ stage and Kohlberg would say that he is in the _____ stage.
    (A) formal operational; postconventional
    (B) concrete operational; preconventional
    (C) sensorimotor; conventional
    (D) preoperational; preconventional
    (E) preoperational; conventional

21. Geoff is a master con artist who frequently steals from his friends and family, showing no remorse for his actions. According to the DSM, Geoff's most likely diagnosis would be
    (A) social anxiety disorder.
    (B) a conversion disorder.
    (C) antisocial personality disorder.
    (D) systemic disorder.
    (E) psychophysiological illness.

22. Chad is a member of the Future Farmers Club at his school. During the last meeting the club discussed how important farmers are to America. Chad and his friends were more convinced at the end of the meeting of the importance of farmers than they were before the meeting started. The more extreme position of Chad and his friends is evidence of
    (A) groupthink
    (B) deindividuation.
    (C) transference.
    (D) group polarization.
    (E) mere exposure effect.

23. The "master gland" of the endocrine system, which also produces the growth hormone, is the
    (A) adrenal gland.
    (B) thyroid gland.
    (C) pineal gland.
    (D) pancreas.
    (E) pituitary gland.

24. Samir attends several loud concerts over the course of a year. At the end of the year he notices that he is having trouble hearing and his doctor diagnoses him with nerve deafness. What part of his ear was most likely damaged by the loud music?
    (A) Eardrum
    (B) Hammer
    (C) Cochlea
    (D) Auditory nerve
    (E) Semicircular canals

25. Which of the following psychologists is most commonly associated with operant conditioning?

(A) John Watson
(B) Carl Rogers
(C) Albert Bandura
(D) B. F. Skinner
(E) Mary Ainsworth

26. Which of the following is the most basic need in Maslow's hierarchy of needs?

(A) Belongingness and love
(B) Safety
(C) Self-actualization
(D) Physiological
(E) Esteem

27. The sentence, "Kevin banana eated" has correct _____ and incorrect _____ .

(A) morphemes; semantics
(B) semantics; syntax
(C) telegraphic speech; semantics
(D) utility; syntax
(E) framing; semantics

28. Which of the following best explains why you can accurately list almost everything that you had to eat yesterday, even though you did not consciously place the menu into your memory?

(A) Mnemonic devices
(B) Implicit memory
(C) Automatic processing
(D) Semantic memory
(E) Working memory

29. Although Carla and her boyfriend are only 19, they have decided to get married. Her friends and family are upset because Carla is "too young." Which psychology principle has Carla and her boyfriend apparently violated?

(A) The social clock
(B) Role confusion
(C) Loss of identity
(D) Deindividuation
(E) Locus of control

30. In which of the following personality tests is a client asked to make up a story based on an ambiguous picture?

(A) MMPI
(B) Myers-Briggs Type Indicator
(C) WISC
(D) Stanford-Binet
(E) TAT

31. Which of the following is the most widely used intelligence test?

(A) The Rorschach Test
(B) The Wechsler Test
(C) Stanford-Binet Test
(D) Dove Counterbalance Test
(E) Langer-Rodin Test

32. An action against a group of people is called discrimination. Typically this is born out of an unjustifiable, often negative, attitude called
    (A) prejudice.
    (B) rationalization.
    (C) aphasia.
    (D) social trap.
    (E) groupthink.

33. Shortly after taking a psychoactive drug, Lydia experienced an increased heart rate, dilated pupils, decreased appetite and an increase in her energy levels. Which of the following did she most likely ingest?
    (A) Methamphetamine
    (B) LSD
    (C) Alcohol
    (D) Marijuana
    (E) Heroin

34. Carla continually washes her hands, even though she knows they are clean. Her behavior is best described as a(n)
    (A) compulsion.
    (B) hallucination.
    (C) delusion.
    (D) obsession.
    (E) phobia.

35. Joyce has been displaying a series of irrational thoughts and fears lately. In an effort to alleviate her symptoms she seeks help from a therapist who has taken a rather tough approach with her. Each time she mentions her irrational thoughts he tells her to "Stop!" and think logically about what she is saying. Her therapist is most likely using
    (A) rational-emotive behavior therapy.
    (B) client-centered therapy.
    (C) psychodynamic therapy.
    (D) a token economy.
    (E) positive psychology.

36. Which of the following statements best represents the correlation displayed on the following scatterplot?

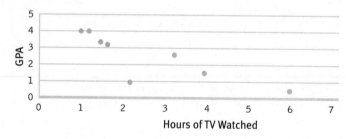

    (A) The graph shows a perfect positive correlation between the two variables.
    (B) The graph shows a moderate positive correlation between the two variables.
    (C) The graph shows a moderate negative correlation between the two variables.
    (D) The graph shows a perfect negative correlation between the two variables.
    (E) The graph shows no correlation between the two variables.

37. The man often cited as the "founder of psychology" because he opened the first psychology lab in 1879 is
   (A) William James.
   (B) Sigmund Freud.
   (C) B. F. Skinner.
   (D) John Watson.
   (E) Wilhelm Wundt.

38. While watching TV with his son, Min is asked to turn up the volume. After doing so, he is asked to turn it up again. Evidently, the first increase was below his son's
   (A) absolute threshold.
   (B) habituation level.
   (C) actualization level.
   (D) ganglion threshold.
   (E) difference threshold.

39. The following graph, which demonstrates a rapid drop in retention that levels off with time, best represents the research findings of which of the following psychologists?

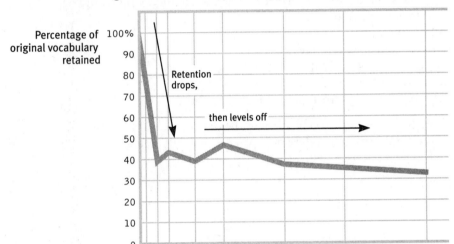

   (A) Hermann Ebbinghaus
   (B) Elizabeth Loftus
   (C) Oliver Sacks
   (D) Daniel Schacter
   (E) Roger Sperry

40. On one day at the mall, Dr. Miele conducted a survey that measured the eating habits of people who were 20, 30, 40, and 50, with 10 people in each age group. Which of the following best describes her study?
   (A) An experiment
   (B) A cross-sectional study
   (C) A case study
   (D) A longitudinal study
   (E) A double-blind study

41. Molley's friends are concerned because she has dropped a significant amount of weight recently. Which eating disorder is she most likely to be diagnosed with?
    (A) Anorexia nervosa
    (B) Binge-eating disorder
    (C) Somnambulism
    (D) Bulimia nervosa
    (E) Agoraphobia

42. Anya has suffered for years with mental illness that has not responded to any drug or psychotherapy. As a last resort, her doctor suggests that she undergo ECT (electroconvulsive therapy). For what disorder is Anya most likely being treated?
    (A) Dissociative identity disorder
    (B) Antisocial personality disorder
    (C) Anorexia nervosa
    (D) Generalized anxiety disorder
    (E) Major depressive disorder

43. While in the 10 items or less line at the grocery store Emily sees that the person in front of her has 17 items. If she makes the fundamental attribution error, which of the following would be the most likely explanation for the other person's behavior?
    (A) "This store is so busy today, no wonder she got into this line."
    (B) "She must be in a hurry to get somewhere today."
    (C) "I guess I could have brought a couple more items into the line."
    (D) "That woman's scarf and shirt don't even match."
    (E) "That woman must pretty selfish to not care about the rest of the line."

44. Han arrives for his AP® Chemistry exam. As he begins the test he notices that some of the questions are not chemistry questions at all but belong on a physics test. His teacher has most clearly violated which of the following in the construction of the exam?
    (A) Standardization
    (B) Reliability
    (C) Validity
    (D) Collectivism
    (E) Algorithm

45. Which of the following brain structures is most involved in the reduction of hunger?
    (A) Hippocampus
    (B) Broca's area
    (C) Lateral hypothalamus
    (D) Ventromedial hypothalamus
    (E) Cerebellum

46. After several failed attempts to escape from her yard, Daisy the dog stops trying. Even when the gate is left open she refuses to leave because she assumes that she will not get very far. Daisy's behavior is best explained as
    (A) classical conditioning.
    (B) learned helplessness.
    (C) compliance.
    (D) neurogenesis.
    (E) hypochondriasis.

47. What is the mode of the following set of scores: 1, 3, 4, 4, 6, 8, 9?
    (A) 4
    (B) 5
    (C) 7
    (D) 8
    (E) 35

48. In Psychology, one of the biggest debates is over what combination of genes and environment contribute to our development and personality. What is the name for this debate?

    (A) Stability and change
    (B) Nature and nurture
    (C) Assimilation and accommodation
    (D) Continuity and stages
    (E) Correlation and causation

49. Nedra is a split-brain patient. As she fixates on a spot in the middle of her vision, a picture of a dog is flashed to her left visual field and a picture of a rabbit is flashed to her right visual field. Which of the following will she be able to do?

    (A) Use her left hand to indicate that she saw a rabbit.
    (B) Use her right hand to indicate that she saw a dog.
    (C) Verbally report that she saw a rabbit.
    (D) Verbally report that she saw a dog.
    (E) Verbally report that she saw both a rabbit and a dog.

50. Luis puts on his seatbelt each time he gets in his car because doing so stops the beeping alarm. Which learning principle explains why he continues this behavior?

    (A) Negative reinforcement
    (B) Stimulus generalization
    (C) Positive reinforcement
    (D) Extinction
    (E) Assimilation

51. The human body attempts to maintain a constant internal state. This is called

    (A) homeostasis.
    (B) gestalt.
    (C) heuristic.
    (D) neurogenesis.
    (E) ganglion.

52. In the midst of a heated argument with his son, Mohammad fell asleep. With which sleep disorder would he most likely be diagnosed?

    (A) Apnea
    (B) Circadian rhythm disorder
    (C) Narcolepsy
    (D) Insomnia
    (E) Cataplexy

53. Which of the following best explains why we are able to touch our finger to our nose with our eyes closed?

    (A) The vestibular sense
    (B) Functionalism
    (C) Biofeedback
    (D) Kinesthesis
    (E) Plasticity

54. Arriving at school for your senior year you find yourself unable to learn your new locker combination. You keep inputting your junior year combination, with no success. The reason for this is most likely due to

    (A) implicit memory.
    (B) retroactive interference.
    (C) transference.
    (D) shallow processing.
    (E) proactive interference.

55. Which researcher below is most closely tied to psychosocial development throughout the lifespan?

    (A) Jean Piaget
    (B) B. F. Skinner
    (C) Erik Erikson
    (D) Lev Vygotsky
    (E) Leon Festinger

56. Which of the following is not one of the generally acknowledged symptoms of schizophrenia?

    (A) Hallucinations
    (B) Delusions
    (C) Paranoia
    (D) Multiple personalities
    (E) Catatonia

57. As part of his therapy, Gulio is asked to share all thoughts that come into his mind, taking care not to avoid saying something because it might be too embarrassing. His therapist will later analyze everything that Gulio has told him. What type therapy is most likely being employed?

    (A) Cognitive
    (B) Psychoanalytical
    (C) Rational-emotive
    (D) Higher-order conditioning
    (E) Behavioral

58. People often behave in more extreme ways when they are in a larger group than they do when acting alone. Which psychological term best explains this behavior?

    (A) Group polarization
    (B) Groupthink
    (C) Deindividuation
    (D) Deinstitutionalization
    (E) Reaction formation

59. After checking into their hotel room, guests often find a card in the bathroom that says, "Most guests choose to reuse towels several times before washing. Won't you join them in conserving resources?" The hotel is trying to influence the behavior of their guests through

    (A) obedience.
    (B) groupthink.
    (C) peripheral route processing.
    (D) conformity.
    (E) eustress.

60. Which of the following best describes Sternberg's theory of intelligence?

    (A) Thought processes and concepts are controlled by language.
    (B) Intelligence is composed of analytical, creative and practical elements.
    (C) There are 8 multiple intelligences that can be found in humans.
    (D) Intelligence is composed of 2 abilities: the s factor and the g factor.
    (E) Intelligent thought requires understanding that there is only one solution to any problem.

61. Upon encountering a barking Rottweiler on her way home from school, Katie noticed that her heart was racing. Which was most likely activated to cause this reaction?

    (A) Sympathetic nervous system
    (B) Somatic nervous system
    (C) Parasympathetic nervous system
    (D) Endocrine system
    (E) Reticular activating system

62. Which of the following is a major disadvantage of the case study method?

    (A) Participants may give answers that are designed to support the researcher's hypothesis.
    (B) Confounding variables may provide inaccurate results.
    (C) The lack of random assignment may result in a stronger experimental group.
    (D) Studying such a large population makes data collection tedious.
    (E) The results may not be applicable to a larger population because the sample is so small.

63. Claire, age 4, watches as her older brother throws the food he does not want to eat on the floor. Later, she does the same thing when given something that she does not want to eat. The fact that she mimics behavior she has seen would be most supported by the research done by

    (A) B. F. Skinner.
    (B) Jean Piaget.
    (C) Lawrence Kohlberg.
    (D) Albert Bandura.
    (E) Carl Rogers.

64. A lawyer wishes to discredit the eyewitness testimony against his client. Which psychologist would he most likely call to the stand?

    (A) John Watson
    (B) Robert Sternberg
    (C) Elizabeth Loftus
    (D) Walter Cannon
    (E) Paul Ekman

65. A deterioration in which of the following neurotransmitters has been linked to Alzheimer's disease?

    (A) Serotonin
    (B) GABA
    (C) Melatonin
    (D) Dopamine
    (E) Acetylcholine

66. What technique is used by experimenters to minimize differences between the experimental and control groups?

    (A) Confounding variables
    (B) Random selection
    (C) Random assignment
    (D) Kinesthesis
    (E) Operational definitions

67. In a bizarre accident, the cones in Li's eyes were damaged. What effect is this most likely to have?

    (A) Li will be unable to recognize faces of her family members.
    (B) Li will be unable to see colors.
    (C) Li will be unable to use her peripheral vision.
    (D) Li will be unable to focus on objects farther away from her.
    (E) Li will be unable to focus on objects that are close to her.

68. Drugs like Zoloft and Paxil are called SSRIs because they work to relieve depression by

    (A) forcing neurons to produce more serotonin.
    (B) inhibiting the amount of dopamine released at the synapse.
    (C) slowing the production of serotonin.
    (D) stopping the activity of regional interneurons.
    (E) causing more serotonin to remain in the synapse after reuptake.

69. Not long after witnessing a horrible accident, Ms. Gonzales lost her vision. In therapy she expresses a great fear that she will witness something tragic again. The best explanation for her blindness would be that
    (A) her rods and cones have stopped working.
    (B) she has a conversion disorder.
    (C) her retina has detached.
    (D) she has developed agoraphobia.
    (E) her ganglion cells are firing too slowly.

70. The excuse "but I was only following orders" attempts to use which of the following to justify behavior?
    (A) Obedience
    (B) Groupthink
    (C) Conformity
    (D) Compliance
    (E) Diffusion of responsibility

71. When he was 10, Ernesto took an intelligence test and scored 125. What would the best estimate of his IQ be at age 40?
    (A) 85
    (B) 100
    (C) 125
    (D) 150
    (E) 500

72. During which stage of Selye's general adaptation syndrome are we actively dealing with the stressor?
    (A) Alarm
    (B) Resistance
    (C) Modeling
    (D) Eustress
    (E) Exhaustion

73. Bandura's reciprocal determinism states that which of the following factors interact to determine future behavior?
    (A) Nature and nurture
    (B) Conservation, friendship groups and intelligence
    (C) Environment, behavior and cognitive factors
    (D) Positive and negative reinforcement
    (E) Unconditional self-regard and sense of identity

74. After dating for 3 years, Suzanne and her boyfriend went through a difficult breakup. At their ten-year high school reunion she fails to remember who he is or that they dated. Freud would suggest that she is making use of the defense mechanism of
    (A) reaction formation.
    (B) sublimation.
    (C) regression.
    (D) repression.
    (E) projection.

75. Yasmine has experienced damage to her Broca's area. With which of the following is she most likely to have difficulty?
    (A) Playing her flute
    (B) Writing her name
    (C) Saying her name
    (D) Distinguishing red from blue
    (E) Drawing a triangle

76. Carl notices that students who are active on Twitter are more sociable than those who do not. If he assumes that tweeting is a result of the student's social ability what error has he made?

   (A) Finding a negative correlation in positive data.
   (B) Applying the representative heuristic too broadly.
   (C) Inferred correlation where there is causation.
   (D) Inferred causation where there is correlation.
   (E) Misapplication of negative reinforcement principles.

77. Jaime's mother consumed alcohol and tobacco while Jaime was in the womb. If Jaime has any negative effects because of her mother's consumption then we would say that those products were

   (A) zygotic.
   (B) stimulants.
   (C) embryonic.
   (D) teratogens.
   (E) monarchic.

78. A disorder in which a person is continually tense, apprehensive, and in a state of autonomic nervous system arousal is

   (A) panic disorder.
   (B) obsessive-compulsive disorder.
   (C) generalized anxiety disorder.
   (D) conversion disorder.
   (E) mania.

79. Janis, a patient with schizophrenia, has recently begun having facial twitches and muscle spasms. These are the symptoms of

   (A) learned helplessnss.
   (B) an avoidance-avoidance conflict.
   (C) a somatoform disorder.
   (D) tardive dyskinesia.
   (E) drug withdrawal.

80. Kevin is set up on a blind date with Jenny, who he has been told is very funny. Over dinner he acts in such a way that elicits jokes and laughter from her, confirming what he had been told about her. This is an example of

   (A) self-efficacy.
   (B) social loafing.
   (C) a self-fulfilling prophecy.
   (D) intrinsic motivation.
   (E) construct validity.

81. The SAT® is designed to predict how well a high school student will do when they get to college. Because of this purpose, the SAT® is classified as a(n)

   (A) aptitude test.
   (B) projective test.
   (C) achievement test.
   (D) sandardized test.
   (E) culture-bound test.

82. Which theory of emotion states that an experienced emotion follows a specific physiological response?

   (A) Two-factor
   (B) Drive reduction
   (C) Cannon-Bard
   (D) Opponent-process
   (E) James-Lange

83. Lisa is described by her boss as someone who pays attention to detail and always submits her work well ahead of the deadline. Which of the following Big Five factors would she rate highly on for this behavior?

    (A) Agreeableness
    (B) Conscientiousness
    (C) Extraversion
    (D) Neuroticism
    (E) Openness

84. Which psychologist below has theorized that humans have an"inborn universal grammar" which will naturally allow a child to develop language under the correct conditions?

    (A) Hermann Ebbinghaus
    (B) Noam Chomsky
    (C) Benjamin Whorf
    (D) B.F. Skinner
    (E) Abraham Maslow

85. Eloisa is a psychologist who works at an electronics company. Her job is to help the designers make their products more intuitive for the consumer to use. What type of psychologist is she?

    (A) Industrial-organizational
    (B) Developmental
    (C) Cognitive
    (D) Human factors
    (E) Humanistic

86. The American Psychological Association has established a list of ethical guidelines that researchers must follow when conducting experiments on people. Which of the following items is not listed in the list?

    (A) Guaranteed financial compensation for participants
    (B) Protection of participant confidentiality
    (C) Protection from harm for participants
    (D) Right for participants to know what will happen in the study
    (E) Right to a debriefing at the end of the study

87. Carlos claims to be able to predict the gender of an unborn baby with near perfect accuracy. He is demonstrating which of the following phenomenon?

    (A) Psychokinesis
    (B) Telepathy
    (C) Precognition
    (D) Bilocation
    (E) Clairvoyance

88. Increased amounts of dopamine have been linked with which of the following?

    (A) Seizures
    (B) Schizophrenia
    (C) Alzheimer's disease
    (D) Parkinson's disease
    (E) Autism spectrum disorder

89. In Watson's experiment with Little Albert, what was the unconditioned response (UR)?

    (A) The white rat
    (B) The flashing light
    (C) The loud noise
    (D) His fear
    (E) The presence of his mother

90.   Which of the following did Erikson list as the major task of adolescence?

(A) Developing an identity
(B) Achieving a sense of integrity
(C) Developing intimacy
(D) Developing basic trust
(E) Achieving formal operational thought

91.   Therapists are trained to accept patients and their thoughts, without any conditions and no matter how the therapist may privately judge the patient. This is reflective of Roger's concept of

(A) temperament.
(B) archetypes.
(C) unconditional positive regard.
(D) self-actualization.
(E) pragmatics.

92.   The variation in intelligence test scores attributable to genetics is known as

(A) maturation.
(B) assimilation.
(C) cognitive universalism.
(D) metacognition.
(E) heritability.

93.   Aggression is different from prejudice because aggression involves

(A) an unjustifiable negative attitude towards a group of people.
(B) behavior intended to hurt or destroy another person.
(C) punishing someone for the mistakes of another.
(D) treating people differently because of the group they belong to.
(E) a set of characteristics that people believe are shared by all members of a group.

94.   Chloe alternates between manic and depressive states. Her physician has diagnosed her with

(A) generalized anxiety disorder.
(B) disruptive mood disorder.
(C) a Somatoform disorder.
(D) bipolar disorder.
(E) major depressive disorder.

95.   Which of the following is the best example of an implicit memory?

(A) The day of your birth
(B) The capital of Sweden
(C) How many feet in a yard
(D) How to ride a bike
(E) Your home address

Questions 96 and 97 refer to the following scenario:

Mr. Amelia had a stomach bug that caused her to get sick after eating her favorite dish, General Gau's Chicken. After this, the smell of the chicken will cause her to feel sick.

96.   In this scenario, the stomach bug is the

(A) conditioned stimulus (CS).
(B) Neutral stimulus (NS).
(C) unconditioned stimulus (US).
(D) conditioned response (CR).
(E) unconditioned response (UR).

97. In the future, Amelia feels sick when she smells fried chicken as well as General Gau's chicken. This is an example of
    (A) stimulus discrimination.
    (B) stimulus generalization.
    (C) response discrimination.
    (D) response generalization.
    (E) an unconditioned stimulus.

98. Alice's doctor has ordered a brain scan because she is concerned that Alice's brain is not using glucose properly. Which of the following tests is Alice most likely undergo?
    (A) MRI
    (B) CT scan
    (C) PET scan
    (D) EEG
    (E) EKG

99. Which of the following parenting styles is demonstrated when parents have a number of strict rules and expect unquestioning obedience from their children?
    (A) Permissive indulgent
    (B) Authoritarian
    (C) Attached
    (D) Authoritative
    (E) Pragmatic

100. Which of the following is the best description of the function of a dendrite?
    (A) Insulate the axon
    (B) Assist with the reuptake of neurotransmitters
    (C) Trigger the release of neurotransmitters from the vesicles
    (D) Receive messages from sending neurons
    (E) Manufacture glial cells to assist in neuron functioning